W9-CBQ-101

THE BEDFORD SERIES IN HISTORY AND CULTURE

Louis XIV and Absolutism

A Brief Study with Documents

Related Titles in
THE BEDFORD SERIES IN HISTORY AND CULTURE
Advisory Editors: Natalie Zemon Davis, Princeton University
Ernest R. May, Harvard University

The Trial of Mary Queen of Scots: A Brief History with Documents
Jayne Elizabeth Lewis, *University of California, Los Angeles*

The Jesuit Relations: Natives and Missionaries in Seventeenth-Century North America
Allan Greer, *University of Toronto*

The English Nationalist Revolution, 1688–1689: A Documentary History
(forthcoming)
Steven Carl Anthony Pincus, *University of Chicago*

Candide by Voltaire
Translated, Edited, and with an Introduction by Daniel Gordon, *University of Massachusetts at Amherst*

The French Revolution and Human Rights: A Brief Documentary History
Edited, Translated, and with an Introduction by Lynn Hunt, *University of California, Los Angeles*

France and the Dreyfus Affair: A Documentary History
Michael Burns, *Mount Holyoke College*

THE BEDFORD SERIES IN HISTORY AND CULTURE

Louis XIV and Absolutism

A Brief Study with Documents

William Beik

Emory University

BEDFORD/ST. MARTIN'S   Boston • New York

For Bedford/St. Martin's
Executive Editor for History and Political Science: Katherine E. Kurzman
Developmental Editor: Molly E. Kalkstein
Production Supervisor: Cheryl Mamaril
Marketing Manager: Charles Cavaliere
Project Management: Books By Design, Inc.
Text Design: Claire Seng-Niemoeller
Map: Richard D. Pusey/Charthouse
Indexer: Books By Design, Inc.
Cover Design: Richard Emery Design, Inc.
Cover Art: Copy by an unknown artist after a work by Claude Lefebvre,
    Louis XIV, King of France and Navarre, ca. 1665–70. Versailles and Trianon.
    © Photo RMN-Gérard Blot
Composition: G&S Typesetters, Inc.
Printing and Binding: Haddon Craftsmen, an R. R. Donnelley & Sons Company

President: Charles H. Christensen
Editorial Director: Joan E. Feinberg
Director of Marketing: Karen R. Melton
Director of Editing, Design, and Production: Marcia Cohen
Manager, Publishing Services: Emily Berleth

Library of Congress Catalog Card Number: 99-62372

Manufactured in the United States of America.

5 4 3 2 1 0
f e d c b a

For information, write: Bedford/St. Martin's, 75 Arlington Street, Boston, MA 02116
(617-399-4000)

ISBN: 0-312-13309-X (paperback)
       0-312-22743-4 (hardcover)

Acknowledgments
Acknowledgments and copyrights appear at the back of the book on page 235, which constitutes an extension of the copyright page.

Foreword

The Bedford Series in History and Culture is designed so that readers can study the past as historians do.

The historian's first task is finding the evidence. Documents, letters, memoirs, interviews, pictures, movies, novels, or poems can provide facts and clues. Then the historian questions and compares the sources. There is more to do than in a courtroom, for hearsay evidence is welcome, and the historian is usually looking for answers beyond act and motive. Different views of an event may be as important as a single verdict. How a story is told may yield as much information as what it says.

Along the way the historian seeks help from other historians and perhaps from specialists in other disciplines. Finally, it is time to write, to decide on an interpretation and how to arrange the evidence for readers.

Each book in this series contains an important historical document or group of documents, each document a witness from the past and open to interpretation in different ways. The documents are combined with some element of historical narrative — an introduction or a biographical essay, for example — that provides students with an analysis of the primary source material and important background information about the world in which it was produced.

Each book in the series focuses on a specific topic within a specific historical period. Each provides a basis for lively thought and discussion about several aspects of the topic and the historian's role. Each is short enough (and inexpensive enough) to be a reasonable one-week assignment in a college course. Whether as classroom or personal reading, each book in the series provides firsthand experience of the challenge — and fun — of discovering, recreating, and interpreting the past.

Natalie Zemon Davis
Ernest R. May

Preface

The cover of this volume portrays a king whose undeniable elegance is nevertheless troubling to the modern eye. Who is this Louis XIV, who looks as if he has stepped out of a baroque opera set, wearing bright red tights and holding an extravagant plumed helmet? The painting, by an unknown artist, was done around 1665–70 at the time of the French conflicts with the Dutch, which may explain the ship that appears in the background. Louis is sitting next to his crown and scepter, both symbols of majesty, and holding a baton, signifying military command. He is flaunting his elegance because he must outshine all others at a court known for its magnificence. But he is also projecting a message of infallibility and domination, because he must persuade the millions of subjects in a large, diverse kingdom, and especially the independently powerful, to accept his direction and obey his ordinances.

Pictures like this convey the mystique of the king but not the reality of his rule. Louis XIV is associated with a setting, the court at Versailles, and a method of government, absolutism, that are both rather foreign to modern perceptions. Louis was part of a society very different from ours, and his personal and political styles reflect that fact. His regime of order was not a foregone conclusion, coming as it did after a generation of civil disorder. Nor was his absolute monarchy anything like the all-powerful reign that is sometimes imagined.

To succeed, Louis XIV had to fashion an image that suited the expectations of the time and develop methods of coordinating the whole governmental apparatus more effectively. In this volume, we will explore the way Louis accomplished those two objectives. Our goal is to examine the meaning of absolute monarchy by looking at the way this king interacted with his society. We must ask how he handled the great nobles, what he offered to provincial elites and what he expected from them in return, how he influenced the economy, and what reaction ordinary subjects had to his rule. Above all, we need to assess the nature of absolutism as one form of European state development.

Each chapter is built around an aspect of the king's internal governance. We will examine the problems of disorder that he faced when he came to power, the nature of his court, his ministers' attempts to grasp the economic and fiscal dimensions of the kingdom, the taming of the rural nobility, the interaction of royal ministers and provincial authorities, popular rebellions, the repression of Jansenists and Protestants, and the creation of the royal image. In each of these areas, I have selected reasonably long documents that tell a story. I have also tried to convey how things looked from the perspectives of the participants, not just from the vantage point of the king and his ministers. These source readings should help students understand absolutism as a process of interaction between the king and powerful social groups in a society that was organized around diverse ranks, each with special privileges. I hope they will also breathe some life into this historical abstraction and help students see it in terms of real people solving concrete problems.

ACKNOWLEDGMENTS

I am grateful to Natalie Davis for suggesting this volume and to Katherine Kurzman for patiently guiding it through to fruition. In planning my own readings on Louis XIV, I have been repeatedly stimulated by the intelligence of the collections that precede this one, notably those edited by H. G. Judge, Roger Mettam, Orest and Patricia Ranum, John Rule, and David L. Smith. I have also been reminded of the pertinence of a number of scholars' work, notably Jim Collins, Sarah Hanley, Albert Hamscher, Sharon Kettering, Andrew Lossky, David Parker, John Rule, Paul Sonnino, and John B. Wolf. Six experts — Sara Chapman, Richard Golden, Albert Hamscher, John Hurt, and two anonymous readers — provided unusually helpful and detailed suggestions for improvement, most of which I have adopted. Amy Enright found and edited the Mazarinade in chapter 1. Students from several generations of History 315 and History 387 at Emory University helped me rethink the problem of how to present Louis XIV to a contemporary audience. Molly Kalkstein has been an extraordinarily imaginative and gifted editor. And above all, I am thankful for the encouragement and companionship of Millie, Carl, and Eric.

William Beik

Contents

Illustrations

Louis XIV and Absolutism

A Brief Study with Documents

PART ONE

Introduction: Louis XIV and French Absolutism

opening paragraph

The name of Louis XIV is inseparably linked to the concept of absolutism. One of Europe's most celebrated rulers, he is noted for reviving the French monarchy after a century of disorder and for consolidating French dominance in Europe. This king epitomizes the height of royal authority, majesty, and, for some, arrogance. The dazzling court at Versailles, his image as the "Sun King," his determination to suppress religious diversity, and his aggressiveness in threatening his neighbors are legendary. But above all, Louis presents us with a picture of successful royal government from the top down. This book aims to explore the reality behind that image.

By personifying absolutism, Louis offers us another way to think about the development of the state in early modern Europe. Absolutism, which means that the king derived his power from God and could exercise it without other constituted bodies having the right to challenge him, appeared to be the normal state of affairs on the continent in the seventeenth century. The king's power, though restricted by traditional practices that we will examine later in this introduction, was otherwise unlimited. Louis XIV could institute new taxes and regulate all aspects of legal privilege and local administration without any constitutional check on his authority. Elite groups increasingly looked to the crown to protect their interests, while the royal court became the social standard setter

rights of Louis XIV

opposite to absolutism

for the aristocracy. This system contrasts markedly with the more familiar British model, in which Parliament progressively assumed power and "English liberties" were gradually extended, while the monarch and the court played a decreasing role in national life. In a rough sense, then, French "absolutism" can be contrasted with English "constitutionalism." But to understand the French situation better, we need to look beyond laws and theories to the way the king's government interacted with the various groups that made up French society.

This book lays out evidence designed to help us explore this problem. We need to penetrate the king's charisma to understand how he managed to rule a large country so effectively after a generation of social unrest. We must explore how his government interacted with the powerful groups in the provinces; how the common people were affected; and how religious groups, Protestant and Catholic, were influenced by the claims of the monarch. We will start with the turbulent days of Louis's youth in order to identify the difficulties the king would face. Then we will explore his relationships with the different segments of society, keeping in mind that government is a process of interaction among many types of agents and many kinds of people.

Our goal is to achieve a deeper understanding of Louis XIV's society and a better grasp of absolutism in practice. The selection of documents is oriented in that direction. Their focus is on the system of government, not the day-to-day events of the reign, and on how the system worked, not on the many changes that took place during the fifty-four years of Louis XIV's personal rule. Louis became king in 1643, when he was not quite five years old, but his government was run by his mother, Anne of Austria, and her favorite and first minister, Cardinal Jules Mazarin, until 1661. His personal rule began then, upon the death of Mazarin. To explore in depth the various aspects of Louis's governance, the documents concentrate mostly on the first thirty years of his personal reign. Those were the years when most of the innovations were initiated and when the myths and images later associated with Louis were created. In the last years of his reign, Louis encountered new problems, new men replaced the original team of leaders, and circumstances changed during Louis's costly wars. Those changes will not be our focus. Instead, we will take a closer look at the nature of French internal governance in the heyday of Louis XIV's rule.

ABSOLUTISM IN THEORY

Absolutism is one of those broad retrospective terms that historians invent to characterize a whole system after it is gone. It denotes a regime in which power was concentrated in the hands of a king who co without any legal limitations on his sovereignty. The term has neg. connotations. It hints at an unfavorable comparison with more desirat. "constitutional" forms of government and suggests overtones of arbitrariness, despotism, and even tyranny. It thus betrays the political orientation of the various constitutionalists who coined it in France after the French Revolution and in England around 1830. We should be aware of this critical perspective. We may well agree in condemning absolutism, but we should avoid the error of confusing it with more recent forms of dictatorial or totalitarian government.[1]

Contemporaries of Louis XIV did not use the term *absolutism* at all, but they did discuss the "absolute power" of the crown, which they understood to mean the concentration of sovereign authority in the hands of the king. This concept can be understood only in the context of a traditional aristocratic society, which operated according to its own values and customs. Absolute power was not totalitarian because early modern kings had neither the inclination nor the resources to direct the lives of their subjects in any comprehensive way. Absolute power was based on the divine right theory that kings were chosen by God to rule and that they should follow divine and natural law in doing so. It did not mean that they were allowed to act arbitrarily or despotically; it meant instead that when they exercised the fullness of their authority, they could not be limited by institutional or social checks. The theory of absolute monarchy thus contradicted any theory saying that the king derived his authority from the people or the aristocracy. It also denied any right of resistance on the part of constituted bodies, such as representative assemblies, law courts, or groups of magistrates.

FRENCH ABSOLUTISM IN PRACTICE

In practice, a French king's power was constrained in several important ways. First, he had to answer directly to God for his actions — no small responsibility in the age of Catholic Reform. Second, he was considered bound by the so-called fundamental laws of the realm. These were unwritten, customary precepts about the nature of the monarchy.[2] Most

---

[1] A *dictator* is one who seizes power arbitrarily and rules without consent. A *totalitarian* regime is a twentieth-century concept implying a government that intrudes into every aspect of citizens' daily lives. Absolute monarchy was neither: It was ruled by a generally accepted, legitimate king according to established norms and procedures.

[2] The three generally accepted fundamental laws were (1) the Salic law, which decreed that the throne passed in the direct male line, excluding women; (2) the rule that the royal

was limited by contemporary concepts of natural
t he was expected to respect the rights, freedoms,
rty of his subjects. He was above the law in the
suspend the rules and change procedures when
l interest. Nevertheless, he was viewed as the de-
......er of a mystical body politic that was understood to include the
existing hierarchical society in which private individuals and groups enjoyed distinctive rights and privileges. This mandate left room for interpretation. The king could act cautiously, consulting powerful groups
frequently and acting as referee in their quarrels. Or he could intervene
more dynamically by organizing new ways to mobilize state power. In either case, he would meet with resistance if he appeared weak or if his
government was divided, and he would find widespread support when
he affected the role of princely protector.

Still, the most important limitation on absolutism was not theoretical
but practical. Whatever their claims, French kings had only gradually established their authority over the territory of France. Through the centuries, they had laboriously pieced together a patchwork of provinces,
sometimes seeing them slip away only to return at a later date. Each
province struck a different deal with the crown when it was incorporated
into the realm. Privileges and laws were confirmed, existing institutions
maintained, powerful groups bought off with favors. Faced with a different situation in each of their provinces and towns, the kings had to work
through existing institutions, or create new ones that duplicated the
functions of the old ones, if they wanted to establish any sort of uniform
control. We will examine specific institutions at the point where they appear in the documents. For now, it is sufficient to note that the government of Louis XIV was superimposed on a complex, preexisting society
comprising many overlapping power centers. Without going into too
much detail, we need to understand those social forces and their relationship to the king.

THE LANDED NOBILITY

The backbone of society was the landed nobility. France had a predominantly agrarian economy in which a large percentage of the wealth was
produced by peasants living clustered in villages and working relatively
small plots of land. Their labors, directly or indirectly, were the source of

---

domain (property) could not be sold off (alienated); and (3) the idea that the king should
uphold the Catholic faith.

much of the wealth of the nobility. Most nobles were lords *(seigneurs)* over estates called *seigneuries,* which included ownership of land and also a bundle of rights over local peasants within their jurisdiction and the ability to collect various fees and revenues. These assets, which varied tremendously in value and scope, sometimes included the authority to collect certain seigneurial dues from the inhabitants, judge disputes in their own seigneurial courts, and make political and economic decisions about the life of the village. The lands a lord personally owned were usually rented out to local villagers in relatively small plots to supplement the peasants' own inadequate holdings. Seigneuries thus represented a bundle of possible revenues. They also represented a source of prestige in that being "lord" over persons was highly regarded, and as the most influential citizen in the community, a lord was the man with money to lend, contacts with outside authorities to invoke, and the power to judge local disputes. To top off this already advantageous situation, persons who were legally noble also received special recognition from society in the form of exemption from the basic land tax, the *taille,*[3] along with exemption from the lodging of troops, special treatment in the courts, and other honorific privileges designed to set them apart from the rest of rural society.

Nobles had traditionally lived on their estates and ruled "their" local villages, but by the seventeenth century this dominant position had been greatly eroded, since most peasants had become rent-paying tenants rather than unfree serfs. Traditional revenues had declined relative to inflation. Many nobles became absentee landlords, who limited their involvement to renting out their land and rights and collecting the revenues. The estates back home nevertheless produced much of the nobles' income and enhanced their family pedigrees. Poor nobles owned small properties in one or two locations and exerted only local influence, whereas the great families owned vast properties scattered over many provinces and had potentially vast regional power.

The nobles were generally regarded as a superior race. To their traditional reputation as those who excelled in warfare, valor, and command over men (and who in reality enjoyed agricultural revenues without having to farm themselves), the greatest of these men had been

---

[3]The *taille* was the king's direct tax, established in the fourteenth and fifteenth centuries. It was levied on the revenues of land and some other revenues. Many groups, notably the nobility and the clergy, were exempt. The taille was collected without anyone's consent. Each year the desired total was established in the royal council and divided among the tax districts of France (and, within each district, among the villages or communities) by royal officers according to various standard procedures. The villagers themselves were then required to raise the requisite sum by apportioning it among themselves. Thus the amount of the taille was not directly determined by the taxpayers' ability to pay.

adding since the Renaissance a new identity as cultivated taste-setters and courtiers. Politically, the nobility was considered to be the second "estate" of the realm (the first being the clergy), and when the king summoned the national consultative body, the Estates-General, or held meetings of provincial estates, the nobles had the right to participate as such.[4]

But outside these bodies, the estate of the nobility had no ongoing corporate organization to express its interests and no right to assemble unless summoned by the king. Informally, however, the nobles could be a powerful force. The more successful families had maintained political influence through their networks of personal connections. The better-placed regional nobles did favors for the followers below them and provided links to the great nobles at court above them. Well-connected nobles also received fiscal advantages and grants of all sorts from the state: military commissions, pensions, or appointments to posts that conferred influence over local patronage. Such posts might include governorships and lieutenancies of provinces, governorships of towns and fortifications, or the lesser judicial posts of *bailli* and *seneschal*.[5] Great nobles might control vast wealth and have bands of loyal followers in key positions in the provinces where they served as governors. When such grandees[6] could also wield influence at court, they could become almost as powerful as the king, and when several such client networks clashed with one another, there was great potential for civil war.

THE ROBE NOBILITY

The second force the king had to contend with was the robe nobility. Through the centuries, the crown had made an effort to establish better

[4] The Estates-General was the national assembly of France, called by the king in times of emergency to approve proposals for special taxes or programs of reform. It consisted of three chambers that met separately — that of the clergy, or first estate; that of the nobility, or second estate; and that of the third estate, which consisted mostly of the representatives of town governments. Kings were not required to summon Estates-Generals, and these assemblies did not pass legislation. They were mostly occasions to discuss serious problems with leading notables in hopes of influencing opinion. No Estates-General met in France between 1614 and 1789.

[5] A *bailli* was a royal officer who presided over the *bailliage* court. A *seneschal* was a royal officer who presided over the *sénéchaussée* court. These two terms were used to refer to the same kind of court in different parts of France. They were regional courts of appeals for a district the size of a county, from which further appeals went to the parlement. The *bailli* or *seneschal* was traditionally a nobleman with local influence who also served as a military commander in times of danger.

[6] The term *grandee* has been borrowed from Spanish history. It refers to the great landed and titled nobility, members of the important families with places at court and important positions in the government.

control in each province by creating companies of royal officers to carry out the two essential functions of justice and taxation. Royal officeholders were usually local figures with powerful connections, but by the seventeenth century they acted in the king's name and thus had more interest in defending royal policies. The monarchy did not have the resources to pay a salary to a corps of civil servants, however, so the distinctive system of *venality of office,* whereby official posts were sold for life, was developed. By the seventeenth century, the major offices in Paris and the provinces were owned by prominent individuals who, in return for putting up substantial sums of money and holding the posts for a period of years, received noble status for themselves and their descendants. Payment of an annual fee called the *paulette* guaranteed them the right to bequeath or sell the office, by then a valuable part of the family fortune, to another party, usually upon the death of the incumbent.

The impact of venality was tremendous. By selling offices in regional bodies to rich local citizens, the crown had in effect created a new kind of property: ownership of the right to exercise the king's authority and borrow some of his prestige. In addition, officeholding provided a new avenue of social mobility for rich commoners: Buy a high office, and you could join the nobility, enjoy exemption from the taille, and enter the privileged elite with your family. Thus was born the robe nobility, so called because these men wore long professional robes when performing their duties. They were distinguished from the traditional nobles, often called the sword nobility, by the fact that they were professionally trained and derived their nobility from their function, not from an ancient pedigree or from a title bestowed on them by the crown.

For the king, the sale of offices had advantages and disadvantages. On the one hand, by drawing many of the richest families in a given region into royal service, the government had created a whole new body of individuals whose fundamental interests lay on the side of the state. Selling them offices was a way of tapping their wealth, which tended to originate in commerce or finance. Purchasing an office was like giving the crown a large sum as a permanent loan. In return, the officer received a small annual stipend *(gages)* that was like an interest payment. On the other hand, venality drew these same people away from productive employment in business, making them part of the undertaxed privileged elite and creating a collegial body of virtually irremovable, powerful figures who might well defend their own interests, even when these clashed with royal policies. In the best of times, the companies of robe nobles would be more loyal to the king than the old feudal nobility; in the worst of times, they would provide another focal point for agitation and resistance.

The most prominent robe nobles were the judges of the Parlement of Paris and the eleven parlements of the various provinces, each of which consisted of an imposing group of some two hundred judges in Paris and fifty to one hundred in the provinces. These parlements must not be confused with the English Parliament, for they were high courts of law with no capacity to initiate legislation, and the judges held office permanently rather than being elected periodically. The parlements, and especially the Parlement of Paris, whose district covered more than one-third of France, were politically significant bodies in three important ways.

First, their judges belonged to powerful dynasties of robe families with connections in government and financial circles, and their legal decisions greatly affected the interests of the greatest families of the realm.

Second, like all old-regime courts, the parlements had considerable authority to regulate public functions and apply the laws. Parlements issued *arrêts* (decrees) concerning the implementation of existing laws and the maintenance of public order; they were thus players in day-to-day government and rivals to other administrative authorities, such as the governor or the intendant.

Third, the parlements registered the king's edicts and ordinances in their books to make them enforceable. This gave them the capacity to delay legislation or petition the king for changes in it. They had no veto power. If the king disagreed with them, he would respond with a *lit de justice,* literally a "bed of justice," in which he paid a personal visit to the court and commanded it to register the legislation without delay.[7] But if the king was weak, the judges could place obstacles in his path and make principled appeals for justice that might affect a wider audience outside the court.

Throughout France, the companies of important royal officers constituted a significant vested interest. Besides these eleven parlements, there were about twenty-five other sovereign courts with more specialized functions and a whole range of financial officers, managers of the royal domain, and various treasurers and receivers responsible for handling the king's revenues.[8] In all, some three thousand to four thousand

---

[7] A *lit de justice* was a royal session of a parlement attended by the king. Since the court was an emanation of his authority, it could not refuse to obey his direct command. In provincial parlements, the king often sent written orders, or *lettres de jussion,* instead of appearing in person.

[8] Including Paris, there were thirteen *cours des aides,* which handled appeals of disputes involving taxation, and twelve *chambres des comptes,* which audited the accounts of royal officers. Many of these courts were joined together or merged with parlements. All these courts were called *sovereign* because they represented the highest court of appeals short

royal offices conferred nobility on their holders, and there were thousands of lesser posts that did not. These robe nobles were looked down upon by the greatest landed families as new arrivals, but they were educated men who knew how to argue legal cases, keep accounts, and organize administrative operations. And they were the ones who monitored much of the routine business of government, all the while looking out for the interests of their regions and themselves.

THE ROYAL COMMISSIONERS

In the seventeenth century, the king began to invent ways of getting around the slow, often self-serving, procedures of his officers. One method was co-option. At the top of the robe hierarchy were men who left their companies to serve the king directly by becoming royal councillors, executing special commissions, or serving as ministers of the king. Posts like these in the central administration had traditionally been held by great nobles and royal family members, but Louis XIV made a point of restricting most governmental functions to legal and administrative experts who came, mostly, from wealthy robe families.[9] Issuing special orders, or commissions, to loyal agents to go to a particular place and see that a specific action was carried out in a particular way became common practice. When these men exercised their special delegated authority in the provinces, they exasperated the regular officers whose jurisdiction was violated. Such missions were the beginning of what can be called an administrative monarchy, the clearest expression of the king's absolute authority to act independently of traditional procedures.

By the 1660s, it was customary to assign commissioners as *intendants*[10] to particular provinces for a period of years. Their job was to act as administrative agents for the ministers at court, collecting information, troubleshooting, and intervening with the regular authorities

---

of the king and his council. These courts were distributed throughout the provinces in a pattern that owed more to historical accident than to deliberate planning.

[9] Many of these agents started by acquiring a venal office called *master of requests (maître des requêtes)*. The company of one hundred masters of requests judged certain kinds of cases that came before the royal council and prepared the materials that were discussed in council meetings. This office was a step toward higher positions in the king's government.

[10] Intendants were royal agents, usually drawn from the company of masters of requests, who were issued a commission to oversee specific operations in a province. Since their commissions were temporary and subject to revocation (unlike venal offices) and their careers were dependent on service satisfactory to the king, they provided a more effective means to implement the instructions of the central government and a vital source of information about provincial conditions.

to see that the king's wishes were carried out. They reported regularly back to their counterparts in the royal administration, producing archives full of letters and reports and providing a base of information that could be used by ministers like Colbert in thinking about the reorganization of national resources. In chapter 5, we will examine a number of these documents.

THE CATHOLIC CHURCH

The third force that the king contended with was the Catholic Church. The church was not really one organization but many. It consisted of an administrative hierarchy of some eighteen archbishops and more than a hundred bishops, each of whom had a cathedral, an episcopal palace, church courts with jurisdictions over certain kinds of offenses, a chapter of resident priests (called cathedral canons), and an endowment consisting of revenue-producing property. Under these bishops were some forty thousand parishes with their various categories of priests, appointed in many cases by church foundations or private individuals. In addition, there were many orders of monks and nuns with their own religious houses and endowments, as well as various kinds of international connections.

The church was a formidable institution for several reasons. First, it represented an information network reaching from the centers of power into every parish church in France — the only such network that existed for communicating with the population. For example, in emergencies local priests could be induced to make announcements from the pulpit. Second, the church was immensely wealthy, and most of its highest posts were filled with well-connected individuals from the most influential noble families, all of whom held their positions for life. In addition to the revenues from its endowment, the church collected its own agricultural tax, the tithe *(dîme)*,[11] which was an assessment of roughly one-twelfth of the harvest, payable in kind by anyone who worked the soil. The tithe was thus a major tax on production. Most of its yield was appropriated by monasteries, cathedral canons, and the church hierar-

---

[11] The tithe, firmly established since the eighth century, was the church tax collected on all crops produced on the land and all newborn animals. Theoretically a tenth of the yield, it varied widely around that figure, and there were infinite local variations as to what was taxed at what rate. The tithe was collected in kind, right in the fields at harvesttime. It was supposed to be used to support the local priests, maintain the church buildings, and help the poor. In reality, most of the revenue from it was appropriated by bishops, cathedral chapters, monasteries, and sometimes even laymen.

chy — organizations which, as a result, had attics full of grain to sell — and very little of it went to support parish churches and their priests. Third, the church was a repository of holiness and the interpreter of God's will in a society where the king claimed to be God's direct agent. Fourth, the church was an international institution whose spiritual leader was the pope in Rome, another man beyond the direct control of the monarchy, who also saw himself as God's direct agent on earth, setting up an obvious source of potential conflicts, which we will explore in chapter 7.

The monarchy's response to this external source of authority was to assert the autonomy of the French church from Rome and to try to control it. The so-called Gallican, or French, church had always claimed a certain autonomy and the ability to manage its own affairs. The kings sided alternately with the Gallican church or the pope as it served their interests. In the Concordat of 1516, a treaty with the pope signed by King Francis I, the king gained additional influence at the expense of Gallican independence. He acquired the right to fill vacancies in almost all the high church posts in France, while the pope would ratify and install those selected. The result was an immense opportunity for patronage, which was used by the monarchy to reward the great families of the realm and sometimes, especially in the seventeenth century, to encourage church reform. Although this was a way to take advantage of the wealth of the church, the fact remained that once those favored by the king became bishops, they acquired a great deal of independence. The clergy, like the nobility, was exempt from the taille, subject to special legal arrangements, and largely irremovable. As the first estate of the realm, the church was always represented in the Estates-General and bishops were immensely influential in several provincial estates. Even though the king controlled its appointments, the church in France remained an autonomous organism with considerable power to mold opinion and obstruct measures it disliked.

In Louis XIV's time, a major preoccupation was the continuing existence of Protestant (Calvinist, often called Huguenot) churches, which had been authorized after the religious wars by the Edict of Nantes in 1598. Louis XIII had removed their military powers and restricted their rights somewhat, but they retained the freedom to hold worship services in designated locations, to maintain their organizational structure of local consistories and regional synods, to enjoy civil rights, and to have special protections in judicial cases. Eliminating this religious minority was a major goal of the bishops and much of the Catholic population as well. We will explore this issue in chapter 7.

THE URBAN BOURGEOISIE

The king also had to consider his relations with what we might loosely call the bourgeoisie — those subjects who were not peasants, nobles, or priests and who generally lived in towns and practiced professional, mercantile, or craft skills. This was a diverse group. The bourgeoisie in the sense of a capitalist, profit-seeking class was not highly developed in France. To be sure, every town had artisans who plied a great variety of trades, usually in small shops where they employed a few journeymen and apprentices and ran family businesses using techniques carefully regulated by their trade associations (*métiers,* or "guilds").[12] Some cities had export industries, such as Lyon's silk-weaving industry. In the most advanced cases, their merchants organized the production process by importing raw materials and passing them through a series of stages carried out by urban or rural artisans in their own shops, after which the merchant arranged for the sale of the finished product. This was called the *putting-out* system. France exported some grains, at least in good harvest years, and substantial amounts of wine, plus smaller quantities of luxury goods such as tapestries and books. The French also imported spices, Italian fabrics, and many raw materials. These import-export operations required merchants with the knowledge and the wherewithal to organize long-term movements of goods and credit. In Atlantic port cities such as Bordeaux and Nantes, trade with the French colonies in America and the Atlantic world was beginning to be important, and in Marseilles trade with the Levant (Middle East) was a major operation.

Nevertheless, much of this activity was small-scale and localized. France was a country of diverse regions, whose cities often competed with one another and jealously held on to traditional techniques. Tolls on roads and rivers kept transit costs high. The wide dispersal of agricultural products required a great many local markets, most of which had their own weights and measures. The cities were small, separate worlds contained within defensible walls, and each had its own governing traditions. French mercantile interests were consequently fragmented, localized, and technologically conventional. The king had a real opportunity here to develop the economy by unifying markets, promot-

---

[12] Guilds were associations of all the masters plying a certain trade in a given town, such as barrel makers, silk weavers, or bakers. They usually operated according to statutes that granted them the exclusive right to exercise that trade in that locality, along with the right to police the members to be sure they adhered to standard procedures and pricing policies. The masters also regulated the training of apprentices and journeymen and controlled the admission of new masters.

ing competitive foreign trade, and standardizing taxes and units of measure. But these activities were not likely to appeal very much to a king like Louis XIV, who focused instead on aristocratic status and military glory.

Moreover, two counterinfluences made bourgeois activities less appealing than they might seem. First was the appeal of royal office. Those who made fortunes in urban pursuits saw that by buying an office for themselves or their children, they might attain a safer, more prestigious form of social mobility that would lead to political influence, noble status, and tax exemption. Merchant trading, by contrast, was riskier and less respected. The second counterinfluence was the attraction of royal finance.

In the years before 1661, the cost of the Thirty Years' War in Germany had caused Cardinals Richelieu and Mazarin to raise taxes to unprecedented heights. Not only did the taille paid by the peasants double and triple, but towns were forced to increase indirect taxes on basic commodities in order to raise the large sums demanded by the king. In addition, all sorts of new fees and surcharges were levied on guilds, corporate groups, and individuals, even as the crown mortgaged its revenues and coerced its officeholders into lending the king large sums. On the one hand, this abrasive taxation angered almost every sector of French society, causing the tensions that led to the rebellion of the Fronde (see chapter 1). On the other hand, because of the insecurity of the king's credit, the funding of the royal enterprise at high rates of interest became the largest "business" in France. Financiers, backed by investments from a wide circle of royal officers and court nobles, advanced the money to the king, using anticipated tax revenues as security. "Tax farmers" contracted to pay a large sum in advance for the right to collect some new lucrative tax using their own agents. Enormous fortunes were made, and it became clear that there was more profit in managing the royal tax and credit flows than there was in risky merchant ventures. So merchant money was diverted into royal offices and into financial deals with the crown, with the same parties often involved in both, to the detriment of real economic development.

Thus the king's relationship with the bourgeoisie was ambiguous. The cities of France — with their trade guilds, merchant enterprises, and markets of all kinds — were the source of considerable wealth and expertise, but they were too diverse and too geographically separated to be able to organize any concerted effort to influence the government at the national level. It would be advantageous for the king to promote their wealth, reduce barriers to economic growth, and develop foreign trade — and at times such efforts, called *mercantilism,* were made under Louis XIV. But a more obvious and attractive option was to take advantage of the fact that the cities were vulnerable to exploitation by the crown in the form of fees for the regulation of guilds, taxes on artisans and markets, and interventions in municipal affairs, usually for money. Faced with the choice of developing the bourgeoisie or taking advantage of it, the king was more likely to take the latter course. Thus he co-opted much of the wealth and economic initiative through sale of office and involvement in royal finance.

THE LOWER CLASSES

Finally, the king had to consider the fate of the masses of the population, the vast majority of peasants in villages, small craftsmen and laborers in cities, and their wives and families. Their position was precarious. While nobles, clergy, and many of the inhabitants of major cities were all exempt from the taille paid by the peasants, these groups in turn collected their own rents and tithes from the same peasants. In the cities, most indirect taxes hit poor consumers the hardest because they were levied on basic commodities such as meat, wine, salt, and market transactions. As we have seen, a significant portion of these taxes never reached the king because money was siphoned off to collection agents and financiers along the way. The funds that did reach the king were spent on warfare, including noble military commanders; the costs of the court, which partly supported the great nobility; interest payments to financiers; stipends to royal officers; and pensions to loyal followers. This process is explored in chapter 3. In a sense, then, the king, his officers, the great nobility, and the clergy were living off the labors of the rest of the population, and the burden of their exactions had increased markedly in the half-century before 1661.

There was no danger of general rebellion from below because the people affected were isolated in their towns and villages. And though each group could rage against a particular burden affecting them, none could analyze the larger picture or come up with an alternative interpretation, unless it was to say that the king's evil advisers should be fired or that oppressive innovations should be eliminated. We should not conclude, however, that the population was passive or unable to make a difference. The first half of the seventeenth century, and to a lesser extent the reign of Louis XIV, was characterized by waves of very serious uprisings in which particular rural or urban populations organized rebellions against those who were exploiting them — agents of tax farmers, royal agents, city officials, grasping financiers — and punished them by threatening bodily harm, pillaging their houses, ripping up their authorizations, chasing them out of town, and sometimes mutilating and killing them. There were hundreds of urban riots during this period, some of which disrupted normal life for days. There were also large-scale rural uprisings — for example, in 1624, 1636, 1639, 1658, 1662, 1675, and 1707 — in which armies of peasants from particular regions fought royal troops. These events genuinely disrupted normal governmental activities and sent a clear message to the ruling authorities that enough was enough and that the authorities would be held accountable for bad treatment. We will encounter some of these events in chapter 6.

This book concentrates on the earlier years of Louis XIV's personal rule. Because we are analyzing his relationships with the various groups in society, we are not looking at his foreign policy. It is worth remembering, however, that the backdrop to this story was warfare. Louis was at heart a military man who wanted his armies to achieve glory in battle and who was determined to make France the greatest power in Europe. To a large extent he succeeded, but at enormous cost. His armies numbered as many as 390,000 at their peak. He fought increasingly massive wars, by the end of his reign holding off most of the other powers of Europe: the War of Devolution (1667–68), the Dutch War (1672–78), the Nine Years' War (1688–97), and the War of the Spanish Succession (1701–14). These wars, along with other lesser campaigns, drained the resources of society, causing severe strains by the end of Louis's reign.

In ruling his kingdom, Louis XIV had to think about conciliating a class of traditional sword nobles with independent landed wealth and enormous prestige, companies of powerful robe nobles whose cooperation was indispensable to effective government, a church hierarchy with independent sources of revenue and international connections, a group of dependent but indispensable financiers, and to some extent the other citizens of revenue-producing towns. He did not have to conciliate the masses, but he had to be careful not to goad them into disruptive rebellion. Most important, he had to watch out for measures that might bring any of these parties together through common grievances. During the reign of Louis XIII and the youth of Louis XIV, every one of these groups had been greatly antagonized and most of them had engaged in some kind of resistance. When Louis came to personal power in 1661, he brought with him memories of his turbulent youth and a determination to restore order and stability by forcing all these groups back into their appropriate places.

A NOTE ABOUT THE TEXT

The documents in this volume are designed to illustrate Louis's relationships with these groups. Whenever possible, I have tried to select descriptive sources, some of them unusual, that bring the people and issues to life by connecting them to actual experiences. Each chapter illustrates a particular aspect of Louis XIV's rule. But instead of trying to cover every topic systematically, which would have required overloading the book with short quotations from many different documents, I have provided longer sets of materials, arranged chronologically within each section. I hope this method will enable you to draw a variety of conclusions from the documents, using evidence that is not entirely predigested. I would like these sources to engage your interest and bring you closer to this unfamiliar era.

The translations are my own, except where indicated. In trying to produce an easily readable text, I have not hesitated to simplify sentences, eliminate redundant phrases, and cut down on the number of formal courtesies that were so dear to contemporaries. Scholars wishing to capture every nuance should refer to the original French.

PART TWO

The Documents

KEY
- pays d'états
- pays d'élections
- Jurisdiction of the Parlement of Paris
- ○ Seats of Parlements

France under Louis XIV

1

Confronting French Society during the Fronde

When Louis XIV assumed personal power in 1661, he was conscious of the fact that the French monarchy had faced rough times for much of the previous century. After the accidental death of Henry II in 1559, the country had been plunged into a series of religious wars in which Protestant and Catholic factions led by great nobles with regional power bases had struggled to control a weak central government presided over by an unpopular foreign queen from Italy, Catherine de Médicis. After the assassination of Henry III in 1589, Henry IV, the first king from the Bourbon branch of the Capetian line, began a restoration of authority, only to be assassinated himself in 1610. Henry IV was a Protestant turned Catholic who began to rebuild the authority of the crown by conciliating the towns and the great nobles and granting limited toleration for Protestants in the Edict of Nantes (1598). In 1610 Henry's death left the throne in the hands of his nine-year-old son, Louis XIII, and the government under the control of the king's mother, Marie de Médicis, another unpopular Italian who was named regent on behalf of her son. The following years were punctuated by sporadic rebellions of the greatest princes of the realm, often led by the prince of Condé, leader of the junior branch of the Bourbon family. There were also rebellions by Protestants who feared the erosion of their rights.

When Louis XIII took power, his authority was undermined for a long time by the lack of a male heir and by his less-than-commanding personality. However, he placed his trust in a talented first minister, Armand-Jean du Plessis, Cardinal Richelieu, a brilliant statesman from a prominent provincial noble family who set out to assert France's power in Europe while strengthening the king's authority. Richelieu's foreign policy was ultimately successful, but at the cost of constant warfare from 1635 to 1659 and the postponement of his plans for internal reform.

These problems provided the setting for the *Fronde,* a complicated civil war that broke out between 1648 and 1653. It is not important for us

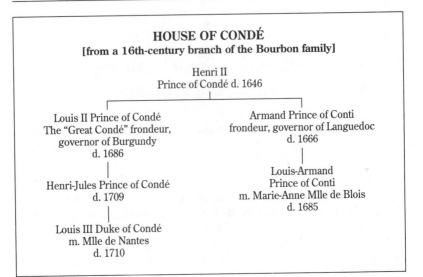

HOUSE OF CONDÉ
[from a 16th-century branch of the Bourbon family]

Henri II
Prince of Condé d. 1646

Louis II Prince of Condé
The "Great Condé" frondeur,
governor of Burgundy
d. 1686

Armand Prince of Conti
frondeur, governor of Languedoc
d. 1666

Henri-Jules Prince of Condé
d. 1709

Louis-Armand
Prince of Conti
m. Marie-Anne Mlle de Blois
d. 1685

Louis III Duke of Condé
m. Mlle de Nantes
d. 1710

to understand all the twists and turns of this confusing series of events, in which rebellions were sporadic and the principal players kept changing sides, but the fundamental conflicts underlying the Fronde illustrate the problems Louis XIV had to solve if he was to become an effective ruler. The Fronde was the formative experience of the Sun King's youth, a lesson he never forgot. Every segment of the population was affected. The Thirty Years' War against the Holy Roman Emperor and Spain led to an unprecedented increase in the basic taxes paid by ordinary subjects. Aggressive tax farmers, who pocketed large sums by levying special excise taxes and fees on behalf of the crown, were widely viewed as leeches sucking the lifeblood from honest citizens for their own profit. Genuine popular discontent provided fertile ground for elite leaders who were equally unhappy, but for different reasons. The judges in the royal parlements were threatened by the creation of new offices in their companies, and their judicial authority was challenged by the interventions of intendants and the rulings of the royal council. The grandees — the heads of the great noble families, including the royal family — felt slighted at seeing a reclusive cardinal exercising authority that they thought should rightfully be theirs.

When Richelieu died in 1642, followed in 1643 by Louis XIII, all these problems got worse. France was once again ruled by a minor king, as Louis XIV was not quite five years old when his father died, and once

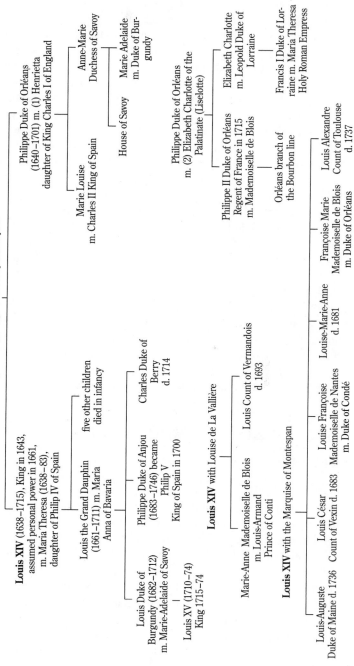

THE ROYAL FAMILY

Louis XIII (1601–43) m. Anne of Austria (1601–66), daughter of Philip III of Spain

Louis XIV (1638–1715), King in 1643, assumed personal power in 1661, m. Maria Theresa (1638–83), daughter of Philip IV of Spain

Louis the Grand Dauphin (1661–1711) m. Maria Anna of Bavaria

Louis Duke of Burgundy (1682–1712) m. Marie-Adelaide of Savoy

Louis XV (1710–74) King 1715–74

Philippe Duke of Anjou (1683–1746) became Philip V King of Spain in 1700

five other children died in infancy

Charles Duke of Berry d. 1714

Louis XIV with Louise de La Vallière

Marie-Anne Mademoiselle de Blois m. Louis-Armand Prince of Conti

Louis Count of Vermandois d. 1693

Louis XIV with the Marquise of Montespan

Louis-Auguste Duke of Maine d. 1736

Louis César Count of Vexin d. 1683

Louise Françoise Mademoiselle de Nantes m. Duke of Condé

Louise-Marie-Anne d. 1681

Françoise Marie Mademoiselle de Blois m. Duke of Orléans

Louis Alexandre Count of Toulouse d. 1737

Philippe Duke of Orléans (1640–1701) m. (1) Henrietta daughter of King Charles I of England

Marie Louise m. Charles II King of Spain

Anne-Marie Duchess of Savoy

House of Savoy

Marie Adelaide m. Duke of Burgundy

Philippe Duke of Orléans m. (2) Elizabeth Charlotte of the Palatinate (Liselotte)

Philippe II Duke of Orléans Regent of France in 1715 m. Mademoiselle de Blois

Elizabeth Charlotte m. Leopold Duke of Lorraine

Orléans branch of the Bourbon line

Francis I Duke of Lorraine m. Maria Theresa Holy Roman Empress

21

again the government was in the hands of a foreign regent, Louis's mother, Anne of Austria, who was Spanish by birth. She came to rely completely on another foreigner, an Italian diplomat named Giulio Mazarini (Jules Mazarin), who had come to France as an envoy of the pope and became a protégé of Cardinal Richelieu. Most historians give Cardinal Mazarin credit for running the government loyally on behalf of the young Louis XIV and his mother, but the cardinal's reputation with the French people sank so low that it endangered the regency. The French could not understand why their country was dominated by a foreign woman and a foreign cardinal, who were believed to be having illicit sexual relations, while the war went on interminably, great nobles and officers were thrust aside, and grasping financiers, closely tied to Mazarin, seemed to rule the day.

This first set of sources highlight the kinds of unrest that would face Louis XIV if he failed to rule effectively. During the years of the Fronde, many individuals and groups were agitating more or less concurrently. If popular crowds, parlements, and grandees could have united around a common program, they might have moved France away from absolutism by instituting some sort of check on the monarchy. As it happened, they rose at different times and places and with a variety of objectives. Still, they provided powerful lessons in the dangers that could exist when disaffected leaders joined forces with popular crowds. The Fronde was a threat to royal power precisely because so many groups were agitating in so many ways. It represented the unraveling of the social ties that bound the polity. Louis XIV would have to weave them back together.

PARIS REBELS AGAINST THE CROWN

The trouble that broke out in Paris in 1648 was the culmination of years of exasperation on the part of the judges in the parlements and other sovereign courts. These judges had seen Mazarin reduce their fees; create new chambers, which diluted the value of their offices; and impinge on their vast regulatory power through the use of royal intendants. Mazarin tried to keep the Paris Parlement loyal by granting it special advantages not given to the other Parisian courts or their provincial counterparts. But the cumulative effect of new taxes on Parisian citizens and new restrictions on the offices of robe officers finally led the judges to act. In early 1648, they began vigorously opposing new Parisian tariffs, thereby endearing themselves to the common citizenry. Then in May the Parlement, led by a much-respected elderly judge named Broussel, joined the other Parisian courts in setting up a joint session, the Chamber of Saint Louis, during which their deputies issued an ultimatum to the government in the form of a list of twenty-seven demands. (It was unprecedented for the Parisian courts to form a committee that criticized the king's policies.) Perhaps the most notable demands were that the king should lower the basic taille by one-fourth, limit special taxes and regulate the financiers who profited from them, abolish the use of intendants, and let the courts audit the royal accounts. These demands were both an expression of self-interest and a declaration of lack of confidence in the government. They were emergency demands, which were not really intended as a constitutional challenge to the crown. But they were wildly popular in the streets of Paris, and the government, with its troops tied up on the frontier, felt obliged to offer conciliatory gestures to maintain order. In August, when the news arrived that the prince of Condé[1] had won a notable victory over the Spanish at the Battle of Lens, Louis XIV's mother, the regent Anne of Austria, decided to use the occasion of the celebrations in Paris to punish this attempt by the Parisian judges to meddle in the affairs of the government. The events that followed are narrated by Madame de Motteville, one of the queen's ladies-in-waiting, who was at court during these events. Her account reflects the perspective of the people at court. Note the way the Parlement interacts with the Parisian crowds, and the way the latter — consisting of groups of artisans, workers, and their wives — intervene in these events. Note especially the deterioration of respect for authorities and the humiliation suffered by some of the king's most distinguished ministers.

---

[1] Louis II of Bourbon, prince of Condé (1621–1686), will appear often in these accounts. The Condés were the younger branch of the Bourbon family, and thus in line to inherit the throne after Louis XIV's brother and uncle. In 1648 the prince of Condé, just seventeen years old, was already establishing a reputation as one of France's great generals. During the Fronde, he started out supporting the crown, but he was later imprisoned by Mazarin. When he was released, he went into rebellion and, when his cause was lost, fled to Spain. As we will see, he was eventually pardoned and returned to serve Louis XIV.

Madame de Motteville's Account of the
Parisian Disturbances in August 1648

Wishing to have a Te Deum[2] service sung at Notre Dame[3] to thank the Lord for this great victory and to present the enemy's conquered banners to the cathedral, the queen decided to take advantage of this day of triumph to solve the problem of the rebellion of the Parlement and punish it for its recent disobedience, which was viewed by everyone as an attempt to conceal criminal boldness behind the false appearance of loyalty. With the approval of the duke of Orléans [the king's uncle] and the Minister [Cardinal Mazarin], she commanded Comminges, the lieutenant of her guards, to arrest President Blancmesnil, President Charton, and above all a councillor named Broussel who had persistently raised the standard of rebellion against the king and initiated discussions that tended to undermine the royal authority.[4] He had made himself the mouthpiece of the people, continually showing the spirit of a man born in a republic and expressing the sentiments of a veritable Roman. . . .

Comminges sent his carriage with four of his guards and a lieutenant to the end of Broussel's narrow street with orders that as soon as Comminges appeared on foot outside the house, this lieutenant should drive the carriage up to the door with the curtains drawn and the steps down. . . . Comminges took possession of the entryway and, leaving two guards there, took two others upstairs with him to Broussel's apartment, where he found Broussel finishing his dinner, surrounded by his family. Comminges told Broussel that he was the bearer of an order from the king for his arrest, but that if he preferred to avoid the discomfort of hearing it read out loud, he had only to follow and obey. This man, more than sixty years old, was troubled to hear the name of the king used this way. . . . He replied that he was not in a condition to obey because he was under medication and needed more time. An old woman of the house be-

---

[2] A Te Deum was a special Mass celebrated to thank God for a military victory or some other notable event.

[3] Notre Dame is the cathedral of Paris.

[4] René Potier de Blancmesnil and Louis Charton were presidents in the Parlement of Paris. Pierre Broussel was a councillor in the same court. These three men were held responsible for the trouble the Parlement had been causing for the queen and Mazarin.

Madame de Motteville, *Mémoires de Madame de Motteville sur Anne d'Autriche et sa cour,* new. ed. (Paris: Bibliothèque Charpentier, 1886), 2:152–70.

gan calling to the neighbors for help, shouting that they were trying to take away her master and showering Comminges with a thousand insults. . . . Hearing this woman's noise, people began collecting in the streets: The first who ran up brought others, and in an instant the street was filled with rabble. When they saw the carriage filled with arms and men, they all began shouting that their "liberator" was being taken away. Some tried to cut the reins of the horses, and others spoke of smashing the carriage, but the guards and Comminges's small page defended it valiantly, threatening to kill anyone who would try anything.

Hearing the noise, Comminges realized that there would be disorder if he delayed any longer. He grabbed Broussel, threatening to kill him if he didn't march, dragged him away from the embraces of his family, and threw him into the carriage whether he liked it or not, with the guards walking in front to hold back the people who were threatening to attack. At this news, chains went up in the streets, and Comminges was stopped at the first blockade. To escape, he kept having to turn the carriage this way and that to fend off the crowds, which were increasing the farther they went. By sheer effort he finally arrived opposite the First President's [head of the Parlement's] house on the quai, and there his carriage turned over and broke. He would have been lost if some soldiers from the regiment of the royal guards hadn't been stationed there with orders to lend him support. He leaped out of the overturned carriage, and finding himself surrounded by enemies who wanted to tear him to pieces with only three or four guards to save his life, he shouted, "To arms, comrades, to the rescue!" The soldiers, who were steadfastly faithful to the king, surrounded him and gave him all the support they could. The crowd surrounded him, too, with very different intentions, and the struggle of fists and insults that followed could have been just as dangerous for the state as one involving steel and gunfire. Comminges held out for quite a while until one of his guards brought up another carriage. . . . As he left, his own carriage was being torn into a thousand pieces by the people out of rage and spite. . . .

When the Parisians had lost sight of their Broussel, they started shouting in the streets like convicts that all was lost, that they wanted their "protector" back, and they would gladly die on his behalf. They assembled in groups, hung chains across the streets, and in a few hours had built barricades in every quarter of the city. Warned of this disorder, the queen sent Marshal La Meilleraye[5] out to calm the people and re-

[5] Charles de la Porte, also known as the duke of La Meilleraye and marshal of France, was military commander of a regiment of cavalry. He was also the cousin of Cardinal Richelieu and had been named to an important financial post in the queen's government.

mind them of their duty. The coadjutor of Paris [the future Cardinal of Retz[6]] was also sent out. . . . The people acted respectfully toward him, but they rejected his reminder that they owed loyalty to the king, constantly calling for their "protector" and insisting that they would never calm down until he was returned. And without considering the duty they owed to Marshal La Meilleraye, they threw rocks at him, assaulting him with a thousand insults, and uttering horrible curses against the queen and her minister. . . .

This same day the First President, upon hearing about the exiles, came to meet with the queen and ask for their release, but she sent him away without an answer. The people, suspecting that he had struck a deal with the court, went to his house. Some enraged rascals shouted insistently that he was a traitor who had sold out his company [the Parlement], so to calm them down he felt obligated to go out on foot and justify himself to these mutineers. Without such a demonstration of firmness they might have gone even further in their insolence. His gentleness calmed their fury, and they accepted his justifications on condition that he go back and appeal again on behalf of Broussel. This he did, with just as little success as the first time.

The next day Chancellor Séguier [the king's top judicial minister] was ordered to go to the *palais de justice* [Seat of the Parlement] and preside over the Parlement to calm people's nerves and fend off disorder, as decided in the council meeting the day before. This uprising had alarmed everyone, and friends of the chancellor told him that his mission seemed infinitely dangerous. . . . He departed at five in the morning for the palais de justice, or more accurately, he left his house with the intention of going there. . . . When he was on the Pont Neuf bridge, three or four tall scoundrels came up to the carriage and insolently asked him to return the prisoner [Broussel], saying that if he didn't do it they would kill him that very hour. Once these desperate men had started an uproar, others arrived, surrounded the carriage, and threatened the same thing.

Not knowing what to do to escape from this rabble, Chancellor Séguier ordered his coachman to drive toward the Augustins monastery, where the house of his friend the duke of Luynes was located, so that he could take refuge inside if he was stopped by the multitude, or proceed on a safer route to the Palais via the Notre Dame bridge, for he believed that the good bourgeois would not let these mutineers pillage him. When he had arrived in front of the Augustins, the crowd had begun to

---

[6] Jean-François-Paul de Gondi, soon to be Cardinal of Retz, was the stand-in (coadjutor) bishop of Paris. An ambitious man, he played a major role in the intrigues of the Fronde and wrote memoirs describing his experiences.

move away, so he decided to leave his carriage at the duke of Luynes's and continue on foot. He had not gone three paces when a large ruffian dressed in gray started shouting, "To arms, to arms! Let's kill him and avenge ourselves for all the misfortunes we have endured." At this, the tumult heated up and the chancellor had to throw himself into the Luynes residence. Very few people had arisen yet in that household. Only an old serving woman received him, and seeing a chancellor of France asking for help, she took him by the hand and led him into a small closet built of pine planks at the end of a room. No sooner had he and his companions gone in, than the rabble arrived with terrifying shouts, asking with a million curses where he was and saying they wanted to get him. Some said, "It will be prisoner for prisoner, and we will exchange him for our dear protector." Others said more maliciously that they would slice him into quarters and display his members in the public squares as testimony to their revenge. They came right up to the closet, and when they saw that the place was largely abandoned, they gave a few kicks against the planks and listened for noise; then they went off to look for him somewhere else. . . . He said confession in the closet to his brother, the bishop of Meaux, and prepared himself for death. . . .

[Troops are sent and Séguier is rescued.]

That's what happened on the morning of the second day, which was no better than the first. When the queen got up about nine, she was given the news. She was furious, not only out of pity that for her sake a person of his stature had been forced to spend two hours in the hands of a thousand rascals worthy of hanging, but also at the damage to her authority caused by this coup, which set a dangerous precedent for the state and might have unfortunate effects abroad. . . .

After the queen had conquered her sorrow, she could see that despite her determination not to yield, she had much to fear. It was necessary for her to get dressed and receive the Parlement, which was coming in a body on foot to ask for the release of the prisoner [Broussel]. She spoke to them vigorously and sensibly, without losing her temper . . . then President de Mesmes, interrupting [the First President], said, "Dare I inform you, Madame, that the people are in such a state that it seems to me that Your Majesty can only avoid the sorrow of seeing this prisoner forcibly freed by graciously giving him back to us herself." The queen, . . . who admitted afterward that she had been well instructed by her minister, retorted that they should think about their duty; that in the future they should display more respect for the wishes of the king; and that, if they did that, she would accord them all the graces they had a right to expect from her. The chancellor then explained what this response meant: that if they promised absolutely to cease discussing affairs of state, she would release the prisoners to them, since she had only been forced to act on account of their revolt and their daily criticism of a royal declaration that showered them with favors and demonstrated perfectly well His Majesty's benevolence and the mildness of his Minister.

At this proposal the whole company decided to return to their palace and deliberate how to respond. They processed out of the building following the same rank order by which they had arrived, but when they had reached the rue Saint Honoré at the first barricade they encountered, crowds surrounded them, shouting and demanding Broussel. Several persons approached the First President and, holding a pistol to his throat, uttered a thousand insults and threatened that if he didn't get Broussel returned, they would kill him. They made it very clear that they would love to mistreat him, but he saved himself by assuring them that he had been working with all his power on this problem. Hearing this, they spared his life on condition that he return to the *Palais Royal* that very hour to consult with the queen, indicating that if he didn't obtain the release [of Broussel], they would tear him into a thousand pieces. The whole [Parlement] turned around in their tracks, shocked to discover that the fury of the people extended all the way to them. . . .

I entered the king's residence shortly after the return of these men in long robes[7], and I saw them go from the queen's large chamber . . . into the king's grand gallery to accomplish what they had intended to do back in their own palace, that is, find some remedy for the current difficulties. They hadn't eaten all day, and it was getting late. Out of pity more than tenderness, the queen had wine and bread brought to them, with some meat, which they must have eaten, it seems to me, with much shame, given that they were themselves the cause of the queen's worries, of the arrest of Broussel, and of the revolt of the people. . . .

When the Parlement had finished its deliberations, the cardinal came to join the queen, who went to receive them in the small gallery, without any ladies-in-waiting. The First President, in the name of his company, delivered a short compliment stressing their fidelity and reporting that they had decided to suspend their deliberations until Saint Martin's Day, when they could once again assemble at will to discuss any issue. In response to this postponement, the queen, pressured by the condition of Paris, granted them the release of their prisoner [Broussel] and imme-

[7] Parlementaire judges wore long judicial robes, hence the term "robe nobility."

diately issued orders to have him brought back in a royal carriage. This concession, extorted by an illusory short-term obedience, which was really obtained at the expense of the state, pained the queen and must have pained the cardinal, too. It caused sorrow in the souls of all good Frenchmen, although there were few of those, for the people from the [Parlement] had poisoned each other with such hate and become so preoccupied with getting rid of the Minister that the sorrows of the queen were great, and few people shared them.

So here is the prisoner Broussel, whom the queen is forced to release; the Parlement is victorious, and the Parlement and the people are the masters. . . . But the bourgeois, who had willingly taken up arms to preserve the city from pillage, were no better behaved than the people. They demanded Broussel just as heartily as the ragpickers. Beyond the fact that they were all infatuated with the common good, which they saw as their particular responsibility, they loved the Parlement too much, and they all hated the Minister. Indeed, they were filled with joy at the mere thought that they might be needed for something. They believed they participated in the government because they guarded the gates of the city. And everyone in his shop had his own opinions about affairs of state. . . . The strength of their outburst against the queen and the Minister was something astonishing. They didn't hesitate to announce that if anyone deceived them, they would come and sack the *Palais Royal* and chase out the "foreigner," and they shouted incessantly, "Long live the king by himself, and Monsieur de Broussel."

A MAZARINADE AGAINST THE QUEEN AND THE CARDINAL

The Parisian riots of August 1648 had forced the queen to conciliate the Parlement and its popular supporters. They had also made it clear that the Paris crowd was a force to be reckoned with, for once the neighborhoods set out to defend their perceived interests, neither *parlementaires* (judges of the Parlement) nor prestigious dignitaries were safe from attack. Furthermore, the peace negotiations to end the Thirty Years' War in the Holy Roman Empire were at a critical stage, and it was imperative to avoid the appearance of weakness at home. So Mazarin played along, granting most of the reforms demanded and biding his time, while the king and the court remained vulnerable to new popular agitation. Then, in the middle of the night of January 5–6, 1649, he secretly spirited the royal family out of Paris to the palace of Saint Germain, where they would be safer, and called on the prince of Condé to besiege and conquer the city. Not only was it shocking for the king to attack his own capital, but the alliance of Condé and the crown aroused jealousies among other great nobles, such as the prince of Conti and the duke of Longueville,[1] who sided with the Parlement and the Paris crowd.

The next document alludes to these events. As various factions vied for power, a flood of pamphlets poured off the presses, criticizing or defending the government, siding with one prince or another, attacking the queen or Mazarin. More than five thousand of these polemical bits of propaganda, called Mazarinades, since many of them attacked Mazarin, appeared during the Fronde. Often published anonymously both in Paris and in the provinces, they spread rumor and gossip and tended to discredit the government or, by extension, all constituted authorities. The Mazarinade reproduced here, which is far from the most insulting, appeared sometime in 1649. Note the way it undermines governmental authority by suggesting the difference between the present situation and an idealized monarchy. Note also its focus on the king, who is portrayed as being innocent of the corruption of those around him. The author is not proposing an alternative system but rather discrediting the queen and Mazarin by suggesting the role that a good king ought to play.

An Intimate Discussion between the King and the Queen Regent, His Mother, concerning the Affairs of the Day

The King Begins: My good mother, why have you taken over the Regency when my father prohibited this at the time of his death?

The Queen Replies: My son, in order to be mistress of all of France, under your authority.

The King: My good mother, why have you driven out the duke of Vendôme and imprisoned the duke of Beaufort?[2]

---

[1] The prince of Conti was Condé's younger brother. The duke of Longueville was governor of Normandy and was married to Condé's and Conti's sister. The three of them — Condé, Conti, and Longueville — are often referred to as "the princes."

[2] In 1643 the duke of Vendôme and the duke of Beaufort had participated in a failed conspiracy to overthrow Mazarin that was called the *cabale des importants.* Beaufort was arrested in Anne's apartments in the Louvre, and the rest of the conspirators fled.

Entretien familier du roy et de la reine régente sa mère sur les affaires du temps (Rouen, 1649), selected, edited, and translated by Amy Enright, with revisions by William Beik. The text has been shortened by about one-third by eliminating some of the questions and answers.

The Queen: My son, because they are too honorable to follow the advice of Cardinal Mazarin.

The King: My good mother, why do you make use of Cardinal Mazarin rather than anyone else?

The Queen: My son, because I love him and he does everything I want.

The King: My good mother, why have you let him live in my palace so close to you?

The Queen: My son, to ensure his personal safety, for I cannot live without him.

The King: My good mother, why have they driven away or put to death so many of the presidents and councillors of the Parlement of Paris?

The Queen: My son, because they didn't want to obey Cardinal Mazarin.

The King: My good mother, why have you driven away Monsieur de Châteauneuf?[3]

The Queen: My son, because he angered me, and Cardinal Mazarin too, by saying that the Parlement could take away my power as regent.

The King: My good mother, why did they erect barricades in Paris at the exit of the Te Deum service at Notre Dame?

The Queen: My son, because I had President Blancmesnil and Councillor Broussel of the Parlement imprisoned for being honest men.

The King: My good mother, why have they driven away and imprisoned so many good preachers?

The Queen: My son, because they preached too frankly and openly against Cardinal Mazarin concerning matters of state.

The King: My good mother, why is it that you take Communion so often and frequent all the churches of Paris, yet you don't value good men?

The Queen: My son, Cardinal Mazarin told me this was necessary as a maxim of statecraft so that I will appear to be a devout and good queen.

The King: My good mother, since you want to be considered a good queen, why don't you nourish me the way the mother of Saint Louis nourished him, for he was a king of France like me?[4]

The Queen: My son, the mother of Saint Louis was a wise and virtuous woman who didn't have a cardinal for an adviser.

[3]The marquis of Châteauneuf had been keeper of the seals but was relieved of his duties after plotting against Richelieu. After the failure of the "importants," he worked against Anne's and Mazarin's leadership. Mazarin blamed Châteauneuf and Beaufort for encouraging the Parlement's stand against new taxes in 1647 and eventually exiled the former in September 1648.

[4]The reign of King Louis IX (Saint Louis) (1226–1270), who had a fine reputation for both piety and state building, had begun with the regency of his mother, Blanche of Castile.

The King: My good mother, tell me who your counselors are so that I can know them.

The Queen: My son, it is Cardinal Mazarin and everyone who does what he wishes — for example, all the relatives of the late Cardinal Richelieu.[5]

The King: My good mother, tell me also who are these henchmen of Cardinal Mazarin whom you love so much?

The Queen: My son, they are the prince of Condé, the count of Argout, the chancellor, the grand master of Guiche, the count of Brienne, Madame de Combalet, abbot of la Rivière, . . . Tubeuf, and all the tax farmers of France.[6]

The King: My good mother, tell me, are all of them truly devoted to my service?

The Queen: My son, yes, you can be sure of it, because Cardinal Mazarin selected them and they are the ones who advise him and who own all the property in France.

The King: My good mother, why do they perform so many plays in my palace in Paris at such exhorbitant cost?[7]

The Queen: My son, that was Cardinal Mazarin's doing, to please me and to show that Italians are better actors than the French.

The King: My good mother, why was I secretly taken from Paris without drums beating, without guards, without light cavalry or soldiers, in the dead of the night?[8]

The Queen: My son, to please Cardinal Mazarin, who wanted it that way.

The King: My good mother, why did the members of the Parlement of Paris come to Saint Germain en Laye so many times?[9]

The Queen: My son, in order to issue a declaration and to show them the authority of Cardinal Mazarin.

---

[5] Richelieu married most of his relatives and clients into distinguished noble families. His brother became archbishop of Lyon; his sisters, nieces, and cousins married dukes; and in 1636 his niece was married to the prince of Condé.

[6] The prince of Condé was at this time allied with the queen. In 1650 he was imprisoned, and in 1651 he went into rebellion. The other names are also well-known supporters. Madame de Combalet, the duchess of Aiguillon, was another niece of Richelieu. Jacques Tubeuf was associated with the treasury and the tax farmers.

[7] Anne greatly enjoyed the theater and appreciated Mazarin's introduction of the Italian opera to France. Rossi's *Orpheus* was the first opera brought to the French stage.

[8] In the early-morning hours of September 13, the king was spirited out of Paris by Mazarin, later to be followed by the queen, and taken to the nearby château of Saint Germain to be free of pressure from the Parlement and the crowd.

[9] The Parlement was negotiating a settlement with the crown. The result was the Declaration of Saint Germain, which once again granted most of the Parlement's demands. After the settlement, the court returned to Paris.

The King: My good mother, why isn't this declaration implemented, since it was so difficult to draw up?

The Queen: My son, we only issued it to deceive the members of the Parlement of Paris and to keep them amused.

The King: My good mother, why then was I taken back to Paris?

The Queen: My son, to employ our time better at deceiving everybody and to rake in fifteen million livres [French monetary unit] there.

The King: My good mother, why was this money taken in, and what did they do with it, when my table was bare for two days?

The Queen: My son, it was deposited with Monsieur de La Meilleraye and Madame de Combalet on the pretext of a loan they made to you, and as for the shortages at your table, they are intended to make the people believe that it is the Parlement of Paris that is at fault.[10]

The King: My good mother, why don't they ever make peace?

The Queen: My son, it's because the cardinal does not think it appropriate. For he says that then he would not be honored and respected the way he is now.

The King: My good mother, why did they wake me up so early on Twelfth Night to drag me out of Paris?[11]

The Queen: My son, to take everyone by surprise and to starve out the city of Paris.

The King: My good mother, tell me what did the people of Paris ever do to you?

The Queen: My son, it's that the gentlemen from the Parlement no longer want to let the cardinal and the tax farmers pillage your people.

The King: My good mother, who are these tax farmers, and what are they good for?

The Queen: My son, they are honorable men whom Cardinal Mazarin uses to gather up all the wealth of France, along with the intendants.

The King: My good mother, what use are the intendants of justice in the provinces?

The Queen: My son, they are to suck away all the money from your kingdom by using your authority and concealing themselves behind the veil of justice.

---

[10]Marshal La Meilleraye, Richelieu's cousin, had been named superintendent of finance in July after the government declared bankruptcy. Madame de Combalet was closely connected to financial circles.

[11]On the night of January 5, 1649 (Twelfth Night, or Epiphany), the royal family again snuck out of Paris so that the reforms could be abrogated and the prince of Condé could besiege the city.

The King: My good mother, why do we make war so often in Italy?[12] Is that necessary?

The Queen: My son, that is for reasons of state to please Cardinal Mazarin.

The King: My good mother, what have you done with the five hundred million livres that you collected since my father died?

The Queen: My son, it has been distributed by order of the cardinal, who has hidden it away.

The King: My good mother, since you have received so much money, why haven't the salaries of my officers and my soldiers been paid for three years?

The Queen: My son, Cardinal Mazarin keeps everything for our necessities and to marry off his nieces the way Cardinal Richelieu did.

The King: My good mother, tell me then, what is Cardinal Mazarin's birthright that he can marry his nieces to French princes of the blood?

The Queen: My son, now you're annoying me, for I am well aware that Cardinal Mazarin is the son of a bankrupt Roman, a lackey, coachman of a courier, a gambler, and a piper, but despite all that I love him, and he should marry his nieces to whomever he wishes, for he has all the wealth of France and my friendship behind him.

The King: My good mother, tell me, since you want to starve out my good city of Paris, what will become of all the good monks and nuns who are dependent on alms for survival, the little babies at the breast, the poor in the hospitals and those all around the city, and all the good people who are in Paris?

The Queen: My son, don't get all worked up, because you have no idea where the passion of a female ruler may lead when someone thwarts her will.

The King: My good mother, then you hardly care about my kingdom.

The Queen: My son, when you are of age, you will look after it, but as for me, I only want to live and die with Cardinal Mazarin.

The King: My good mother, King Henry IV, my ancestor, said that he was a great king because his people were rich. What will I say since you are ruining mine?[13]

The Queen: My son, King Henry IV was a man who did not have a favorite to do good things for, as I do.

---

[12] France was still at war with Spain, which controlled much of Italy.

[13] Henry IV (1589–1610) was France's most beloved king. He had a reputation for looking after his people.

The King: My good mother, when everyone in Paris dies of starvation, I will lose many millions that are collected in tariffs and subsidies on goods that enter the city.

The Queen: My son, Cardinal Mazarin has all he needs to make himself pope, and he will set us up in the kingdom of Navarre that the pope caused you to lose, which is worth more than Paris, and we will go from there to Pamplona; the king of Spain would like that very much.[14]

The King: My good mother, I would much rather have Paris than the kingdom of Navarre, but the duke of Beaumont, my tutor, says that I should want whatever you want.

The Queen: My son, that is well said; God will bless you. Let's stop and go to the council meeting.

––––––

THE PARLEMENTAIRES OF AIX STRIKE BACK, 1649

In many provinces, discontented officers, jealous nobles, and angry crowds soon seized the opportunity provided by the confusion at court and the clashes over authority in Paris to pursue their own rivalries and grievances. In Aix-en-Provence, some four hundred miles from Paris, the Parlement of Aix had been greatly angered by the government's creation of a new "semester" chamber that would sit for half the year and introduce ninety-five new positions that were sold for large sums. The original councillors, here referred to as the "original officers," were thus facing a humiliating blow to their influence and revenues. In retaliation, they subjected the "semester officers," those individuals bold enough to purchase the new offices, to harassment and intimidation. The man responsible for enforcing the king's orders was the well-connected governor of the province, Louis of Valois, count of Alais, who was viewed as an ally of Mazarin. Alais installed the new semester court in January 1648, expelling the original officers from their chamber. These officers, many of whom belonged to powerful noble families with extensive influence in the city, were already seething with rage at the government when the Fronde broke out in Paris.

In this account of the uprising in Aix, we get a clear picture of the deterioration of public order and the damage that could be done by disaffected royal officers far from the king, ensconced in a province they

––––––

[14] Mazarin had come from Rome, where he was a protégé of the Colonna family. France was at war with the king of Spain, who was the queen of France's brother. Pamplona was a city in Spain not far from the French border.

controlled. The potential allies in the defense of the private interests of these officers are the crowds of citizens independently concerned about taxes. Their enemy is the governor, who has the hapless job of supporting the semester interlopers and is therefore considered a "Mazarin." The narrator here is Pierre-Joseph de Haitze, a seventeenth-century local historian who wrote from eyewitness accounts. On January 18–19, 1649, there had already been an uprising against Alais. The rebels occupied the streets and cornered Alais, who agreed to a truce whereby he promised to remove his troops from the city. Haitze takes up the story from there.

Haitze's Account of the Uprising in Aix, 1649

This arrangement was just a step toward a total breakdown of relations, because the original officers began to realize that they had better control of the city than the governor. This idea emboldened them to the point where they began telling the people that the governor's reluctance to pressure them demonstrated that he had recognized his error and they had been right to resist his conduct; that it was the role of parlements to monitor the king's situation during royal minorities, and for this reason they had decided that when they were restored to their offices, they would join the other organs of the state in punishing the extortions of the Mazarin. Hearing that the issue was reform for the benefit of the public, the people applauded and indicated that they were ready to support any efforts to make this plan succeed.

Meanwhile . . . as a result of bad advice or as a precautionary measure, the governor decided that he should seize the city hall, in order to protect the weapons stored there and to control the bell tower, which could dominate the city because of its location. To accomplish this, he introduced eighty or a hundred men from his regiment into the city on the twentieth of January, the morning of Saint Sebastian's day. . . .

No sooner had this detachment of soldiers been seen entering the city hall than the emissaries of the original officers set out to arouse the people. They spread the rumor that the governor had decided to close the gates as soon as that day's Saint Sebastian procession had gone outside the walls so that the marchers would not be able to help the rest. Then he would carry out his plot to hang the parlementaires and their

Pierre-Joseph de Haitze, *Histoire de la ville d'Aix* (Aix: Makaire, 1891), 5:12–67.

supporters and take revenge on the people for the uprising of the previous day by carrying out a general massacre. . . .

Almost all the crosses and banners of the confraternities[1] [in the procession] were already outside the Notre Dame gate between nine and ten in the morning when this spreading rumor . . . caused panic in the Saint Sauveur square, where lots of people were assembled, and the alarm spread into the church, where multitudes of people had gathered for the procession. People said that there was no time to lose if they wanted to save the town. Meanwhile a peasant who had fought on the side of the parlementaires in the preceding days . . . caught sight of several soldiers in the city hall, and imagining that they had come to arrest him and carry out the punishment that the governor was threatening, he fled at top speed toward Saint Sauveur from those who he imagined were chasing him, shouting, "Help, help, we are all lost!" right up to the door of the church. . . .

The confraternities and guilds parading outside the city immediately turned around, and the Notre Dame gate was closed. The tocsin [warning signal] was rung by means of the big bell on Saint Sauveur, and it was soon answered by the city's many other bells. Alarm spread through every quarter because of the widely circulated rumors about treachery. All you could hear were confused and tumultuous voices. Each person was urged to take up arms to oppose the imagined treason. At this odious word *treason,* the great and the small armed themselves — some with halberds, some with firearms, some with iron-tipped clubs — running here and there around the city wherever there were clumps of people. You could even see disheveled women, as furious as bacchants[2] (they are always outrageous in their mannerisms), running through the streets to arouse the people, some with pistols or naked swords in their hands, others with sacks of money to win them over; some shouting loudly, "Long live liberty and no taxes," while the least courageous armed themselves at home with rocks to throw from their windows at the unfortunate semester officers and their supporters. . . .

Meanwhile the consuls,[3] who were hated by the people because they had not selected them and who were in the Saint Sauveur church for the

---

[1] Confraternities were religious societies of laypeople devoted to honoring a particular saint.

[2] In the ancient world, bacchants were priestesses of Bacchus, the god of wine, and were therefore thought of as wild, frenzied women.

[3] The government of Aix was headed by three consuls who were selected annually in an "election" that was really a process of co-option. The consuls of 1649, however, had been appointed by Alais and were therefore unpopular with the crowd.

procession, were surrounded by insolent people who showered them with insults and curses, with no respect for the house of the Lord. They were called traitors and betrayers of their country, and the hat was even snatched from the shoulders of one consul. Seeing the people's fury . . . the unfortunate magistrates, who were not guilty of anything at all, escaped into the sacristy, escorted by du Chaine, canon of the cathedral, whose presence deterred the people, who were loudly threatening to kill them and hack them to pieces. . . .

Someone had begun to batter down the door when, fortunately, young du Chaine, the popular leader who had started the outcry, learned that his cousin [canon du Chaine] was in the sacristy and was in danger of being killed if the people should break down the door and pour into the room. . . . He approached the door firmly with his sword raised so that no one could get in front of him, got his cousin to open the door, and, with a marvelous presence of mind, grabbed the hoods of the consuls and threw them into the middle of the church in order to get the people to withdraw. Within a minute this furious populace had abandoned the door of the sacristy and converged on these sacred symbols, which they ought to have respected, like an animal attacking its prey. These hoods were raucously torn, dirtied, attached on the end of a pike, and paraded derisively in front of the city hall, where they were displayed as if they had been defiled by those who had worn them. Some people peppered them with musket fire, others tried to tear them to pieces, accompanied by terrible growls and cries as if they were exterminating something monstrous. . . .

That morning the governor had gone out to say his customary devotions, and from there went to visit Cardinal Antoine Barberin, who was lodged in the Capuchin monastery. Hearing the noise of the uprising and the sound of the tocsin, he hurriedly returned to his palace. There, to his amazement, he found that the uprising had occurred so rapidly that his friends were already taking refuge in his house, since they had no safe haven anywhere in the city. . . . Meanwhile the tocsin kept ringing on all sides, creating as much panic as the clash of weapons or the sound of a brawl. This was all it took to induce the semester officers, along with their families and everyone who had sworn loyalty to them, to flee to a place of exile. A large number reached the governor's apartments in the palace, until there were two hundred persons there who were not part of the governor's entourage, with a large number of gentlemen, including the duke of Richelieu and certain galley captains. Intendant de Sève and President Gaufridy [from the Parlement of Aix] had hastily abandoned their houses and taken refuge there, too, with their families, bringing nothing else with them. . . .

The original officers, seeing that their game was more successful than they could ever have hoped, moved through the city in red robes[4] and gave speeches to the people. They explained that the purpose of their movement was to protect themselves from the governor's plot to slaughter them and from the schemes of Cardinal Mazarin, who had introduced the semester court just so that he could get all the edicts he wanted ratified and overburden the province; that it was up to the people to reform this injustice; that in the future there would be no more taxes; and that to achieve this admirable goal all they had to do was continue what they had been doing so effectively. . . . These actions led the people to believe that the original officers were truly liberators and guardian angels and that since they were acting on behalf of the public good, it was only proper for the people to acknowledge them.

At the sight of these red robes, the riot heated up all the more, each person trying make more noise than the next. . . . The most agitated were Councillor de Bonfils and Solicitor General de Cormis. The former, sword in hand, ran through the streets dancing up and down to the point of frenzy to stir up the people. The latter kept stopping people on street corners to utter invectives against the governor, whom he called a tyrant, and against the consuls, who were characterized as the valets and dastardly creatures of Mazarin. Never had so many speeches been delivered to persuade people to do what they wanted to do anyway. . . . The people were so aroused by the anticipated treason, the prospect of exemption from taxes and fees, the speeches of the original officers, that in less than three hours the whole city was barricaded by twelve [thousand] to fifteen thousand armed men, who headed for President d'Oppède's neighborhood.[5] They placed white handkerchiefs in their hats to demonstrate their sincerity and express opposition to the blue, which was the color of the count of Alais [the governor]. From there these men fanned out into all corners of the city to guard gates, occupy squares and street corners where assemblies were possible, and defend the barricades. . . .

[More parleys take place between the governor and the original officers. It is agreed that the original officers will immediately be restored to their posts, that the governor's soldiers will leave the city, and that the governor will be held hostage until all this is accomplished.]

After the departure of the governor's troops, the original officers donned their red robes and assembled again in the city hall to discuss

---

[4]These red robes were the professional robes of the parlementaires.
[5]President d'Oppède, one of the original officers, was the leader of the opposition to Alais.

what should be done. They began by restoring public order. They issued an ordinance forbidding anyone to pillage the houses of the semester officers or any other inhabitants, on pain of death. This was essential because the real reason the common people take arms is to pillage, and they always think that the rich are holding their property. They were, in fact, very disappointed that the day had been so fruitless for them. The same ordinance commanded all inhabitants to put a light in their windows all night long. As a further precaution against pillagers, a company of guards was stationed near all the houses where there was reason to be concerned, with instructions to repel anyone who came to steal by force of arms. After these orders had been issued, the original officers, still dressed in their red robes, along with Count Carcès, marched that very night in a ceremonial procession to the palace — preceded, accompanied, and followed by an unbelievable multitude of people — to resume possession of their posts.

AGEN IS SEDUCED BY THE PRINCES

If the narrative about Aix illustrates the danger of factions within a provincial parlement getting out of hand and unleashing the pent-up rage of an urban population for their own purposes, this selection demonstrates the dilemma faced by the citizens of a provincial city when a rebel army demanded their allegiance. Condé, who appeared in earlier documents on the side of the crown, has now gone into rebellion and wants his troops admitted into Agen, which for the citizens of that city would be tantamount to committing treason against the king. Agen was a small city on the Garonne River, upstream from Bordeaux. The dilemma of the inhabitants was increased by the fact that Condé was the governor of their province of Guyenne and had many friends in the city. His rebel forces were at that time being chased by a superior royal army led by the count of Harcourt. At this later point in the Fronde, Condé and his brother the prince of Conti were in full rebellion against Louis XIV, with support from the king of Spain, who was then at war with France. The people of Agen were split: Some wanted to support a popular governor, while others feared the consequences of going against the king.

Note how the citizens are split into two camps, for and against admitting Condé's troops, how Condé woos them, and how they respond both politically and militarily. Although the town remained loyal to Louis XIV, their civic insurrection was hardly the kind of experience the king would have wished for his cities. Many French towns faced similar dilemmas during the Fronde.

An Account by Bru, Bookseller, 1652

On Thursday, March, 21, 1652, Condé appealed to the consuls of Agen to allow him to station a garrison in the city. Some of the consuls[1] did not dare refuse his demand, but others, such as d'Espalais and Labouroux, protested that the people would not readily accept a garrison in Agen, which angered him greatly. Condé threatened Labouroux that he would take revenge upon him and his family up to the fourth generation and commanded the consuls to let him consult the neighborhood militia captains, the sergeants, and the heads of all the guilds in order to find out how they felt about the garrison. These were immediately summoned. . . . The prince spoke to the captains and sergeants and gave them a long harangue about the exigencies of his situation and how he needed to depart, leaving behind the prince of Conti, his brother, along with four hundred men for his protection. . . . Monsieur de Lescazes, royal prosecutor and captain of the quarter of Saint Étienne, spoke on behalf of the captains, saying that if it were up to him, he would blindly obey the orders of His Highness [Condé]. Then Bru, sergeant from Saint Étienne, reported, in accordance with his comrades' instructions, that the people were grumbling loudly at the word *garrison* and would not willingly tolerate one. . . . Condé got very angry at Bru and spoke harshly, calling him a Mazarin. . . .

The prince thought he had matters under control, and to further consolidate his position . . . he went promenading around town accompanied by a large number of nobles. When he encountered crowds, he asked seductively whether they loved him or not and whether they wouldn't like to do whatever he wished, without explaining further, and they responded with cries of "Long live the king and Monsieur the prince," yet most of them added, "But no garrison!" He concluded that he could

---

[1] In Agen, as in Aix, the consuls were selected each year to run the city government.

"Récit au vray de ce qui se passa dans la Ville d'Agen le jour que Monseigneur le Prince de Condé y voulut establir garnison," written by Bru, bookseller, a participant in the events described and a partisan observer on the side of the crown. [From Archives Municipales d'Agen 2J 67: a nineteenth-century copy.]

succeed and secretly gave orders to have Conti's regiment, five hundred men lodged at Boé, begin advancing. . . .

Learning the news, the rest of the city barricaded all the streets and alleys, and the women gathered large quantities of rocks behind the windows and prepared boiling water. There were 133 barricades built with incredible speed by everyone from men and women down to small children. Observing this uprising, His Highness gathered all his noble followers and his councillors from the Parlement and started going from barricade to barricade, requesting that each one be dismantled and saying that if the garrison were not admitted, he and his followers would be at risk. Some dismantled them to let him pass on condition that he command the garrison to leave the city. Others refused, saying that they would never remove their barricades as long as the garrison was still there and that those who did would rebuild them stronger than ever as soon as he and his party had passed. He walked virtually every street without getting anything accomplished and became extremely angry. . . . The next day, March 22, the regiment left Agen and went to lodge at Clermont Dessous by order of His Highness. . . .

On Good Friday, March 29, the [royal] army of Harcourt[2] arrived at Passage d'Agen [just outside the city], frightening many inhabitants. A group of them gathered at the city hall. . . . Meanwhile Laugnac, Galapian, and Moncaut,[3] with their servants and some ill-intentioned inhabitants, went around the city shouting, "Long live the king and Monsieur the prince." They assembled as many armed men as possible at the houses of Laugnac and Galapian and had tables set out so they could invite everyone from their party who would shout "Long live Monsieur the prince" to drink and eat. Certain other distinguished persons who had assured Monsieur the prince of their loyalty did the same. While these men were busy enticing people to their party by means of the fine spread they were offering, certain distinguished ladies who supported the same party as Monsieur the prince decided to give presents to those who would support their party. They distributed light brown and blue ribbons [Condé's colors] to induce those who received these insignia to go out and shout "Long live Monsieur the prince" all over town. . . .

When the town's deputies returned [from an embassy to negotiate with Harcourt], they emphasized that Harcourt had received them with

---

[2] Henri de Lorraine, count of Harcourt, was commander of the royal forces that were chasing the princes of Condé and Conti.

[3] Laugnac, Galapian, and Moncaut were clients of Condé who were orchestrating the pro-Condé faction.

every sign of friendship and courtesy and had indicated that, as long as they maintained their obedience to the crown, nothing would be refused them. This encouraged the loyal citizens and caused the disloyal to redouble their efforts. Through the whole night from Good Friday to Saturday, [the rebels] never stopped trying to debauch the carters and butchers, most of whom let themselves be blindly won over.[4] But along with some of the consuls, Saint Gilis, and several good and loyal inhabitants from the rue de Garonne, other inhabitants remained faithful: Monsieur de Sevin the younger from the parish of Saint Hilaire did wonders holding on to the loyalty of those from his quarter, as did Monsieur Ducros the elder, attorney, in the Porte Neuve quarter. Dufort, a priest, held those from Carné loyal, and in Pont de Garonne [a district] Messieurs de Maurès and de Loret seized and held the church of the Jacobins, aided by some faithful people from their neighborhood who had taken refuge there. [On the other hand], almost everyone at the du Pin gate and in the rue de Saint Jean was seduced, and in the parish of Saint Caprais almost everyone was in the other party except for several captains and sergeants. . . . The ladies of the other party and their band continued to circulate through the streets distributing their ribbons to attract the simpleminded to their party, which caused a great problem in that the common people revolted against the consuls and magistrates. These mutineers threatened that they would come and cut the throats of everyone in the city hall, crying "Long live Monsieur the prince" and claiming they would perish before they would allow Harcourt to enter the city.

On Easter Sunday, March 31, 1652, the loyalists and all those who supported the party of the king, finding that they were not safe among this mutinous population, reported to the city hall, where they were determined to die for their country. Coquet, captain of the city's regiment, led his company from the palais to the city hall to reinforce the guard, expecting to be attacked. Bressolles, councillor in the presidial court [and] captain in the quarter of Saint Hilaire, kept his quarter loyal and brought ten of his soldiers to the city hall when they heard it was going to be attacked. Bru, a sergeant, stationed musketeers in all the approaches to the city hall and in the windows, posting ten men at Madame de Roques's house, eight at Castaing's, eight at Meuraille's; Laplace and some friends

---

[4]The rest of this paragraph cites the names of many citizens known personally to Bru, some of whom sided with the Condé faction while others supported the crown. Their identity is not important. But note the phenomenon of prominent citizens lining up whole streets and neighborhoods for one side or the other, and note how personal such relationships were in a seventeenth-century town.

also took up positions in his windows. Learning this, the enemy did not dare try anything. . . .

On Tuesday April 2, Galapian decided to attack the city hall. He came out of his house with twenty men, leaving another eighty behind. All he could do was circulate through town to assemble as many men as he could and try to form a critical mass to seize the city hall, telling them that "nothing could be easier; that there were only a few rascals inside who would not resist." In many areas he was denied passage. . . . He headed toward Saint Caprais, past the clock tower and straight to the du Pin gate and the rue de Saint Jean, inviting everyone to follow him. But people were beginning to come to their senses, and they replied that they wanted to maintain their barricades. All he could do was draw in sixty or so youths who were induced to shout "Long live Monsieur the prince." He came past the palais and headed straight for the city hall, where everyone was prepared to give him a suitable reception. . . . Seeing that he was in no condition to occupy the city hall as he had imagined, he returned to his house. . . .

On Thursday, April 4, His Highness Harcourt, followed by the great nobles, entered by the Saint Antoine gate and was met by the consuls and the parishes standing at attention. The parishes of Saint Caprais and Sainte Foy had not wanted to send anyone. As soon as he had entered, he went to the cathedral of Saint Étienne, where a Te Deum was sung by the choir and there were shouts of "Long live the king."

A REVOLUTIONARY PARTY IN BORDEAUX: THE ORMÉE

Bordeaux was a large, strategically important city, seat of a major parlement and home of a major port that communicated easily with Spain, France's enemy, and with Cromwellian England. Opposition to the crown during the Fronde had been led by judges from the Parlement of Bordeaux, who, like the "original officers" in Aix, had helped organize resistance to an oppressive governor, the duke of Épernon, in 1649 and 1650, with considerable popular support. In 1651, however, after enduring two sieges by royal armies, a group of citizens began to resent the hardships placed on them by the leaders of the Parlement, who refused to let lesser citizens share in the decision-making process. The parlementaires seemed to be extorting money, using it badly, and then capitulating and signing treaties with the king when the common citizens wanted to go on fighting. The result was the emergence of a popular party called the Ormée, after the elm trees under which they originally met.

The Ormée was the only group in all of France that successfully took over and held a city against both a parlement and the king. It was aided by the fact that Condé, who was made governor of the province of Guyenne in 1651, made Bordeaux his center of operations. (Bordeaux and Agen were both in Guyenne, but whereas Agen held out against Condé, Bordeaux joined his rebellion.) But Condé could never entirely control the Ormée, which maintained its independence and dominated Bordeaux for about two years, from the spring of 1651 to the summer of 1653.

The rise of the Ormée demonstrates the ultimate danger presented to the crown by the Fronde. Rebellions of princes might provide citizens with a vehicle for expressing their grievances. Even more alarming, if they were pushed far enough, influential urban groups, such as merchants, lawyers, and lesser royal officials, might begin to demand representation on their own behalf or institute constitutional reforms that would damage the claims of absolutism. The Ormée movement became increasingly radical. It soon began to terrorize eminent citizens who opposed it and to throw the parlementaires out of the city.

The first document, the "Apology," is from a printed Mazarinade commissioned by the Ormée and written by a local man named Lartigue in late 1652. Notice the nature of the ormistes' claims, the way they defend themselves, and especially the care with which they protest their loyalty to the king. Their attempt to replace the existing authorities was revolutionary in the context of local power, but they would ultimately fail because they offered no broader critique of the monarch or his society.

Apology for the Ormée

by a Member of the Assembly of Messieurs the Bourgeois,
Dedicated to Monseigneur the Prince of Conti

The head of the Gorgon[1] was so remarkable that it appeared terrifying to those who gazed upon it from afar, but as soon as you approached, it

[1] The Gorgon was a terrifying monster described by Homer, Hesiod, and other ancient authors.

Excerpts from "Apologie pour l'Ormée," reproduced in Eckart Birnstiel, *Die Fronde in Bordeaux 1648–1653* (Frankfurt am Main: Verlag Peter Lang, 1985), 269–98. Christian Jouhaud has discovered Lartigue's reimbursement in the Bordeaux municipal accounts: Christian Jouhaud, *Mazarinades: la Fronde des mots* (Paris: Aubier, 1985), 203.

displayed such beauty and grace that it attracted as many admirers as there were people capable of feeling and understanding. The Ormée, by its vision of ancient truths and its inspiration drawn from new virtues, has likewise produced opinions that are anything but indifferent: From a distance it seemed to be an assembly filled with horror and impetuosity, a confused body without intelligence, a monster without eyes or head, the object of the condemnation of edicts and the denunciation of gazettes; when [in fact] its children were demonstrating their esteem and affection by sacrificing their lives for its defense and spilling their blood to engrave its maxims in the hearts and memories of men. My personal knowledge of this body, down to the smallest details, obliges me to paint a more accurate picture that will bring it closer to the gaze of people wherever the sun shines. . . .

Several years ago Guyenne was disturbed by all sorts of movements: It was the regular operating ground of armies, a theater of carnage and cruelty. The city of Bordeaux, capital of the province, had to suffer the biggest shock of the war by taking on debts for all the expenses normally caused by war. . . . Still, these misfortunes did not rule out all possibility of amusement on the part of these unhappy people. The most respectable individuals from the bourgeoisie, those who do not necessarily have to work in the shops, got in the habit of taking walks at one corner of the city on an elevated platform, which provided an unobstructed view of the countryside and offered the shade of several rows of elm trees, which shielded it from the noonday sun. Their discussions took exactly the form you might expect at gatherings of this nature — talk of everyone's common misery, of exactions, taxes, the way they were being misused, how one person who had been receiver of the funds had used them to buy a piece of land worth six thousand livres of rent, how another had paid off a debt of forty thousand livres that he had incurred earlier. In this way everyone established a common feeling of rapport, without artificiality or premeditation. As people's curiosity caused the assembly to grow and the meetings to become more frequent, [these meetings] aroused the hatred of the Parlement, which called the assembly the Ormée to mock it and prohibited its meetings. But these upright bourgeois, who were already deeply angered at so many losses and extortions, could no longer tolerate losing their liberty along with their property, and since it is natural for desires to become aroused when prohibited, they reacted by insisting that they were motivated by reason and would therefore continue to assemble more enthusiastically and persistently than before by forming a regular organization bound by all kinds of oaths and promises. They would maintain close bonds and aid one another mutually, persevere in their common cause of defending their privileges, and demand an accounting of the sums levied [by the city] and the other financial arrangements. These beautiful maxims conquered the souls of our brave bourgeois so powerfully that, mastering all fear, they began marching around the city, displaying such unusual confidence and making such an extraordinary impact that many lost their lives at the murderous hands of their enemies. But their party was strengthened by these violent agitations, and drawing strength from being watered with their blood, the Ormée extended its roots and spread its branches so widely that, in a short period of time, it covered the whole city with its shade. There was a general rush of people clamoring to sign this declaration of "union"; they established committees, regulations, and carried out a thousand remarkable deeds, the details of which would extend my narrative to a boring length. . . .

The Ormée Abolishes the Parlement of Bordeaux

Unlike the "Apology," the next document is apparently a private letter written by a notable of Bordeaux to a friend, presumably in Paris. The letter, dated May 23, 1652, was written at the moment when the conflict between the budding Ormée and the Parlement was just reaching its climax. A month later, there were bloody confrontations in the streets. The anonymous author is dubious about the Ormée and speaks ironically.

You will no doubt be surprised to learn that our Ormée is strong enough to outlaw our Parlement and force it to cease dispensing justice — something that the king with all his power and his many declarations has not been able to achieve. That isn't all: They claim to have suppressed the parlementaires' offices, abolished venality, and arranged for sovereign justice to be dispensed by persons of probity and recognized qualifications. This is the first step in the reformation of our city, undertaken by a movement imbued with Divine Inspiration. I pray that the Holy Spirit will guide them to a happy conclusion. Seriously, though, they will have difficulty disentangling the two objectives that were set in recent assemblies of the Ormée: first, to get an accounting for the immense sums that

Anonymous letter, from Bibliothèque Mazarine, ms. 4360, item 36, reprinted in *Archives Historiques du Département de la Gironde* 58 (1929–32): 29–31.

have been levied during the recent troubles, no matter who was responsible; second, to get an automatic transfer of all the legal business of the bourgeois of this city [to another outside court]. . . . I have learned that most of the bourgeoisie have come together and signed a unity pact ["union"]—that is how edified we are by the good government of our "senators." And I can assure you that our ormistes have so little support in the Parlement that they will be easily led astray. Monsieur Lenet[1] was sent Friday on behalf of Monsieur the prince of Conti to the Jacobins church, where the Ormée assembly was meeting to present a proposal concerning reconciliation, but they would not listen to him. They decided with a single voice that there would be no further deals between the Parlement and the Ormée. What aggravated them was that Friday morning a straw dummy was discovered, dressed in a parlementaire robe and a judge's bonnet, hung from a great elm tree in front of the chateau of Puypaulin, which they say was put there by the men of the Parlement in order to make the Ormée look odious and criminal. . . .

[Added at the end] Everyone here is talking about the victories of our fine Fronde of the Ormée and about the daily progress it is making against our Parlement. It marches around every day pompously and triumphantly to the sound of fifty or sixty drums inviting the people to take part in the joy and erect a maypole in honor of Monsieur the prince of Conti and Madame the princess [of Condé]. Our city officials appeared, leading five thousand or eight thousand men decorated and crowned with ivy branches, to the great delight of Madame de Longueville [Condé's sister] and to the despair of the Parlement's "little fronde" party.[2] [The latter] had to remain hidden in the shadows during this day of celebration and joy, and they will try to evade the decrees the assembly has issued against them by choosing voluntary exile. It is true that Monsieur de Conti is opposed to their being banished and cannot consent to have the friends of Monsieur his brother [Condé] chased away so ignominiously. But in the end resentment and rage will win out over the respect owed to their highnesses, and three or four at least [of the judges from the Parlement] will be the victims of the others.

---

[1] Lenet was Condé's chief agent in Bordeaux.
[2] The "little fronde" party was the more conservative group from the Parlement, which supported rebelling against Mazarin but not the Ormée's rebellion against the Parlement.

The crown finally defeated the Ormée, which was the last, dramatic episode of the Fronde, in the summer of 1653. Condé fled to Spain, and the other grandees submitted to royal authority. Mazarin and Anne of Austria continued to rule France in the name of Louis XIV, who was then fifteen and legally old enough to rule. The Fronde had not accomplished anything of significance in constitutional terms, but it had demonstrated to France's elites who lived through it how much they needed the king's strong support. And the king had learned how hard it would be to rule if the grandees, the robe nobles in the parlements, or the angry crowds in urban centers were unwilling to accept the premises of absolutism. There had been no revolutionary movement because these groups had no common program other than their hatred of Mazarin. Grandees and parlementaires were mostly interested in defending their privileged situations, but they had difficulty joining forces because their pretensions conflicted. Local leaders needed help if they were going to keep their discontented populations in line. Putting the genie back in the bottle would be difficult for everyone. The only thing this weary collection of diverse rebels knew — from the citizens of Agen to the greatest princes, from the original officers of Aix to the exiled parlementaires of Bordeaux — was that they needed the young Louis XIV to bring them a society in which each could shine and mobilize his special prerogatives without clashing with the rest.

2

The King and the Aristocrats at Court

When Louis XIV came to personal power in 1661 after the death of Cardinal Mazarin, he was determined to eliminate the problems France had experienced during the Fronde. His methods at court have been both admired and criticized by historians. Standard accounts always start with the king assuming personal power, working hard at government business in his councils in conjunction with bureaucratic ministers such as Colbert and Louvois, and building a rational, effective system of national rule. This is the positive picture the king himself painted in his memoirs, which we will sample in chapter 8. But there is another, negative view of a self-indulgent Louis, who reduced his grandees to idle, decadent courtiers in the "gilded cage" at his palace of Versailles. It will be up to you to assess the advantages and disadvantages of Louis's court on the basis of the evidence provided. One thing is clear: During the minority of Louis XIV, the system worked badly because the king was not in control. After 1661 it functioned more effectively because he played his expected role brilliantly.

Since Louis's power depended on good relations with the grandees at court and in the provinces, the monarch's personal ties with them were important. The court served three functions that would later be kept separate in modern governments: It was a household where the king's family lived, a social center where the highest nobles participated in the rituals surrounding the king's daily life, and a seat of government where administrative officers ran the affairs of France. Louis did not invent court life, which was a feature of all early modern monarchies, but he brought it to a level of perfection that was highly unusual. Earlier monarchs had filled their governments with family members, great nobles, or first ministers, and thereby ran the risk of being dominated by favorites or weakened by factions struggling for control. Louis demonstrated early in his reign — by his strength of personality, his clever distribution of resources and privileges, and his capacity for hard work — that he was capable of controlling these divisive energies and using them to his advantage. By reducing the elites' quarrels and personifying their expectations, he became the king that they had been hoping to see.

Louis's personal reign lasted for a remarkable fifty-four years, during which he changed from a gallant young man of twenty-three to a seventy-seven-year-old great-grandfather who had outlived most of his generation. Before 1682 the court spent much of its time at the palace of Saint Germain en Laye on the outskirts of Paris, with stays at Louis XIII's small château at Versailles for recreation, trips to the war front in Flanders, periods in the Louvre Palace in Paris, and forays to Fontainebleau and other palaces in the Paris region. Only gradually was the stolid life seen in the later years at Versailles introduced, as the king moved from a series of amorous affairs to a lasting domestic partnership with his last mistress (and later wife), Madame de Maintenon. Thus the court of Louis XIV should not be imagined solely in terms of the colossal palace of Versailles, since the formative years were mostly spent elsewhere. Still, it is striking how much of the later ritual existed in the early days of his personal reign. From the first, life at Louis's court was compelling in its glamour, its hold on the lives of the participants, and its intimate connection to the royal person.

As the king moved around the Paris region, his family, followers, staff, and government moved with him. Prominent at his court were the immediate royal family, including Louis's eldest son, the Dauphin, and eventually the Dauphin's wife, the Dauphine, and their sons the dukes of Burgundy and Anjou, along with the king's brother the duke of Orléans (Monsieur) and Orléans's wife (Madame). The queen, Maria Theresa, daughter of Philip IV of Spain, had her own household, which was tightly controlled by the king. Next in the hierarchy after the royal family came the princes of the blood, notably the princes of Condé and Conti and their offspring, once they were reintegrated after their rebellious exploits during the Fronde; the princes "reputed to be foreign," such as members of the Houses of Lorraine, Savoy, Gonzaga, and Mantua; and finally those with the title "duke and peer," plus the wives, families, and servants of all these people. In an ambiguous category were the king's illegitimate children, who were ultimately legitimized and inserted into the court hierarchy by the king himself. Cardinals and bishops, often from the same noble families, also had high ranking at court. In addition, the great officers of the crown (chancellor, grand master of artillery, grand chamberlain, grand admiral, marshals of France, grand squire) and the great officers of the king's household (grand master of the wardrobe, grand master of the hunt, and so on) played a major role. The king usually bestowed these posts on great nobles already at his court, so they did not constitute a separate group of persons.

These individuals were the high aristocracy of France, or the *grandees*. They were invariably wealthy individuals whose fortunes were made up of revenue-producing estates in the provinces, real estate, and investments in state financial operations such as tax farms or loans to the crown. In addition to their rural lands, they usually owned residences in Paris, and the greatest of them eventually built town houses in Versailles near the palace. They did not necessarily live at court, nor were they strangers to Paris or the provinces, but they had to appear regularly before the king to be taken seriously. The royal day followed a regular schedule of business and pleasure, and at every step of the way the courtiers were expected to appear in the king's retinue. If they were lucky enough to hold an official post at court, they also had considerable ceremonial duties to perform. In return, the king honored them with his favors, appointments, and support. He awarded pensions, forgave debts, helped with marriage alliances, and distributed titles, not only for ceremonial positions but also for lucrative church posts, military commands, and governmental posts, such as governorships of provinces and delegations to foreign courts. Louis honored the grandees by maintaining a strict court etiquette that recognized their subtle differences of rank. He also had informers who kept him abreast of what was being said and done outside his presence, and he was good at manipulating the lives of his courtiers, punishing indiscretions or poor conduct with exile or humiliation, and making it clear at all times that his favor had to be constantly earned.

It is a historical myth that Louis isolated the entire nobility at Versailles, since these positions concerned only the top aristocrats and even they had lives beyond the court. What his policies did do was make it impossible for such persons to develop independent spheres of authority that might compete with those of the king. In all there were some 200,000 nobles in France, of whom only several hundred of the most important were regulars at court. The palace of Versailles at its height contained some 220 apartments and some 450 rooms, housing at the most 3,000 people, many of them family members and servants.[1] Whereas the greatest nobles had to make regular appearances, most of France's middle-level nobles were expected to come to court only once in a while, and the majority of poor country nobles never left their provinces. Some

[1]The best analysis of Louis XIV's court is Jean-François Solnon, *La cour de France* (Paris: Fayard, 1987), 253–417.

distant provinces, such as Brittany and Provence, still had important families who stayed quietly at home.

As we have seen, France also had a powerful robe nobility. These royal officers — who had connections to a whole class of lawyers, financiers, and government bureaucrats — were legally privileged and very well connected, although socially they were considered a step beneath the traditional sword nobility. It was from such circles of legal practitioners and administrative agents that the king drew his ministers, including Jean-Baptiste Colbert, Michel Le Tellier, and Le Tellier's son the marquis of Louvois, along with many other men who ran the administrative business of France. They also appeared at court, but only on their way to and from council meetings, since the king used devoted servants from the robe to manage the administration of the kingdom and kept government business out of the grandees' hands. Despite the king's determination to stay on top of all important business himself, such men wielded great influence and, like the courtiers, received favors in the form of family advancement and multiple positions of responsibility. In particular, the families of Le Tellier and Colbert produced whole dynasties of royal administrators, but the king made a point of never depending exclusively on one family or the other. It is evident in the accounts in this chapter that the Colberts and Le Telliers married well, had influence at court, and tended to move in ever more exalted circles. Nevertheless, Louis maintained a clear distinction between the honorific function of the courtiers and the governmental functions of his ministers and agents.

Much of the gossip at court concerned the king's love life, which was important to everybody in terms of daily social relationships and the future of the royal family. No sooner was Louis married in 1660 than he began to show an interest in Henrietta (Madame), who was not only his brother's wife but also his cousin and the sister of the king of England. The ruse of pretending to visit one of Henrietta's ladies-in-waiting, the seventeen-year-old Louise de La Vallière, led to a serious relationship with Louise that produced four children between 1661 and 1667. The court was full of intrigue over keeping the queen and the queen mother in the dark, at least officially, about this scandal.

Meanwhile, everyone noticed that Louis was falling for another lady-in-waiting, the more beautiful and sophisticated marquise of Montespan, who gave him eight children between 1667 and 1681. She caused much friction between the three "wives," who often had to be seen together, until La Vallière retired permanently to a convent in 1674. This relationship was a further embarassment to Louis because Montespan was married and her husband, who stayed away, was known to be unhappy about the relationship. Madame de Montespan engaged Françoise d'Aubigné to bring up Louis's "bastards" in a hideaway in Paris. But to Montespan's increasing despair, d'Aubigné gradually attracted the king's attention. Montespan held on until 1691, when she finally left the court permanently. The king also enjoyed a brief interlude (1679–81) with the twenty-year-old Mademoiselle de Fontanges.

Madame de Maintenon, as d'Aubigné came to be called after Louis made her marquise of Maintenon, was the widow of the poet Paul Scarron. She had been brought up in poverty, lived in Martinique in the Caribbean (which led to the incorrect belief that she was born in America), and maintained a respectable salon in Paris before bringing up the king's children. Louis seems to have chosen her as his companion for his old age, and she inaugurated a new era of piety and seriousness, to the disgust of many people at court. She was the only "queen" who presided over the permanent court at Versailles, where the king moved in 1682. Louis secretly married Maintenon in October 1683.[2]

To assess life at Louis's court, we will examine the memoirs of people who were there in the first half of the reign, mostly before the final move to Versailles. By looking at a variety of accounts and situations, we can begin to understand the role of the king, his family, and the ladies and gentlemen around them. Watch for the role of the great nobility in the government and the larger society. Note the role of women at court. As it happens, our reporters are mostly foreigners, because they brought an intelligent outsider's point of view to their observations. We have omitted the better-known memoirs of the duke of Saint Simon because they were written at the very end of the reign by a bitter man whose prejudices often colored his prose. Remember in reading these accounts that the authors are repeating what they saw and heard in a tone that incorporates their own biases and points of view. You can learn a lot about how the king and the court functioned without necessarily believing everything these observers reported. Some of the names cited will be unfamiliar, but it is not necessary to know who everyone was to figure out how these courtiers treated one another.

[2] Ibid., 306.

THE KING AND HIS FAMILY

Mademoiselle de Montpensier

When Louis took personal power, all eyes were on him. Here is a description of the twenty-one-year-old Louis written in 1658 by his cousin Mademoiselle de Montpensier, who was thirty-one and sounds infatuated. Note her expectations about the role the king should play.

... His manner is elevated, refined, proud, and pleasant, with something sweet and majestic in his face. He has the most beautiful hair in the world both in color and in the way it is curled. He has fine legs, a robust bearing; all in all he is the handsomest and best built man in the kingdom, and probably in all other kingdoms. He dances divinely well.... He throws himself into all sorts of physical exercises and excels at them, firing at fowl more adroitly than anyone.... He expresses the greatest passion in the world for warfare and is in despair that he is kept from going to battle as often as he would like.... His health suits his inclinations, for he is as strong and vigorous as he would need to be to resist the fatigues of war. His manner is cold; he speaks little, but he speaks effectively to familiar persons; he talks precisely and says nothing inappropriate, jokes pleasantly, has good taste, discerns and judges as well as anyone in the world.... He is well suited for gallantry and inclined in that direction. But I think what inhibits him is that he has such delicate taste that he does not find ladies to his liking, and those of today are not attractive enough for him.... He has considerable piety and devotion: It is exemplary and edifying and sets a fine example, being neither too austere nor too strict.... Finally the king is worthy of being beloved by his people, the object of veneration by the whole court, and the terror of his enemies.

Anne Marie Louis Montpensier, *La galerie des portraits de Mademoiselle de Montpensier,* ed. Edouard de Barthélemy (Paris: Didier, 1860), 495.

Saint Maurice

Three years later, after the death of Cardinal Mazarin, young Louis took power and proceeded to delight the public. Tales of his hunts, horse shows, and love affairs began to circulate, along with news of his diligence in council meetings and his prosecution of tax farmers. The court was now the place to be, as we can see from any number of eyewitness accounts. Our first reporter is the marquis of Saint Maurice, who was at court between 1667 and 1673 as ambassador of the duke of Savoy, to whom he sent these letters. He was an important dignitary with close relations to a number of figures at court. We will follow him on his first visit there and sample some of his later reports. Note how the movements of the king are the focus of everyone's attention.

[1667] We left this morning at 6:00 A.M. [from Paris for Saint Germain]. Everyone of stature from Piedmont and Savoy came along, all wearing fine new suits. We arrived at Saint Germain at nine o'clock. When we descended from the carriages, we encountered M. de Bonneuil, the introducer, who conducted us to the chamber where you await the hour of the king. At 10:30 I was taken to the audience, and I learned from M. de Bonneuil that I would be permitted to speak with the king about my business since he was expecting to depart soon and wanted to be free of obligations. I was conducted into the king's bedroom in the accustomed manner. I found him seated in the space between the bed and the wall, his hat on his head, dressed in a black velvet jerkin with a gilded vest and a cane in his hand. At the railing were the duke of Bouillon and count of Lude and beyond it, at the entrance, M. Lionne and M. Charost, captain of his guards, and the bedroom was so full of people that I could scarcely get through. I made a deep bow to the king; he raised his hat, then put it back. I presented the compliments of Your Royal Highness and gave him your letter. . . .

There are many distinguished ladies here [at Compiègne], and people are thinking about nothing but pleasure and entertainment, but I find the amusements mediocre. They consist of certain promenades and gambling in the evening in the queen's chamber. On promenades the king rides in a carriage with the queen, with both of them in the back; in

Marquis de Saint Maurice, *Lettres sur la cour de Louis XIV,* ed. Jean Lemoine (Paris: Calmann-Lévy, 1910), 1:18–21, 85–87, 156–57, 162, 221–22, 406–7, 409; 2:3–5.

front are Mademoiselle de Montpensier and the princess of Baden; at a door by the king is Madame de Crequy; . . . next to her is seated the duchess of La Vallière. . . . Sometimes they get out to have refreshments; other times they eat in the carriage; when they return, the queen and the ladies gamble and the king works with M. de Louvois. He sometimes goes to visit the duchess of La Vallière before supper and sometimes after. I still think she is holding her own, although everyone says she is not; and people speak about it freely here; she is still very thin and tries to pass for pretty but with too much affectation. I find her a bit fussy. She looks people over from head to foot and is not annoyed when they look her over. . . .

. . . After entertaining himself well at Versailles, the king has finally returned to this city [Paris]. He arrived on Wednesday and lodged in the Tuileries, a truly royal palace, but the apartments in my opinion are not as beautiful or as richly ornamented as those of Your Royal Highness. As for the furniture, it is sumptuous and unusual. . . . At the king's *lever*[1] the court is the most beautiful thing in the world. I went yesterday. There were three rooms full of distinguished men and a crowd so thick that it is unbelievable how hard it is to get into the king's bedroom, and more than eight hundred carriages were waiting in front of the Louvre.

. . . Now that the court is here, there is talk of nothing but business. The king works incessantly the whole day. During his hours of relaxation he plays *jeu de paume,*[2] reviews his household troops on horseback, and makes a few visits, and in the daytime he goes to visit Madame de La Vallière, and from time to time there are balls or a comedy at the Tuileries. He must have some special reason for joy, since in the last eight days he has appeared completely cheerful and in a satisfied mood.

[1668] . . . It is true that one can be entertained at court, but the king does not deviate for a moment from the hours he has scheduled for official business. He works regularly for three hours every morning and an equal amount in the afternoon. Council meetings are set up for each day [of the week], thus everyone knows when to go to Saint Germain according to the nature of his business, and the ministers each come to Paris on a certain day each week. M. de Lionne arrives on Saturday or Sunday and returns [to Saint Germain] on Tuesday morning. M. de

---

[1]The *lever* was the ceremony when the king got out of bed in the morning and got dressed in the presence of certain great nobles, upon whom he had bestowed the right to participate, which was considered a great honor.

[2]*Jeu de paume* was an indoor game rather like tennis.

Colbert is [in Paris] every Wednesday and Thursday; the council comes on Monday and returns [to Saint Germain] on Friday, and this sequence is regularly observed. The king has no morning free, and the time after his midday meal is only free on Sunday, Wednesday, Thursday, and Saturday. On those days he plays at *jeu de paume,* goes to the encampment, hunts, or goes to Versailles. After four or five in the afternoon he no longer does anything, except under extraordinary circumstances. He spends the evenings gambling or with the ladies. Thus he does not shrink from work. He loves it, and his hours are regulated like a monk's, even including the times for Mass and meals, for going to bed and for getting up. . . .

[1670]   . . . The duchess of La Vallière is surely pregnant. All her and the king's efforts are directed toward hiding this from Madame de Montespan until she has given birth, for fear that this news will anger her and do some damage. The king's confessor, weary over all this, decided to withdraw completely [from court]. The king has consented and taken on another Jesuit confessor named Father Ferrier, fearing that it would cause a great scandal if the reason for the previous one's withdrawal were known.

. . . There have been tears from the "favored" ladies because the recently arrived one has discovered the pregnancy of the other one; it is said that their "gallant" has had great difficulty consoling them and that he has been immensely embarrassed.

. . . The king seems to have great consideration for the queen now. They say this stems from a quarrel they had when it was believed that Mademoiselle [Montpensier, quoted above] would get married. The king was angry at her and at Monsieur for criticizing this plan too much. . . . She retorted to His Majesty that she was astonished he should question her conduct at a time when he should be praising [her forbearance] like the rest of the kingdom. She said that she had acted only in the interest of his glory and reputation; indeed she had no other goal in this world, for she loved only God, the king's person, and her children. . . . She knew perfectly well that he was filled with hatred toward her and that he had never approved of anything she had done, even though she had indulged him against her very conscience and reputation. . . . It is certain, My Lord, that this good queen has more spirit than people think and that no woman has ever possessed so much virtue, piety, and good conduct. She scorns the "favored ladies" because they have no virtue, but she feels no hatred or jealousy. She just makes little gallant jokes about them, which are never offensive.

Primi Visconti

Our second reporter is Jean-Baptiste Primi Visconti, count of San Maiolo, who observed the court between 1673 and 1683. Thus he watched the consolidation of the royal system in the years after Saint Maurice had left. Primi was an Italian nobleman who worked his way into Parisian courtly society by establishing a reputation as a reader of handwriting and a soothsayer. He was well connected at court, and his observations are quite reliable.

[1673] . . . I went [to Saint Germain] in the month of February. I caught sight of the king on his way to Mass. Although I had never seen him before and he was lost in a crowd of courtiers, I immediately recognized him. He had a grand, majestic air, and by his stature and demeanor you could tell that if he hadn't already been a king, he would have deserved to be one in the eyes of the beholders. . . .

The king does what he can to demonstrate that he is not at all dominated by his ministers, and no prince was ever less dominated. He wants to know everything: from his ministers about affairs of state, from his presidents about affairs of the parlements, from his judges about even the most insignificant matters, from his favorite ladies about gallantry. In short, in any given day there are few events about which he is not well-informed, and there are few persons whose names and habits he does not know. He has a discerning eye, he knows intimate things about everyone, and once he has seen a man or heard him talked about, he always remembers him.

In addition, his life is very regulated. He always gets up at eight o'-clock, stays in his council meeting from ten to half past noon, when he always goes to Mass with the queen and his family. Thanks to this intense desire to preside over all the affairs of government, he has become skillful. Each question is digested by the time it reaches him because it has been drawn up in advance by the interested parties, then prepared by the clerks, and finally studied by the ministers who report on it [in the council meeting]. But with his marvelous talent he often manages to clarify something that neither the ministers nor their clerks had been able to untangle. . . .

Primi Fassiola di San Maiolo, *Mémoires sur la cour de Louis XIV,* 2nd ed., ed. Jean Lemoine (Paris: Calmann-Lévy, 1908), 3–4, 31–36, 44–45, 175–76, 206–10, 214, 267–69.

Figure 1.   *Louis XIV at the Château of Vincennes near Paris, by Adam Frans van der Meulen* (1632–1690).
Note the elegance of the king and his companions as they take a leisurely ride through the park.
© *Photo RMN—Gérard Blot.*

At one in the afternoon after hearing Mass, he visits his favorites until two, the hour when he always dines with the queen in public. In the course of the afternoon he goes hunting or promenading [see Figure 1], or holds another council meeting. From dusk until ten o'clock he converses with the ladies, gambles, or goes to a play or to balls. At eleven o'clock, after supper, he goes down again to his favorites' apartment. He always sleeps with the queen. Thus he has divided up the hours of the day and night among business, pleasure, devotions, and duties, in such a way that the courtiers can always tell you what he is doing and where to go to pay him court.

In public he is full of gravity and very different from the times when he is on his own. Often when I have been in his bedroom with the other courtiers, I have noticed that if the door accidentally happens to be open or he steps outside, he adopts a different expression as if he were going to appear on a stage; in short he knows well how to play the king. In addition, he has destroyed the chieftains and their factions and abolished the practice of patronage. The least positions at court and in the kingdom are now at his disposal. There are no intermediaries. If you want something, you have to go directly to him and not to anybody else. He listens to everyone, receives reports, and always replies with grace and majesty, "I will see," and everyone goes away satisfied.

How very different is the response of the ministers. The king wants them to bring all requests before the council because he wants the government to function with perfect harmony. For war, Louvois is the designated successor of Le Tellier; for finance, it is Jean-Baptiste Colbert; for foreign affairs, Arnauld de Pomponne; for the Huguenots it is Châteauneuf. Louvois is a hard and violent character with a severe expression. You would think he was mistreating you when he talks, so many people are afraid to approach him. As for Colbert, he is cold and dry with a somber air: He freezes petitioners. Pomponne is sweet and Châteauneuf very ceremonial; but the latter is a simple secretary of state, and Pomponne is not as vigorous a minister as Colbert and Louvois.

They have reason to worry because the king has an extraordinary memory and he expects that every appeal, no matter what it is, will be reported to him so that he can issue a pardon or do justice; therefore they enter every council meeting trembling. A simple glance from the king if they are imprecise is a reproach that leaves them devastated, for the king does not talk very much. The ministers have subordinates called clerks *[commis],* and it is harder to get an interview with them than with the ministers. They work day and night: The king wants everyone in his service to be continually active, each according to his calling. Laziness has never had a more powerful enemy.

He is always doing something — reviewing the troops, parading the soldiers, building fortifications, moving earth. He encourages navigation and keeps friends and enemies all over Europe in constant motion. He has a strong constitution and good health, and his health and good fortune seem to compete with each other, keeping the whole world out of breath. It is a beautiful sight to see him leaving the château with his guards, carriages, horses, courtiers, valets, and a multitude of people in great confusion, running noisily around him. It reminds me of the queen bee when she goes out into the fields with her swarm.

[1674] . . . The king treats [the queen] with all the honor befitting her status: He eats and sleeps with her, fulfills all his family duties, makes conversation with her as if he had no mistresses. As for her, she spends most of her time at devotions. Her entertainment consists of the half dozen silly people she surrounds herself with. She addresses this one as "my heart," another as "poor boy," and yet another as "my son." With them are a multitude of little dogs, but the dogs are better treated than the fools. They get a carriage and valets to take them on walks. They share the scraps from the table. I don't know who told me once that those little animals cost 4,000 écus a year. As for the fools, they can hardly scrape together a pistole.

[1676]   . . . I wish you could see the king: He has the manner of a great dissimulator and the eyes of a fox. He never speaks of public business except with the ministers in council. If he speaks a few words to the courtiers, it is about nothing more than their respective positions or professions; but everything he says, even the most frivolous things, make it seem as if an oracle were speaking. At meals and whenever he is required to chat, he speaks gravely and clearly; when he opens his mouth, all the courtiers around him lower their heads and press in as close as they can to hear him. The passion of the courtiers for being noticed by the king is incredible. When the king deigns to glance toward one of them, the person noticed believes his fortune is made and tells the others, "The king looked at me." You can bet that the king is a rogue. He rewards so many people with just a look!

[1678]   The king had just turned forty. I believe he had been influenced by the scandal his conduct had caused and he was planning a secret liaison with Mademoiselle de Fontanges. Marsillac, who loved Mademoiselle de Poitiers, was in on the intrigue. He had no trouble carrying it out since Mademoiselle de Fontanges was eager to comply, and the king told Marsillac how to proceed. At that time people played *la bassette* [a gambling game], and one evening when Madame de Montespan was with the king, she lost three million, but she won it all back later by persuading the courtiers to play right through until the next morning. The king . . . let Madame de Montespan go ahead so that she would be lulled to sleep and would not discover his plans with Mademoiselle de Fontanges. That night he traveled to Paris, escorted only by several guards and went to the Palais Royal [residence of Monsieur and Madame]. Mademoiselle des Adrets opened the door to the apartment of Madame's ladies-in-waiting, and that was the first time His Majesty enjoyed Mademoiselle de Fontanges. Despite the darkness [of the dawn], those who rise early saw the king returning. . . .

They gave Mademoiselle de Fontanges the apartment next to the king's study. A lighted lamp was always left there. She had been assigned a bedroom in the wardrobe above the king's bedroom, and sometimes the king went up — or she came down — a little staircase that went between the study and the bedroom. In public the king pretended not to know her. Later she became pregnant and gave birth to a boy who died. Her childbirth was followed by losses of blood that caused her death, and thus she died as a martyr to the king's pleasure. He treated her very differently from Madame de Montespan. The latter was treated like a queen, whereas Mademoiselle de Fontanges was treated like a servant. Still, he made her a duchess at Easter in 1680, a reward that signaled her service was over and the king's repentance was sincere.

The king treated his favorites like members of his family, each in a separate category. The queen received their visits along with those of the [king's] natural children as if it were a duty she had to fulfill, since everything functioned according to each person's station and the wishes of the king. When they attended Mass at Saint Germain, they [all] positioned themselves in plain view of the king: Madame de Montespan with her children at the platform on the left facing everyone, and the other one on the right, although at Versailles Madame de Montespan sat on the side where the Gospels are, while Mademoiselle de Fontanges sat on the raised seats on the side where the Epistles are. There they prayed, rosary or missal in their hands, raising their eyes in ecstasy like saints. Assuredly, the court is the best comedy in the world.

[1680]   The whole court was astonished at the preference shown for [Madame de] Maintenon, an unknown person, widow of the poet Scarron, born in America, for whom the post of governess of the natural children of the king appeared to be the height of good fortune. Before too much time had elapsed, Madame de Rochefort was considering it an honor to treat her as a companion, since the king was spending most of his time at Madame de Maintenon's side, at the expense of his visits to Madame de Montespan and Mademoiselle de Fontanges. No one knew what to think, for she was old. Some regarded her as the king's confidante, others as an intermediary, others as an able person whom the king was using to write his memoirs. . . .

THE WORLD OF THE COURT

Now that we have a picture of Louis XIV in action, we will turn to the chroniclers to observe the life of the courtiers around him. Remember that these were the most distinguished nobles in the realm — the same sorts of grandees who caused so much trouble during the Fronde. Think about their relationship to the king and to each other, their sources of prestige, and the role they played at court. Watch also for differences between the functions of women and men.

[1667] Yesterday the king spent almost eight hours in council. A quantity of cavalry and infantry commissions were issued because the army has been greatly weakened by deserters, by disease, by those who have been killed, and by the garrisons left in the conquered fortifications. Ten new regiments of cavalry are being created; I don't know how many of infantry. . . .

. . . The duke of Mazarin[1] is going to preside over the Estates of Brittany. He has asked the king to command his wife to follow him. This duchess is staying with the nuns near this city, where an aunt of her husband is abbess. The king has told her to accompany her husband to Brittany or else to withdraw to the convent of the Daughters of Saint Marie on the rue Saint Antoine. She replied that she would go anywhere His Majesty commanded except with the duke of Mazarin. She wanted nothing more to do with him, and she implored the king to have pity on her children and to look into the state of the duke of Mazarin's property, for an investigation would reveal that in addition to his bigotry, he had horribly dissipated [his fortune]. It is believed that the duke took advantage of M. Colbert's absence to obtain this [royal] command about his wife, since she is [normally] protected by that minister.

[1668] . . . Day before yesterday we went to the celebrations at Versailles.[2] . . . Your Royal Highness will read accounts of this pompous festival elsewhere, and I will limit myself to matters concerning the foreign ministers. There has never been such an influx of people or such great disorder. . . . The foreign ministers were pushed, repulsed, beaten, and badly placed. They were able to see the play and the fireworks, but not the meal served in the alleys nor the superb machinery at the spot where the king entertained the ladies for supper and a ball. . . .

After the comedy we were taken to sup in the grotto, which was pretty and well lighted. There were three tables of twenty places each for us

---

[1] Charles-Armand de la Porte, marquis of La Meilleraye, duke of Mazarin, was the nephew of Cardinal Mazarin. He was the son of the duke of La Meilleraye, mentioned in the Mazarinade on page 33.

[2] This was one of the famous festivals put on by Louis at Versailles. It was the occasion for the first performance of *Georges Dandin,* a play by Molière.

Marquis de Saint Maurice, *Lettres sur la cour de Louis XIV,* ed. Jean Lemoine (Paris: Calmann-Lévy, 1910), 1:97–98, 134–35, 200–204, 214–17, 360–61, 374–76, 2:14–16.

and our followers. We were treated very well in comparison to the king's tables. Sieur de Bonneuil did not take us to the ball. It's true that it lasted only a short time because they wanted to start the fireworks, which were the most beautiful I have ever seen. . . . As for me, I went promenading in the gardens, which were marvelously well lighted with great statues and vases. Distinguished persons and ladies were standing here and there, most of them not knowing where they were going or what they were doing. Then I retired to the apartments in the château, where the best company had gone. The king and the queen had departed for Saint Germain after the fireworks, about two-thirty in the morning.

. . . A rumor from a reliable source claimed that the king was dissatisfied with his ministers and had listened to their enemies. . . . It is true that the children of M. Le Tellier do not have a cooperative attitude, but they have a hold over the whole court through self-interest: Louvois distributes military posts, and his brother the abbot controls the nomination of a quantity of ecclesiastical benefices that are dependent on his abbeys, including the benefices of Cardinal d'Este, for whom he is the grand vicar, and the benefices of the archbishop of Reims, for whom he is the coadjutor [stand-in archbishop]. He has recently received the bulls from Rome [for the post of coadjutor], and the issuance fees were waived, which would have cost him 15,000 écus. He had also thought of purchasing the post of grand almoner from Cardinal Antoine by offering him 400,000 livres, but the bishop of Orléans, brother of the duke of Coisin, grandson of the chancellor [Le Tellier], who is first almoner, broke off this negotiation. He spoke to the king about it and received encouraging words that gave him great hopes. . . .

[1669] . . . There is nothing new at court. They are following their usual pattern. The ladies are pretty, proper, and in good humor because they are well entertained and rich. They are the only ones. Everyone else grovels, and there is neither joy nor contentment at Saint Germain, where their majesties will spend the winter. This decision annoys me greatly because to get [to Saint Germain] in time to see the king or his ministers, you have to leave [Paris] an hour before dawn in this weather. It is also very expensive to stay at the inns there. But one must be resigned and not mention it because the king makes love there.

. . . The court passed the week at Versailles, where no one thought of anything but pleasure and hunting. The ladies rode horseback every day, including the "beautiful one" [probably La Vallière], who has turned out not to be pregnant, which will be a reason for the court not to come to Paris. Monday evening, while the queen was gambling, Madame the countess of Soissons, who was seated next to her, left the room, and the countess of Gramont, who was croupier, sat down on the stool next to her. When Madame the countess returned, she said to the other one that that was her seat; the other replied proudly, "We will see about that," without getting up. The countess only responded with a laugh of contempt. Then the count of Gramont spoke up and said, "Madame, the chairs are not nailed down here; my wife will stay put. We are from as good a family as you are." The queen heard the whole thing, but she did not dare say a word, even though Mademoiselle d'Elbeuf did everything she could to get her to settle the issue. Hearing about the incident, the king criticized the conduct of the count and countess of Gramont, calling them extravagant and ordering them to ask Madame the countess's pardon. Gramont opposed this and appealed to the marshals of France.[3] They sentenced his brother and sister-in-law to do what the king had ordered. He had to say to Madame the countess that he greatly regretted having failed in showing respect, that he did not believe he could have said that their family was as good as hers, but that since she claimed to have heard it, he asked her pardon. The countess of Gramont is English. She makes much of it because she is related to the [English] king, but here they make fun of her. . . .

There is still talk of some changes in posts at court. The governorship of Guyenne will be given to the duke of Crequy and his post of gentleman of the chamber to the marquis of Charost; his post of captain of the guards of the king goes to M. Colbert, brother of the minister, who was in Candia; and the black musketeers that he commands to the count of Marsan, son of the late count of Harcourt. The king also gave the governorship of Brittany to M. de Chaulnes when he left for Rome, with permission to sell the lieutenant generalship that he had purchased from the duke of Mazarin for 400,000 livres. Since I have been here, all the posts in the king's household have changed except master of the hunt. The king promotes all those who serve near his person, with the result that he is very well served. All the great lords rush to purchase posts; therefore the court is impressive and filled with distinguished men.

[1671] . . . I am sending Madame Royale one of the booklets describing the ballet that was danced here [the tragedy *Psyche,* performed at the Tuileries]. I must confess that I have never seen anything better executed or more magnificent. Such things cannot be done elsewhere be-

---

[3] Gramont was also a marshal of France, which was a military title giving him the right to judgment by his peers in matters of honor.

cause of the number of dancing masters. There were seventy of them dancing together in the last entrance. What was also marvelous was the number of violins and musicians — over three hundred, all magnificently dressed. The room is superb, specially built; the stage is spacious, marvelously well decorated; the magnificent machines and changes of scene were all well performed. Vigarani [the designer] outdid himself this time. The last scene was easily the most astonishing thing imaginable, for suddenly you see more than three hundred persons suspended either in clouds or in an aureole, making the most beautiful symphony in the world with violins, lutes, harpsichords, oboes, flutes, trumpets and cymbals. It is easy to see that in these sorts of events they are reduced to following the taste of the Italians. . . .

Primi Visconti

[1674]   Speaking of Versailles, the palace seemed to me to be inferior to many others in Paris, and yet it is of unprecedented size. . . . The garden and the fountains are marvelous [see Figure 2]. A certain Le Nôtre was the designer, and the most amazing part is that he planned it all without training, entirely from his own genius, since he had previously been a simple gardener. The fountain designer is a certain Francini, son of a Florentine, a man heavy of body and even more of mind. He costs the king a lot of money because he is ignorant of how to implement the plans of Le Nôtre. For the aqueducts alone he has had more than seven million [livres] worth of lead [pipes] put underground. There is no mine in the world as valuable as Versailles. The cost of bringing the water for the basins is worse. Windmills have been built, but to supply just a small jet of water on the expanse in front of the king's apartment, it takes a hundred fifty horses to pump the water. This is truly grand for the king, but the fountain maker cuts a really stupid figure.

Back in Paris, when the news spread of the attention I had received at court, I was besieged from morning to night: pursued by carriers, pages, and porters bringing messages to the portal of the Hôtel de Vendôme; accosted in the churches where they wouldn't let me hear Mass, in the Tuileries where ladies called to me, pursued me, pointed at me with their

Primi Fassiola di San Maiolo, *Mémoires sur la cour de Louis XIV,* 2nd ed., ed. Jean Lemoine (Paris: Calmann-Lévy, 1908), 67, 83, 104–5, 250–53, 255–56, 258–60, 271–72.

Figure 2.   *The Château of Versailles as seen from the gardens, by Israël Silvestre the Elder.*
This engraving shows the palace in its final form, as we see it today. Note the courtiers strolling on the grounds.
© *Photo RMN.*

fingers, pulled me by the clothes and by the hand. I no longer had a voice; I saw nothing further; my head was broken.

[1675]   On the evening of the last day of January, Mademoiselle d'Elbeuf got me in to see the queen, who had already retired to her bedroom. The queen said that I was a good man and that she wanted to ask for an abbey for me. I was transported to the skies, all the more so because I wasn't trying to acquire anything. The next morning I arose convinced that the deal was done. I went to thank Mademoiselle d'Elbeuf, who was in front of her mirror fixing her teeth with white wax. I recounted my good fortune to the countess of Soissons. She broke out laughing, then laughed some more, and finally told me that the queen didn't dare as much as move her lips to ask for anything in the presence of the king. Mademoiselle d'Elbeuf was a liar, she said, even though she was from the house of Lorraine, and neither of them had the slightest influence. In fact, an expression of their good will would probably ruin my own [good reputation].

[1679]   . . . At court they want only humble persons who have no secret intentions. The princes of Savoy and Lorraine and other princes from great houses, who were dangerous to the crown because of their factions and because of the civil wars they fomented, have now been reduced to living like simple, unhappy knights. Even the princes of the blood are allowed nothing more than a simple recognition of their birth. In every other matter, including government business, the ministers are the only ones who are taken seriously. I wish you could see the court: It is a real confusion of men and women. Known persons are allowed entrance everywhere. Since the nation [of the French] is loose in character, it produces a mixture of people and a constant buzzing, to such an extent that the duke of Pastrana said to me one evening, "Monsieur, this is a complete bordello!" On the other hand, when Cardinal Maldacchini came to France for the first time and saw all the knights and ladies together, he exclaimed, "Oh, what a land of cocagne! Oh, what a land of cocagne!"[1]

. . . Still, I am amazed at the way marriages are arranged. Everyone wants money. They often cheat one another, and consequently it is no surprise that separations are so numerous. I tell you, there is no country more turbulent than this one. Since they are of a sanguine temperament, every household is in revolution; there is not a single house, property, family, or honor that is permanent. You get up in the morning without knowing who you will be that evening; everything is in the hands of Providence. . . .

The great nobility are subject to even more upheaval, for whether they are in the country, at court, or in the army, they inevitably ruin themselves with their expenditures. They avoid living in towns other than Paris, so that they will not have to dispute issues of precedence with the members of the parlements and the other judges. A citizen who devotes himself to the law receives no consideration, and the only persons who appear noble are those who follow a military career. I have noticed that many bourgeois families are not considered noble, even though they have provided distinguished service as councillors and presidents [in parlements] for two, even three hundred years.[2] In a sense this is proper because such posts are venal and open to purchase by the first person to arrive. But to hear the most distinguished Frenchmen talk, no one considers any family to be respectable except the king's and his own. As for the rest, they constantly reproach one another for some defect. I knew a genealogist named Bouchet who told me that the most distinguished houses are the ones that give him gifts.

---

[1] The land of cocagne was a mythical paradise that might be translated as "the land of milk and honey."

[2] Primi means that robe nobles were not well viewed by the aristocracy; they were legally noble without question.

There are four [captains of the royal guard], who replace one another every three months, like all the officers in the royal household, except the first gentlemen of the bedchamber and the masters of the wardrobe, who each serve for a year. The holders of the great offices serve continuously, like the grand master, who is the duke of Enghien; the grand almoner, who is the cardinal of Bouillon; the grand chamberlain, who is the duke of Bouillon; and the grand squire, who is the count of Armagnac. These are called officers of the crown. There are other posts that aren't as important: the grand master of the wardrobe [and] the master of the royal hunt, both of which belong to the prince of Marsillac; the grand provost, who is the marquis of Sourches; the grand master of ceremonies, who is the marquis of Rhodes; the grand falconer, who is the seigneur of Marets; the grand furrier, called the grand marshal of the house, who is the marquis of Cavoie; the grand master of the wolf hunt, who is the seigneur of Heudicourt; and the grand master of the bread — but these last two don't have the splendor they had in former times. The first squire is the count of Beringhen. These offices enable their holders to belong to the Order of the Holy Spirit[3] if they are noble. For that matter, there are many creative ways of making oneself appear noble.

All the court posts are venal, even those in the army. Indeed, the French bankrupt themselves with their desire to obtain them. If they happen to take a round of musket fire, they lose both their life and the money that the post is worth; thus their sons end up in the poorhouse. Ambition is the greatest passion of the French. The duke of Chaulnes told me that the [financial] embarrassment everyone faces as a result of the cost of acquiring offices is the reason the women remain faithful, in order to enjoy the advantages attached to these posts [which have been acquired at such expense]; . . . for it is through [court] offices that titles, governorships, abbeys, bishoprics, benefices, and jobs are obtained, according to the rank of each person. I have noticed that the king follows certain rules in all this. As for the seigneurs who stay in the provinces, they live in obscurity. . . .

[1680]   [The Dauphine, wife of Louis XIV's eldest son,] loves Fontainebleau, but she has a great aversion for Versailles. There is constant construction work going on there, and as a result of the great displacements of soil, the air is bad. In addition, the waters, which are putrid, infest the air so completely that in the month of August everyone fell sick — the Dauphin, the Dauphine, the courtiers — everyone who was

---

[3]The Order of the Holy Spirit was a chivalric society, created by the monarchy in 1578, consisting of great nobles and clerics who swore a special oath to the king.

there except the king and me, I think. Still, the king insists on living there. No one dares talk of leaving the place because he loves it as his handiwork. The very landscape is unpleasant. There is nothing but sand and smelly swamps, and you could say that the king has introduced novel elements by bringing in woods, trees, and water. I heard Monsieur say that the king had spent a hundred million francs up to 1680, and not even a tenth of it is completed. Just to maintain the gardens; fountains; a grand canal with ships, galleys, and all kinds of boats; and numerous personnel of all sorts, he spends a million per year; and if Versailles were abandoned for only two years, not a trace of it would be left.

The Princess Palatine

We have a different perspective of court life from the duchess of Orléans, who felt trapped and victimized by the hypocrisy of the court. She was Elisabeth Charlotte (Liselotte), the daughter of Karl Ludwig, ruler of the Palatinate, a small state in Germany. Raised as a Calvinist, she had been brought to France in 1671, when she was nineteen years old, and hastily converted to Catholicism so that she could become the second wife of Philippe, duke of Orléans, Louis XIV's brother. (As mentioned previously, Philippe was referred to as "Monsieur," and each of his two wives was referred to as "Madame.") Liselotte's position at court was far from enviable. Monsieur's first wife, Henrietta, daughter of King Charles I of England, had died mysteriously in 1670, some said of poison. Liselotte's husband, known for his homosexual proclivities and male favorites, was denied most political responsibilities by the king, although he possessed a vast fortune. Liselotte's children became pawns in the marital games of the court. Finally, to her horror, she had to remain silent while French armies destroyed her beloved Palatinate on the pretext of defending her interests. Liselotte was a great correspondent, whose letters to her relatives in Germany give us the outlook of a woman, a mother, and an outsider at court.

PARIS, MAY 22, 1675
. . . The unbelievable crowd of people who came to see me every day has kept me from writing before now. Then I went to court, where for eight

Elisabeth Charlotte Orléans, *A Woman's Life in the Court of the Sun King: Letters of Liselotte von der Pfanz, 1652–1722,* trans. Elborg Forster (Baltimore: Johns Hopkins University Press, 1984), 11–12, 13–14, 16, 38–40, 53–54, 55–57, 63, 74.

days in a row there were leave-takings for those who joined the army. And with all that, one only arises at half past ten around here; around twelve one goes to Mass; after Mass one chats with those who have attended and around two one goes to table. After dinner the ladies come; this lasts until six, and thereafter come those of the men of quality who are still here. At this time Monsieur plays bassette and I also have to play at another table . . . or I must take the others to the opera, which lasts until nine. When I return from the opera, I must play again until ten or half past ten, and then to bed. So, Your Grace can imagine how much time I have had to myself. But henceforth I shall be more assiduous. Saturday next we shall go to Saint Cloud, where I will not have so much company that keeps me from writing.

VERSAILLES, AUGUST 22, 1675
I have here two wild characters [her children] who all day long make such noise with their drums that one can neither hear nor see; however, in the last two weeks the oldest has become a little more quiet, for in this time he has cut five teeth, including the eye-teeth.[1] This autumn he is to be weaned, for he already can happily devour a big chunk of bread from his fist like a peasant. The littlest one is even stronger; he is already beginning to walk on his leash and wants to jump like his brother, but he is still a bit scaly-pated. But I think this is enough talk of the little fellows. Monday next we will go to Fontainebleau, where the king wants to take me because I have never been there. I hope we will have a good time, for all the hunting equipment is being sent there, as well as the comedians. The lovely weather we are having also makes me hope that we will take many carriage rides.

SAINT CLOUD, APRIL 20, 1676
I have been quite unable to answer you before now, for I was too stricken by the unexpected disaster God Almighty has visited upon me; I simply cannot get over it [her son had died on March 16]. Now you see that it was not for nothing that I wished my children were in your hands, for I saw my misfortune come from afar. They have strange ways here with children, and unhappily I was only too aware that they would not work out well in the long run. My misfortune is that I have no idea how one must handle children, having no experience in this matter, and therefore I must believe all the drivel they tell me here. . . .

---

[1] Her two sons were Alexandre Louis, two years old, and Philippe, one year old, who became regent of France in 1715.

SAINT CLOUD, OCTOBER 10, 1676

Although today I have already written a long letter to Ma Tante [her aunt], one of the first I have written since my confinement, I do not wish to let this mail pass without thanking you for all the good wishes you sent me and my newborn child. As for me, I have been feeling exceedingly well, thanks be to God, ever since I was delivered and so far have not suffered the slightest discomfort, although this time the labor was harder than the other two times: I was in strong labor for ten hours and this, to tell the truth, has so put me off that I do not wish to build up a set of organ pipes, as you say in your letter; it is just too painful a business. And then if they stayed alive, that would be one thing, but if one sees them die as I sadly experienced this year, there is no pleasure in it at all. As for my remaining de Chartres [the living son], whom I so often wish to be with you, he is now, thank God, in quite perfect health, as is his baby sister, who is as fat as a stuffed goose and very big for her age. On Monday last both of them were christened and given Monsieur's and my names, so that the boy is now Philippe and the girl Elisabeth Charlotte. Now there is another Liselotte in the world; God grant that she may not be more unhappy than I am, for then she will have little to complain about. . . .

VERSAILLES, DECEMBER 6, 1682

My dearest sister, I had meant to write Your Grace a great big letter through Count Schomberg, but this has turned out as the proverb says, "Man proposes and God disposes." For he came here the day before yesterday and said that he would have to leave by Tuesday night, and that I would have to give him my letters on Monday. On that day I was unable to write because people kept coming in until six o'clock, and at six o'clock I had to go upstairs to the queen's rooms, for it was *jour d'appartement*.[2] Your Grace does not know what this means, but I will tell her as soon as I have done with what I am saying. Yesterday I wrote to my brother and to Katherine, and just as soon as I was about to start writing to Your Grace as well, my chambermaids came in to dress me, for at seven there was a confounded ball which I had to attend against my will and without pleasure, for of all entertainments I have come to hate dancing more than anything else. Today I gave an audience to an envoy of Parma, thereafter I had to write a long letter to the Queen of Spain [Liselotte's stepdaughter], and at eight I must go to see a new play with

---

[2]*Jour d'appartement,* or "day of the apartment," refers to Louis XIV's practice of holding open house in his suite in the palace on certain days of the week. This was a major social event, which Liselotte describes.

Madame la Dauphine. So I have only this hour to write, for tomorrow, right after the king's Mass, I must go hunting with His Majesty and after the hunt it will be a bit late to write, for it is again *jour d'appartement.* And so that Your Grace can understand what this is, Your Grace must know that the king is having a great gallery built here, which goes all the way from his apartment to that of the Queen. But since this gallery is not quite completed yet, the king has had the part that is done and painted partitioned off and turned into a salon. Mondays, Wednesdays, and Fridays are *jours d'appartement.* Then all the men of the court assemble in the king's antechamber and all the women meet at six in the queen's room. Thereupon everyone goes to the salon of which I spoke, and from there to a large room where there is music for those who want to dance. From there one goes to a room where the king's throne stands. There one finds various kinds of music, concerts, and singing. From there one goes into the bedchamber, where three tables for playing at cards are set up, one for the king, one for the queen, and one for Monsieur. From there one goes to a room that could be called a hall, where more than twenty tables, covered with green velvet cloth with a gold fringe, have been put up for all kinds of games [see Figure 3]. From there one goes to a room with four large tables for the collation, all kinds of things like fruit cakes and preserves. This looks just like the children's table on Christmas eve. From there one goes into yet another room, where there are also four tables as long as those for the collation, and on these there are a great many carafes and glasses and all kinds of wines and liqueurs . . . so that those who want to eat or drink can make a stop in these two rooms. After one is done with the collation, which is taken standing up, one goes back to the room with the many tables; now everyone sits down to a different game, and it is unbelievable how many varieties of games are being played: lansquenet, trictrac, picquet, l'hombre, chess, . . . summa summarum, every conceivable game. When the king and the queen come into the room, no one gets up from the game. Those who do not play, like myself and a great many others, just stroll from room to room, now to the music and now to the game room, for one is allowed to go wherever one wishes; this lasts from six until ten, when one goes to supper, and this is called *jour d'appartement.* But if I should now tell Your Grace how magnificently these rooms are furnished and what great quantity of silver dishes are in them, I should never finish. It is certainly worth seeing. All of this would be delightful and most entertaining if one came to this apartment with a happy heart. . . . But here they are calling me to go to the comedy with Madame la Dauphine; that is why I must close for this time. . . .

Figure 3. *One of a series of engravings depicting the entertainments in the king's apartment described by the Princess Palatine on page 74.*
Here is the third room, where "all kinds of games" are played, including this variation on billiards.
1694 Collection Grosjean, Paris, France. Giraudon/Art Resource, NY.

SAINT CLOUD, OCTOBER 1, 1687

I am bound to tell Your Grace that court life is becoming so dull that one can hardly stand it any longer. For the king imagines that he is pious when he sees to it that everyone is properly bored and bothered. His son's wife [the Dauphine] is being harassed so much by the old women with whom she has been surrounded that it is almost unspeakable. Here is an example: her children are ill, and therefore the good Princess wanted to stay here a few more days in order to be with them. For this she is scolded and told that she wants to stay here because she does not wish to be with the king. Then, when she says that she will go along, the women bruit it about that she does not care for her children and does not love them, summa summarum: whatever one does is wrong. I for my part cannot believe that loving old women and being cranky can be pleasing to our Lord; if that is the way to heaven, it will be hard for me to get in. It is a wretched thing when a man does not want to follow his own reason and lets himself be guided by calculating priests and old courtesans: this makes life quite miserable for honest and sincere people. But what is the use of complaining: nothing can be done about it. Those of us who are caught in this tyranny, like the poor Dauphine and I, we can see that the thing is ridiculous, yet we do not feel like laughing at all.

SAINT CLOUD, APRIL 14, 1688

... I did not want to let this good and safe opportunity go by without unburdening my heart to Your Grace and telling her all the things that plague me and which I cannot entrust to the ordinary mail. And so I must confess to my dearest Ma Tante that I have been most distressed lately, although I try to show this as little as ever I can. I have been made privy to the reason why the king treats the Chevalier of Lorraine and the Marquis of Effiat [her husband's male favorites] so well; it is because they have promised him that they would persuade Monsieur to ask the king most humbly to marry the Montespan's children to mine, that is, the limping Duke of Maine to my daughter and Mademoiselle of Blois to my son. In this case the Maintenon is all for the Montespan, since she has brought up these bastards and loves the limping boy like her own child. ... Now Your Grace can imagine how I would feel to see only my daughter so badly established, considering that her sisters are so well married.[3] Even if the Duke of Maine were not the child of a double adultery but a true prince, I would not like him for a son-in-law nor his sister for a daughter-in-law, for he is dreadfully ugly and lame and has other bad qualities to boot, stingy as the devil and without kindness. His sister, it is true, is rather kind, but extremely sickly; her eyes always look so dim that I fear she will go blind someday. But most of all, they are the children of a double adultery, as I said before, and the children of the most wicked and desperate woman on earth. I leave it to Your Grace to think whether I would wish this to happen. And the worst part of it is that I cannot properly discuss this matter with Monsieur, for whenever I say a word to him, he has the delightful habit of passing it right on to the king, to add to it, and to make all kinds of trouble for me with the king. So I am in terrible straits and do not know how I shall go about averting this disaster. Meanwhile I cannot help fretting inside myself, and whenever I see these bastards my blood boils over. ...

VERSAILLES, MARCH 20, 1689

... Your Grace says that they can take away everything but a happy

---

[3]These were the two daughters of Monsieur's previous wife, who were respectively queen of Spain and duchess of Savoy.

heart. As long as I was in Germany, I would have thought so, too, but since I have come to France I have learned, alas, that they can take that too. As long as those by whom one is chagrined are below oneself and if one is not dependent on them, one can save oneself by despising them, but when they are one's lord and master and when one cannot ever do one step without their permission, this is rather more difficult than one might imagine. If my children were in my power, they would give me great pleasure; but when I think that my daughter is already surrounded by such people that I cannot say a word in her presence from fear that I will get into trouble, and when I see that Monsieur is bound and determined to make the Marquis of Effiat my son's governor, even though this man is my worst enemy and will set my son against me as much as he has set Monsieur against me, then I must confess that the children are giving me more chagrin than pleasure. The king has not permitted Béthune to leave Poland in order to become my son's governor, so I am very much afraid that it will be the above-mentioned Marquis, who is the most debauched fellow in the world, and particularly in the worst respect. If he becomes my son's governor, I can be quite sure that he will teach him all the worst vices, and this gives me little pleasure. As for my daughter, I fear, as does Your Grace, that this wretched war will prevent her from marrying the Electoral Prince of the Palatinate. Nonetheless I cannot give up this wish, for it would be a great comfort to me to think that the grandchild of His Grace the Elector, my late father, would once again rule the Palatinate and that my daughter would not have a limping bastard for a husband. . . .

VERSAILLES, JANUARY 10, 1692
Although my eyes are so thick and swollen that I can barely look out of them, since I confess that I was foolish enough to bawl all night, I do not wish to let this Friday mail pass without telling Your Grace about the most upsetting thing that happened to me yesterday, when I was least expecting it. At half past three Monsieur came in and said to me, "Madame, I have a message from the king for you, which will not be too pleasing to you, and you are to give him your answer in person by tonight. The king wishes me to tell you that since he and I and my son are agreed on the marriage of Mademoiselle de Blois to my son, you will not be foolish enough to demur."[4] I leave it to Your Grace to imagine how

---

[4]Mademoiselle de Blois was the king's illegitimate daughter by Montespan. This marriage to Liselotte's son, who became the duke of Orléans and the regent in 1715, linked Mademoiselle de Blois to the illustrious Orléans family. Liselotte's descendants were prominent in the French Revolution. During the July Monarchy from 1830 to 1848, her descendant Louis Philippe ruled France.

much this dismays and also grieves me. That night, shortly after eight, the king had me called into his study and asked me whether Monsieur had informed me of the proposition and what I had to say to it. "When Your Majesty and Monsieur speak to me as my masters, as you are doing, I can only obey," I said, remembering what Your Grace once wrote to me through Monsieur Harling, namely that if they really insisted on this marriage, I should give in. So now it has come to pass; this morning the king and all the courtiers called on me in my room to compliment me on this lovely affair, and I did not want to wait any longer to report this (I almost said misfortune) to Your Grace. My head hurts so much that I cannot say more. . . .

Exéchiel Spanheim

To sum up, we turn to Exéchiel Spanheim, a learned, well-traveled German Protestant who represented another important German prince, the elector of Brandenburg, at the French court from 1680 to 1689. In 1690, immediately after his return to Germany, Spanheim wrote a long, detailed report titled Account of the Court of France. *This excerpt contains his conclusions about the court in the late 1680s when it was under the influence of Madame de Maintenon. Note the change in tone as the king grows older and settles down with a permanent partner who influences life at court in significant ways. Note also how formal the king's ceremonies have become.*

My first observation is that although the custom has been established that devoted courtiers attend the king's *lever* [getting-up ceremony] every morning, there are nevertheless various levels of admission. First come those who have the right to be admitted to the *petit lever*.[1] They are summoned and then allowed to enter — the officers of the chamber such as the first gentleman of the chamber on duty, the grand master of the wardrobe, the first valet of the bedroom serving for that quarter, and the king's readers, who are summoned if any are present. . . . Thus even

---

[1] The *petit lever* was the earlier, more intimate ceremony of the king's rising, as opposed to the *grand lever,* when more people were admitted into his presence.

Exéchiel Spanheim, *Relation de la cour de France en 1690,* ed. Ch. Schefer (Paris: Librairie Renouard, 1882), 145–57.

if princes of the blood, cardinals, or other great lords who do not have this right of first entrance are present in the antechamber, the door to the king's *lever*— and at Versailles the entire apartment where the king sleeps and dresses — remains closed to them. I have seen this happen to the late prince of Condé, the present prince, and similar persons. The courtiers nevertheless gather in a crowd, waiting for the door to be opened up.

The *second entrance* is ordinarily reserved for princes and lords of the above-mentioned first rank, the captain of the king's guards who is serving that quarter, and the first butler. They are summoned by name by the usher, and the door is opened when they present themselves and then closed again. After a certain length of time it is reopened, and the courtiers are allowed to enter freely, some of whom are first summoned by name in accordance with their reputation at court before the others are admitted. . . . If you enter in time and it is possible to get near, you can see that the king gets dressed from foot to head in the presence of the onlookers. His shirt is handed to him by a prince of the blood if there is one, or by the grand chamberlain if he is present, or, in his absence, by the first gentleman of the bedchamber in attendance. When the king is almost dressed, his hair is done in front of the onlookers on the days scheduled for this. He dines, and afterward he goes into the next room to his prayer stool, which is next to his bed, and says his prayers on his knees in plain sight of the courtiers, accompanied by the bishops or chaplains present, who are also kneeling behind him on the same platform. When this is done, the king retires into the chamber where he customarily holds council meetings, unless he has some public audience to give to the foreign ministers or to deputies from the clergy or the provinces who have been instructed to harangue him at such a meeting.

The *petit coucher*[2] of the king, as it is called, is less frequent than his *lever,* and there are usually only a small number of courtiers present, given the fact that the king always goes to bed late. It should be noted that the king usually gives the *bourgeoir* [a small chandelier with a lighted candle for undressing] to a person in attendance of his choice, and that he gives it only to persons of a certain rank and distinguished status. This also represents a mark of honor and favor for the person who receives it.

A [second] observation is that, as presently constituted, the French court is so submissive to the king that it would be impossible to imagine

---

[2]The *petit coucher* was the corresponding ceremony when the king went to bed.

greater eagerness to pay him court or more dedication in performing each person's assigned functions with complete regularity — something that was not seen during the previous reigns or even during the minority, when absolute power over the government was in the hands of a first minister like Cardinal Mazarin or Cardinal Richelieu. The result is that all the courtiers, down to the least of them, make a special effort to see the king and be seen [by him] on every possible occasion, such as at his *lever,* when he leaves the council meeting and goes to church, or when he takes his meals in public, as he ordinarily does; and this can only be . . . because he has mastered all the graces and everything related to political, military, or ecclesiastical affairs. All of this has caused the French court to become enormous and to be packed with all kinds of people, especially those who have business at court and therefore follow it wherever it is, not to mention those drawn to it by the entertainments that take place from time to time or by the very habit of going there. . . .

[Another] observation is that thanks to the salutary abolition of duels and the rigor with which it has been enforced, we no longer see those disorders, quarrels, and deadly consequences that made so much noise and damage under previous reigns; to which could be added the order restored through policing, resulting, among other things, in the renewed security of life at Versailles and the other places where the court stays. . . . And what will appear no less laudable is that debauchery, dissolute lifestyles, blasphemy, and other scandalous vices that were previously so common at court are no longer tolerated with impunity. Or at least they present an insurmountable obstacle to the advancement of those who indulge in them. . . .

My last observation is that despite everything I have said about the court of France, there is still a great deal of constraint and deception in many people's conduct. Since most of them are motivated only by self-interest or ambition, they must avoid the appearance of anything that might work against this interest, and they must appear attached to the things that conform to the taste and temper of the present reign. This tendency is reinforced by the natural submissiveness of the French nation, to the point that they are slavelike toward their king when they believe that he rules by himself. . . . Everything is more planned, more constrained, less free, less open, less joyful than the habitual genius of the French nation [would suggest], especially its courtiers, with the result that even the entertainments and festivals that the king gives for the principal ladies of the court seem all the less enjoyable in that they appear to be organized to please Madame de Maintenon, and they still seem to be governed by constraint. . . . I might add, finally, that most of the great lords and courtiers one sees, except for a small number like the prince of Condé, live off of the benevolence of the king or the revenues of their posts, and thus they are cautious in their expenditures, less exalted in their manner, and subject to a blind, submissive dependence on the wishes of the court.

3

Managing France

Life at court was the focal point of French absolutism because it was the place where the king interacted with the most important figures in the kingdom. But if we restricted our gaze to the frivolous social life described in chapter 2, we would be missing much of the real work of government. This was carried out in royal council meetings and in the agencies that prepared those meetings, as well as in the provinces, where people sent out from the king's government interacted with regional dignitaries and their companies of officers.

We have already encountered the royal ministers, who were both disdained and feared at court—the "cold and dry" Colbert, the "hard and violent" Louvois, "sweet" Pomponne, and "ceremonial" Châteauneuf, to quote Primi Visconti on some of Louis XIV's chief collaborators in 1673. From the beginning, the king relied heavily on three or four important men who held multiple positions: Jean-Baptiste Colbert handled finances, the economy, and the king's building projects. Michel Le Tellier handled military affairs and was succeeded in that role by his son, the marquis of Louvois. Hughes de Lionne handled foreign affairs, succeeded by Arnaud de Pomponne. In the later years, as these men retired, their successors were often drawn from the same families.

Thus the running of France was cleverly concentrated in the hands of the king and a few trusted ministers, backed up by various agencies, which prepared the business of the meetings. Correspondence was handled by four secretaries of state, each of whom was responsible for one part of France and one type of business—finance, war, foreign affairs, or the special status of Protestants. Each secretary of state had assistants who helped with writing and record keeping. These persons were in close touch with the intendant stationed in each province and with other agents on mission, who sent back detailed reports concerning their assigned projects and the state of their provinces. The secretaries digested this information and reported to the councils. After receiving orders from the king or a minister, they wrote back to the provinces with further instructions. In this way, information and instructions flowed back and forth between the court and the provinces on a regular basis.

The king had a financial bureau consisting of *intendants of finance* and their assistants. In addition, a company of *masters of requests,* who were legally trained agents well versed in judicial issues, prepared dossiers on key issues. This company was the proving ground from which future intendants were often chosen. The king presided in person over his council, which took on several different names and procedures depending on the day of the week and the type of business. He also consulted for hours with particular ministers. In addition to the so-called ministers of state — Colbert, Le Tellier, and Lionne — council meetings typically included secretaries of state, intendants of finance, and masters of requests, as well as the chancellor, who was the top judicial official. Reports or letters were read, points of policy were debated, and the king ultimately made the decision (see Figure 4). There were also lesser councils that Louis did not personally attend. All of these government officials, who were sharply distinguished from the courtiers, were intelligent, educated experts drawn from the robe nobility — that is, from important judicial and financial families. They were notable for their talent and service but inferior in status to the grandees at court.

These men had a comprehensive grasp of the process of government and the state of the country. They wrote well-crafted, analytical letters and exercised a keen sense of how to invoke the royal reputation to achieve their objectives. Louvois handled the army, which had its own intendants and hierarchies, while Lionne corresponded with foreign ambassadors. The best-known minister was Colbert, a methodical man who was constantly pressing his correspondents to send more information and write with greater precision. Colbert's economic philosophy is best described as *mercantilism.* He believed that Europe had a limited amount of wealth, which he equated with precious metal, and that the various countries were competing for shares of it. If Louis XIV was to triumph, he needed to stimulate French manufacturing and promote exports, while heavily taxing imports, so that more coin would flow into the realm. The French people would then be richer, and the king could draw more taxes from them. Historians debate how successful these mercantilist policies were, but at least in the short run, most of them failed because the initiative came from Colbert and his financier allies rather than from the merchant or manufacturing communities.

Figure 4. *Louis XIV attends a council meeting in the Palace of Versailles.*
Note the elegant surroundings and the way attention is focused on the king.
© *Photo RMN—C. Jean.*

Colbert had an imperfect understanding of the reasons for the success of France's rivals. The Dutch and the English were cornering international markets with superior navies, cheaper and better products, and more advanced credit systems. Their governments gave voice to merchant interests and thus made policy decisions that favored commerce. In France, by contrast, Louis XIV was surrounded by privileged nobles who valued landed wealth above capitalistic enterprise and thought in terms of traditional noble values. Colbert wanted Louis XIV to establish protective tariffs, subsidize new industries, and form large monopolistic trading companies modeled on the English and Dutch companies. But this program was hard to sell to a traditional king who thought in terms of divine right, royal splendor, and the glories of land warfare and who had difficulty getting excited about merchants and production techniques.

Colbert's Instructions for the Commissioners Who Have Been Sent into the Provinces, September 1663

This memorandum by Colbert gives a sense of the scope of his intentions and the way his mind was working. He is instructing intendants and other special agents on location to gather a comprehensive set of data on every aspect of economic and political life in the provinces. His questions read like a catalog of the complexities of ruling a large, decentralized country. This document suggests the kind of rational information gathering that was going on in the royal council. Note the sort of plans that are suggested by Colbert's questions. Note also how conscious he is of the important people who need to be conciliated or managed. Remember that these ambitious intentions were not necessarily realized. Most of this information had to be gathered in a limited period of time by a single agent in each province who had very little assistance and hardly any staff. This agent was dependent on information passed along by third parties of varying reliability. Nevertheless, Colbert's agents were capable of prodigious amounts of effort. Information poured in, making Louis XIV's government better informed than any previous administration. The actual document is considerably longer than what is reproduced here, but these excerpts do provide a clear and detailed look at Colbert's instructions.

Wishing to be clearly informed of the state of the provinces within his realm, His Majesty has ordered that this memorandum be sent on his behalf to the masters of requests so that they can investigate carefully and exactly all the items contained below, each within the confines of his district.

Maps.   These gentlemen must seek out any maps that have been made of each province or tax district, checking carefully to see whether they are accurate; and if they are not correct or even not detailed enough, they are to see if they can find some capable and intelligent person to redraw them, in the same province or in the surrounding ones. His Majesty wants them to require these persons to work continuously and without interruption. . . .

Pierre Clément, ed., *Lettres, instructions et mémoires de Colbert* (Paris: Imprimerie Impériale, 1867), 4:27–43.

His Majesty wants [the masters of requests] to draw up accurate reports about everything he wants to know, namely:

Ecclesiastical. As regards the church, the name and number of bishoprics; which cities, towns, villages, and parishes are subject to their ecclesiastical jurisdiction; the nature of their temporal seigneurial holdings and which cities and parishes lie within them. In particular, if the bishop is temporal lord of the cathedral city, indicate the name, age, estate, and disposition of the bishop; whether he is from the region or not; whether that is his normal place of residence; how he performs his episcopal visitations; what influence he has in his region and what impact he might have in times of trouble; his reputation among his people. . . .

The name and number of all the secular and regular ecclesiastical houses in the province; the name and number of abbeys founded; the [religious] order they belong to; what monks inhabit them; whether they are reformed or not; how many monks there were in each of them at the time when the reform was introduced as well as thirty or forty years earlier. . . . The same process must be followed for the endowed abbeys for women and then for the mendicant orders of both men and women, so that His Majesty can learn accurately and comprehensively from this complete listing how much revenue the church enjoys in each province; how much it gets from its temporal possessions; how many vassals and subjects it has; the nature of the conduct of the principal persons who are in charge of the salvation of the others; and generally everything concerning the ecclesiastic order, which is the first order of his kingdom.

Military. As for the military administration, which concerns the second order of his kingdom, the nobility, His Majesty is already familiar with the talents of the governors and lieutenant generals of his provinces. Nevertheless, in order to perfect these reports, he wants the masters of requests to begin their inquiry on the nobility by naming the governors; their ancestry and family ties in the province; whether they currently reside there; their good and bad conduct; whether they are accused of taking money or vexing the people in any other way; whether such accusations are credible; whether the people are complaining about them; what influence they have among the nobility and the people. And since His Majesty believes that the greatest concern of the provincial governors should be to stand up firmly for justice and prevent the oppression of the weak caused by the violence of the powerful, His Majesty especially wishes to be informed about the past conduct of these governors, in order to be able to evaluate what he should expect from them in the future. . . .

His Majesty desires to be especially informed about everything relating to the nobility — that is, the principal houses of each province: their family ties; their possessions; the extent of their lands and seigneuries; their morals and behavior; whether they do violence to the inhabitants of their lands, and in the event that some notable act of violence has been committed that went unpunished, he would be very glad to be informed of the details; whether they facilitate or hinder the functioning of the royal courts; also their influence in the region either with other gentlemen or with the people. . . .

For the lesser nobility, it would be good to know how many of them there are and the names of the most respected; whether, in general, many of them have been to war or not; whether they cultivate their lands themselves or rent them out to tenant farmers. This is one of the most essential indications of their interest in going to war or staying at home. . . .

Justice. As far as justice is concerned, if there is a parlement or another sovereign company in the province, the masters of requests must examine closely those who sit on the court, both as a group and as individuals. The conduct of the whole court during His Majesty's minority must be examined, what impulses it followed, and what means were used by the principal members when they led it in evil or good directions. If its conduct was bad, find out whether its motives for improving since then are strong enough to suggest that in a similar situation they would hold firm, or whether there is reason to fear that they would relapse into the same errors.

And since this is surely the most important thing to be examined in the province, it is essential to identify in detail the interests and talents of these companies' principal officers, in particular whether those who led them astray are still alive. . . .

His Majesty has frequently received complaints that the officials in the sovereign companies in various localities use force to require the sale of landed property that they want for themselves. He would especially like to be informed of where this occurs. It is also necessary to indicate all the landed property that is owned by each of the officials of such companies. . . . The same thing must be done for the *bailliage* courts, *sénéchaussée* courts, and présidial courts. . . .

Finances.   As for finances, in the provinces where there is a cour des aides,[1] indicate the names of the officials, their attainments, and their family ties in the province. . . .

In addition, examine whether the people suffer harassment, either through the [excessive] length of trials or through unwarranted legal fees. Appropriate remedies must be sought for all these abuses, and the simplest ones possible. Also, the greatest surcharges endured by the taxpayers are the result of having such a large number of false nobles in the provinces, some of whom were created by royal letters and some by simple decrees of the cour des aides. It is important to seek out appropriate remedies for both these problems. . . .

The King's Revenues.   It remains to examine matters concerning the king's revenues. They consist of the crown lands, which are all alienated and which therefore produce no revenues; and of the import and export duties, sales tax, salt tax, other duties, and tailles. For each of these five kinds of revenues, investigate carefully how much His Majesty collects each year from each province. . . .

After having learned the value of these various types of revenues and thus of everything the king draws annually from the province, examine in detail all the difficulties encountered in levying and collecting them, either by decreasing the revenues or by harming the people. . . .

The Situation in the Provinces.   After explaining everything that is to be done to delineate the four kinds of government in the provinces of the realm [ecclesiastical, military, judicial, and financial], it remains only to examine what advantages His Majesty can offer to each. For this purpose, the commissioners must carefully examine the inclinations and spirit of the people of each province, each region, and each town: whether they are inclined toward warfare, toward agriculture, or toward commerce and manufacturing; whether the provinces are on the coast or not, and, if so, whether there are numbers of able seamen available and what kind of reputation they have as sailors; the condition of the land — whether it is completely under cultivation or whether there are some uncultivated regions, and if the soil is fertile or not and what sort of crops it produces; whether the inhabitants are industrious, whether they attempt to cultivate their land effectively, and, even more, whether they try to put their land to its best use and whether they are good man-

---

[1]A cour des aides was a regional sovereign court that handled financial matters on appeal.

agers; whether there are forests in the province and what condition they are in (on this point it should be noted that the king has issued a memorandum dealing with everything involving forest reform in the realm); and what sort of trade and commerce is carried out in each province and what sort of manufacturing is there.

Commerce.   And, on these two points, which are surely the most important since they concern the industriousness of the inhabitants, His Majesty also wants to be informed of the changes that have taken place in the past forty or fifty years in each province's trade and manufacturing; among other things, whether during this period, or even before, there was foreign trade that has since ceased, the reasons for the cessation, and how to reestablish that trade. If manufacturing has been abandoned, why this has happened and how manufacturing can be reestablished.

His Majesty wants the commissioners to pay particular attention to commerce and manufacturing, which he considers to be the two sole means of attracting wealth into the kingdom and enabling an infinite number of his subjects to subsist easily. Their numbers will increase considerably every year if it pleases the Lord to maintain the peace that Europe is currently enjoying.

Navy.   To this end, they must find out the number of ships owned by His Majesty's subjects; they must strongly urge each city's chief merchants and traders to buy more, to form companies for foreign trade, and to undertake long sea voyages. They must promise them all the protection and help they will need. . . .

Manufacturing.   The same thing must be done with regard to manufacturing, not only to reestablish all the manufactories that have been lost but also to establish new ones. And since His Majesty is very attached to this question, if the commissioners find cities that are truly eager to implement these reestablishments but lack the means, not only will His Majesty give them his protection, but he will even assist them with certain sums of money proportionate to the [scale of the] proposed plans. . . .

Canals.   Furthermore, His Majesty would like to be informed about all the navigable rivers. He has already ordered the suppression of all [river] tolls, which were considerably reducing the advantages that river navigation ought to provide, but he still wants the commissioners to work diligently to uncover any obstacle that might hinder the navigation of the rivers, along with the method of eliminating them and facilitating trade and the transportation of merchandise, both within and outside the kingdom.

With regard to nonnavigable rivers, His Majesty wants his commissioners to inspect them personally, assisted by experts and persons familiar with them, and summarize all the methods that could be used to make them navigable; the necessary expenditures and the compensations that would have to be paid; which regions would benefit; and whether all or part of the expense could be levied upon the benefiting region.

Bridges and Roads.   Furthermore, His Majesty wants the commissioners to inspect the paths, bridges, and structures that have fallen into ruin in each parish. They are to have summaries drawn up by intelligent and economical persons, so that he can order that repairs be undertaken and provide for the necessary funds, according to the degree of public need. In fact, if the commissioners should decide that new projects are necessary to facilitate commerce and the transportation of merchandise, he would like them to draw up reports and cost estimates.

Horse Breeding.   Finally, His Majesty desires to have stud farms reestablished in the realm. They are necessary not only for public utility during peace and war but also to prevent considerable sums from leaving the country for foreign horses. He wants to be informed of the reasons all those who used to raise mares, whether they were peasants using them for their daily work or gentlemen and persons of quality using them for their service and pleasure, stopped doing so, causing the importation of foreign horses into the realm. . . .

The masters of requests are informed that the king intends them to make their visits and carry out all the points included in these instructions within the period of four or five months' time, at the end of which His Majesty will send them orders to go to another province, leaving [behind] memoranda and instructions concerning all the work they have not been able to finish, which will be carried on by the person who succeeds them. His Majesty would like them to put forth assiduous work and extraordinary diligence so that the masters of requests can visit the entire kingdom in a period of seven or eight years' time. As a result they will become capable of the highest employment. His Majesty is reserving for himself the judgment as to who has done the best work, as seen in the reports they will deliver in his council, and he will reward them with tokens of his satisfaction.

Figure 5. *Jean-Baptiste Colbert in 1666, painted by Claude Lefebvre* (1632–1675).
The king's best-known minister is elegantly dressed, but his outfit is still rather
plain by comparison with the fashions of the aristocrats at court.
© *Photo RMN—Gérard Blot.*

Financial Memorandum by Colbert,
Addressed to the King in 1670

*Seven years later, Colbert drew up another lengthy report in which he dis-
cussed the problem of budget deficits (see Figure 5). We can begin to see here
how the king's love of grandeur and war would jeopardize Colbert's economic reforms. Shortly thereafter, in 1672, Louis XIV entered a six-year*

Pierre Clément, ed., *Lettres, instructions et mémoires de Colbert* (Paris: Imprimerie Nationale, 1873), 7:233–56.

war against the Dutch that was to be only one in a long series of ever more expensive wars.

Here we get a sample of Colbert's thinking about France's economy and his mercantilist assumptions. He sees the kingdom as a producer of wealth and the taxation process as skimming off a proportion of that wealth. He would like to keep these riches inside France and generate even more by promoting new industries. Note how Colbert talks to the king. He has everything figured out, but he must get Louis to see things his way and induce him to make the right decisions of his own volition. This selection also indicates the impressive scope of the projects Colbert had undertaken since 1663. Note, however, that even Colbert realizes that these industries are in their infancy and very vulnerable. (Many of them in fact failed.) Think of this document as a testament to the kind of thinking that was going on in the king's council, however removed it may have been from the realities out in the countryside.

Sire, the state of Your Majesty's finances has caused me to do a close study to find the reasons for the changes I have observed, and then to present [my findings] to Your Majesty, so that you can use your great prudence and insight to provide whatever solutions you deem necessary and appropriate.

Everything I tell Your Majesty on this subject is based on nine consecutive years' experience in a rather successful administration, and on mathematical and demonstrable truths which cannot be denied, if Your Majesty will only be kind enough to devote the necessary time and patience to understand them well. . . .

[Colbert goes on to review how during the past nine years taxes have been lowered and yet revenues have increased through better collection methods. A period of prosperity once made it possible to increase expenditures as well, but in 1670 there was hardship that needed to be analyzed. Colbert states that the problem was that taxes were too high relative to national wealth.]

From everything that has just been said, it follows that the recovery of the people will consist of making what they pay into the public treasury proportionate to the amount of money circulating in commerce. This ratio has always been 150 million to 45 million. It is currently 120 million to 70 million. Consequently, it is much too high, and a logical conclusion is that the people will fall into great misery.

We should have done one of two things to prevent this problem: either decrease taxes and expenditures or increase the amount of money circulating in commerce.

For the first, the taxes have been decreased, but thanks to the king's immense authority and the great respect that the people have for his orders, greater tax revenues have been taken in, despite the great reductions [in rate] that have been made. . . . This can be clearly seen in the taille receipts, which used to produce only 16 million for the public treasury out of 56 million levied, whereas at present 32 million levied produce 24 million. . . .

The second solution would consist of three goals: increasing the amount of money in public commerce by attracting it away from the countries that have it; keeping it within the realm and preventing it from leaving; and giving men greater capacity to derive profits from it.

In these three points lie the grandeur and power of the state and the magnificence of the king, because of the expenditures that great revenues will allow him to make. And he will be all the more exalted in that this process will simultaneously humble neighboring states. There is only a fixed quantity of money circulating in all of Europe, which is increased from time to time by silver coming from the West Indies. It is demonstrable that if there are only 150 million livres in silver circulating [in the kingdom], we cannot succeed in increasing [this amount] by 20, 30, or 50 million without at the same time taking the equivalent quantity away from neighboring states. This results in the double effect that we have seen so markedly during the past several years: Your Majesty's power and grandeur are increased, while your enemies and those who envy you are humbled. . . .

The Dutch, the English, and other nations used to carry wines, liqueurs, vinegar, linen, paper, notions, and wheat out of the kingdom in time of need, to such an extent that, out of every ten units of commerce, nine were handled by the Dutch. In return they brought us fabrics and other merchandise made of wool and down; sugar, tobacco, and indigo from the American islands; all the spices, drugs, oils, silks, cotton fabrics, leathers, and an infinity of other merchandise from the Indies; the same merchandise from the Levant; all the materials necessary for the construction of ships, such as wood, masts, iron from Sweden and Galicia, copper, tar, cannons, hemp, rope, tin, brass, piloting instruments, cannonballs, anchors, and generally everything needed in the construction of vessels for the navy or the merchant marine; powder, wicks, muskets, bullets, lead, pewter, fabrics, and serge from London; silk and woolen stockings from England; barracans, damasks, camlets, and other fabrics from Flanders; laces from Venice and Holland; trimmings from Flanders, camlet from Brussels, carpeting from Flanders; cows and sheep from Germany; leather from every nation; horses from every country; silken fabrics from Milan, Genoa, and Holland. . . .

By all these means and an infinite number of others that would be too long to enumerate, the Dutch, English, Hamburgers, and other nations brought a much greater quantity of merchandise into the realm than they took away and withdrew the surplus in circulating coin, causing both their own affluence and this realm's poverty, and indisputably enhancing their power while promoting our weakness.

We must examine the means we have used to change this destiny.

First, in 1662, Your Majesty supported a tax of fifty sous per ton of freight from foreign vessels. This produced such great results that we have seen the number of French vessels increase yearly, and in seven or eight years the Dutch have been practically excluded from port-to-port commerce, which is [now] carried on by the French. The advantages enjoyed by the state from the increase in the number of sailors and seagoing men, and from the money that has remained in the realm, are too many to enumerate.

At the same time, Your Majesty ordered that work be done to abolish all the tolls that had long been levied on every river in the kingdom, and he initiated an investigation into which rivers could be rendered navigable, in order to facilitate the transport of commodities and merchandise from the interior of the realm toward the sea, and from there into foreign lands. . . .

Finally, after having thoroughly studied this matter, Your Majesty established the tariff of 1664, which sets duties according to a completely different principle — that is, to favor markedly any merchandise or manufactured items coming from the realm, while pricing foreign merchandise higher, but not excessively high, since there were still no established manufactures in the realm. If this increase in duties had been excessive, it would have greatly burdened the people, because of their need to buy foreign products. But this change began to provide some encouragement for the development of equivalent manufactures inside the realm:

The cloth manufactory of Sedan has been reestablished and enlarged to 62 from the 12 looms that were there before.

The new establishments in Abbeville, Dieppe, Fécamp, and Rouen have been built, in which there are presently more than 200 looms.

The manufactory for barracans was next set up at La Ferté-sous-Jouarre, made up of 120 looms;

That of smaller Flemish damasks [a type of cloth imitating a style from Flanders], at Meaux, consisting of 80 looms;

That for carpeting, in the same city, made up of 120 looms;

The styles of Bruges and Brussels, at Montmorin, St. Quentin, and Avranches, with 30 looms;

For fine Dutch linens, at Bresle, Louviers, Laval, and other places, with 200 looms;

Serge of London, at Gournay, Auxerre, Autun, and other places, with 300 looms.

English woolen stockings, in the Beauce, at Provins, in Picardy, at Sens, Auxerre, Autun, and elsewhere, with a total of 32 cities or towns. . . .

To reduce the importation of animals into the kingdom, the entrance duties were greatly increased and the orders given to tax collectors forbidding their seizure of animals throughout the kingdom; these measures at the same time reduced the importation of leather. . . .

[Colbert lists many more accomplishments.]

The setting up of the manufacture of muskets and of weapons of all sorts in Nivernois, and the reestablishment of the same in Forez;

The distribution of stud horses, which will certainly result in the reestablishment of stud farms and will considerably decrease or eliminate altogether the importation of foreign horses.

Your Majesty wanted to work diligently to reestablish our naval forces, and [this project] has required very great expenditures because all the munitions and manufactured items formerly came from Holland and the countries of the north. It was, therefore, absolutely necessary to find or create inside the realm everything needed for this great project. . . .

[Colbert lists tar, anchors, cannons, sailcloth, lumber, ropes, and other items.]

In addition, to keep the Dutch from profiting from the American islands [Dutch West Indies], which they had seized and from which they had excluded the French — [a practice] that was worth at least a million in gold to them every year — Your Majesty established the West Indies Company, in which he has to date invested four million livres. But he has also had the satisfaction of snatching from the Dutch that million in gold, which supported and maintained more than four thousand of their subjects who continually navigated among the islands in more than two hundred vessels. . . .

[Colbert describes other trading companies.]

It is with [foreign competition] in mind that Your Majesty has worked to make the Aube, Lot, Tarn, Agout, Drôme, and Baise Rivers navigable and has considerably increased [navigation] on the Seine, Marne, Allier, Garonne, Somme, and other rivers. He is also expending great care and money to repair his ports, so that his subjects' vessels will find it more convenient to dock; and it is with this in mind that he is having work done on that grand project, the [building of the] canal connecting the seas,[1] which has always been one of the grandest ambitions of the greatest princes in the world, but which had to wait for Your Majesty to see its realization. . . .

All these great projects and an infinity of others are in a certain sense novelties, whose realization Your Majesty ordered seven or eight years ago. They are still in their infancy and can only be brought to perfection with hard work and stubborn effort. They can survive only as long as the state is prosperous, since considerable expenditures will always be necessary to support all this great machinery. . . .

Colbert goes on for many more pages, reviewing the need to decrease expenditures for war and increase expenditures for the trading companies and for economic development. This was to be a losing battle in the next decades, as Louis XIV began to spend vast sums on Versailles and intervene militarily in a series of major European conflicts.

Louis XIV's Tax Flows

Colbert's concerns remind us that the tax system was an essential part of French absolutism. By examining where the king acquired his revenues and what he did with them, we can gain important insights into the values of the society and the nature of its social structure. It is often said that Louis XIV taxed without consent. This means that the king collected the direct tax on land, the taille, by simply deciding, in council, how much to levy in a given year. He then commanded royal officials on many levels to distribute the burden among provinces, districts within

---

[1]Colbert is referring to the Canal des Deux Mers, which connected the Atlantic to the Mediterranean by linking the Garonne River at Toulouse with the Mediterranean Sea at Sète, near Montpellier.

provinces, and communities, after which the communities themselves divided the burden among individual inhabitants. Many French cities were exempt from the taille, but they usually had an arrangement whereby they paid an annual amount to the crown, which they collected themselves either as a head tax or through sales taxes. Other royal indirect taxes were farmed out to private companies to collect. Groups of financiers would pool their resources and pay a large sum up front to the king in return for a contract authorizing them to collect a certain type of tax using their own employees. The king received his money right away but lost control of the collection process, while the "tax farmers" collected a nice profit at the public's expense.

Thus the king had the authority to initiate almost any tax, but, practically speaking, he could collect only by negotiating, directly or indirectly, with any number of corporative interest groups. The key to understanding this system is to realize that it was based on a principle of unequal treatment. France had what might be called a corporative legal structure. Individuals and groups were defined in terms of their place in a hierarchy of levels, each enjoying distinct privileges, rights, and duties. Some individuals, such as nobles, received a certain status by birth. Others, such as the clergy, obtained it from their occupation. People were classified not as equal individuals but in terms of the status they held and the groups to which they belonged. Privilege, which might be defined as legal advantage, was acquired in a variety of ways. It was attributed to individuals because of their status as nobles or priests; to occupational groups, such as the silk weavers of Lyon or the judges of the Parlement of Paris; to persons with titles such as duke or cardinal; and to geographical entities, such as towns and provinces. Thus the province of Brittany enjoyed certain privileges, such as the right to observe its own laws, as did certain towns, such as Toulouse's right to be exempt from troop lodgings. People and groups were treated differently according to the privileges they could claim. In one way or another, the king could usually get money from most constituencies, but only by acknowledging their special rights, exemptions, and privileges. A modern relationship between an administrative state and a body of equally treated, taxpaying citizens was impossible because of the corporative structure of society.

Absolutism can be defined as the king's authority interacting with all these diverse and privileged entities. For taxation, this arrangement had two significant consequences. First, from the king's perspective, it made it impossible to tap the nation's wealth effectively — that is, in an evenhanded, consistent manner. Second, from the perspective of the economy, it created gross inequalities that impoverished some groups while unduly benefiting others. These inequalities were not easily corrected because they were built into the nature of French society and into its various members' identities. If the king pushed too hard to change things, he was likely to undermine the social supports that kept him on the throne, as the successors of Louis XIV were to find out.

The tax system was even more complicated than the social system, but we can understand its basic structure if we look at some statistics calculated by Louis's bureaucrats. Jean-Roland Mallet, a clerk of Nicolas Desmaretz, who was one of Colbert's successors, drew up a set of government accounts based on actual records that have since been destroyed. When these were published in 1789, they provided a lasting record of Louis XIV's receipts and expenditures.[1] Mallet did not use modern accounting methods, and his figures are subject to interpretation, but they can serve us as a rough guide to Louis's tax system.

Receipts.   Table 1 shows the receipts for some of the years we have been covering, from the days of Colbert's survey in 1663 to the era of Madame de Maintenon. The figures represent gross receipts — that is, the sums actually paid before local costs were subtracted. They can best answer the question of where the taxes came from.

(1) *Taille from pays d'élections.* The *pays d'élections,* constituting two-thirds of the kingdom, were the provinces where the taille was collected directly by royal officers and not by regional assemblies. The taille was essentially a land tax, sometimes with other mobile wealth included. It was supposed to be paid by all propertied inhabitants, but — here we begin to note the inequalities — members of the clergy and the nobility were exempt. City residents were supposed to pay, but most larger cities had substituted some other form of tax that they controlled, or they had bargained themselves into some kind of exempt status. Thus the taille, the king's chief source of revenue, was levied largely on the peasants in the countryside. As indicated above, the sum to be imposed in a given year was set in the royal council and then divided among districts, communities, and individuals. The proportions imposed were to some extent traditional and did not necessarily correspond to the ability of a given district to pay, although Colbert's agents worked hard to make the

---

[1]J. R. Mallet, *Comptes rendus de l'administration des finances du royaume de France* (London, 1789). My figures are from the original edition. Mallet has been republished with commentary and modern apparatus: Margaret and Richard Bonney, *Jean-Roland Mallet premier historien des finances de la monarchie française* (Paris: Comité pour l'Histoire Économique et Financière de la France, 1993).

Table 1. Source of Louis XIV's Tax Revenues in Livres

DATE	1. *PAYS D'ÉLECTIONS*	2. *PAYS D'ÉTATS*	3. FORESTS	4. VENALITY OF OFFICE	5. INDIRECT TAXES	TOTAL GROSS REVENUE
1663	37,935,610	6,274,735	297,709	2,041,948	41,634,000	88,184,002
1665	35,345,219	5,934,726	909,618	1,817,220	44,644,595	88,651,378
1667	36,742,162	8,232,073	617,966	1,354,667	44,928,407	91,875,275
1669	33,832,240	9,235,580	649,433	458,936	47,334,600	91,510,789
1671	33,845,797	12,221,041	667,478	1,945,169	51,248,335	99,927,820
1673	36,645,510	7,038,421	1,017,639	3,806,924	53,043,926	101,552,420
1675	38,122,834	12,687,857	887,852	9,686,640	57,965,500	119,350,683
1677	40,435,347	10,069,327	711,122	5,610,879	59,635,166	116,461,841
1679	34,761,420	10,685,477	717,435	2,906,665	59,363,255	108,434,252
1681	34,153,457	8,826,536	914,976	2,577,188	66,893,298	113,365,455
1683	37,908,244	9,830,019	1,411,313	1,966,798	64,937,000	116,053,374
1685	34,508,216	11,127,333	1,564,808	7,493,117	66,043,250	120,736,724
1687	32,439,655	10,840,322	1,557,857	3,055,665	65,881,234	113,774,733

burden more equitable. Two peasants with identical wealth, who lived in different communities or different districts, might be taxed at very different rates. The same was true of residents of the same village, because local tax rolls were based on land assessments that remained fixed for generations. If a taxpayer defaulted, the rest of the community was expected to come up with the difference so that the village could fulfill its quota. In the end, the sum chosen by the king bore no necessary relation to the country's ability to pay. As Colbert pointed out in 1670, it was possible to ruin the rural economy by setting too high an initial figure.

(2) *Taille from pays d'états.* The *pays d'états,* the provinces that formed the other third of France, had regular assemblies of nobles, clergy, and towns called estates. The most important were Brittany, Burgundy, and Languedoc. In these provinces, the taille was deflected through the provincial assembly, which usually had its own collection system. Certain routine sums were collected every year. In addition, a larger sum, the "free gift," was arrived at through negotiations between the king's representatives and the estates. Under Louis XIV, this gift was hardly free, as the king applied intense pressure to get what he wanted. But there was a certain amount of bargaining, which it was the privilege of these provinces to perpetuate. The free gift and the regular sums were levied on taxpayers using repartition methods that were similar to those in the *pays d'élections* but were run by the province's own officers. The *pays d'états* were historically undercharged relative to the *pays d'élections* (another inequality), but the revenue figures we see are misleadingly low because they do not reflect grants for provincial projects such as roads and canals, which were spent directly in the province.

As an added complication, much of the south of France paid the *taille réelle.* Exemptions were based on whether the land you held was considered "noble" or "common," not on the status of the owner. Thus, all over France there were "noble" exemptions (remember the inequality principle), but they were applied in different ways in different areas. In principle, the clergy was always exempt from taxes. However, the Catholic Church met periodically in general assemblies that, like the provincial estates, were expected to grant large "gifts" to the crown. Although the church was hardly tax-free, its contributions were handled in a special way.

(3) *Forests.* This revenue was derived from commercial transactions, either through renting out forest lands or forest rights or through the sale of timber.

(4) *Venality of office.* These sums derived from the sale or resale of royal offices, the tax on offices, or special fees levied on officeholders. In

general, think of these sums as a tax on the officer class. The most important members of this group were exempt from direct taxes because their offices conferred nobility.

(5) *Indirect taxes.* These were revenues from the many different tax farms. They included the gabelle (salt tax); other aspects of the royal domain besides forests; excise taxes on goods transported across provincial or municipal borders; sales taxes on commodities such as meat, wine, other beverages, foodstuffs, or manufactured products; and duties on imported goods. Every city and province had a different set of tolls and rates, making the transporting of goods across the country costly and erratic. Colbert worked on simplifying this system, with some success, but it remained an obstacle to rational planning.

In general, indirect taxes affected poor consumers, especially in cities where basic supplies had to be purchased. Nobles and other wealthy city dwellers were not exempt from them, but the produce of their country estates could be brought in free of charge, so they tended to supply their households with tax-free goods.

Now let's consider these same revenues as percentages of the king's total gross receipts (Table 2). About a third of the tax burden was borne by the people who paid the taille, especially the peasants in the *pays d'élections.* This was not a homogeneous group, since it included rich as well as poor farmers, nobles and bourgeois who owned land in the region of the *taille réelle,* and even urban artisans who owned rural land. City residents in many places paid a share of the taille, but the masses of

Table 2.   Percentage of Gross Receipts*

YEAR	1. *PAYS D'ÉLECTIONS*	2. *PAYS D'ÉTATS*	3. FORESTS	4. VENALITY OF OFFICE	5. INDIRECT TAXES
1663	43.0	7.1	0.3	2.3	47.2
1665	39.9	6.7	1.0	2.0	50.4
1667	40.0	9.0	0.7	1.5	48.9
1669	37.0	10.1	0.7	0.5	51.7
1671	33.9	12.2	0.7	1.9	51.3
1673	36.1	6.9	1.0	3.7	52.2
1675	31.9	10.6	0.7	8.1	48.6
1677	34.7	8.6	0.6	4.8	51.2
1679	32.1	9.9	0.7	2.7	54.7
1681	30.1	7.8	0.8	2.3	59.0
1683	32.7	8.5	1.2	1.7	56.0
1685	28.6	9.2	1.3	6.2	54.7
1687	28.5	9.5	1.4	2.7	57.9

*Because of rounding, some rows may not add up to 100%.

the middling to poor peasantry paid the bulk of it. This is not surprising, as they constituted the bulk of the population, but it is generally agreed that they were greatly overtaxed relative to the rest of the population. They were grouped in easily identifiable villages, and their property was impossible to hide.

Even more striking were the indirect taxes, which constituted more than half of the proceeds in most years. Again, these taxes loomed largest for modest people who had to pay taxes on necessities such as basic food and drink, although they affected everyone to some extent. In urban contexts, there was often an attempt by local authorities to shift the burden of royal taxes onto consumption taxes and away from taxes on property or households, which they themselves would have to pay. Also note that indirect taxes channeled profits to the financiers who invested in collecting them, although these funds are not included in the amount the king actually received.

Table 3 illustrates this point by totaling the charges, or sums from the royal tax flows that were paid out in the provinces before the money reached the king.[2] Mallet was careful to list these for each category of revenue; here we have only the totals, which represent a striking third of the gross revenues. These payments were commitments the king had made to repay someone out of local tax funds. The money went largely

Table 3. Share of Revenues Distributed in the Provinces

YEAR	GROSS REVENUE TO CROWN	DISTRIBUTED IN PROVINCES	NET REVENUE TO CROWN	PERCENT DISTRIBUTED IN PROVINCES
1663	88,184,002	37,725,554	50,458,448	42.8
1665	88,651,378	29,805,242	58,846,136	33.6
1667	91,875,275	32,554,913	59,320,362	35.4
1669	91,510,789	26,833,338	64,677,451	29.3
1671	99,927,820	26,873,720	73,054,100	26.9
1673	101,552,420	27,619,121	73,933,299	27.2
1675	119,350,683	30,483,358	88,867,325	25.5
1677	116,461,841	33,397,690	83,064,151	28.7
1679	108,434,252	32,926,035	75,508,217	30.4
1681	113,365,455	36,834,504	76,530,951	32.5
1683	116,053,374	27,376,952	88,676,422	23.6
1685	120,736,724	35,287,560	85,449,164	29.2
1687	113,774,733	30,610,076	83,164,657	26.9

[2]On tax flows and charges, the essential work is James B. Collins, *Fiscal Limits of Absolutism: Direct Taxation in Early Seventeenth-Century France* (Berkeley: University of California Press, 1988).

to royal officers and financiers to pay the returns on their investments in offices, to pay interest to those who had loaned the government money under various auspices, and to provide profits to tax farmers for their services. In a sense, this money represented a cost of government: It was the amount paid for the parlements, the lower royal courts, the tax collection apparatus, and even some practical projects here and there, such as Colbert's subsidies to manufacturing and his efforts to develop rivers and canals. It is important to understand, however, that very little of this money actually went for what we would consider government operations. The men who handled public business were receiving interest on the money they had paid for their offices, and they recouped their losses by charging fees for judicial services and exercising influence in their regions. Royal government comprised a set of arrangements between the king and certain privileged groups and individuals, rather than a set of services provided. The money went to men who had, in a sense, purchased a piece of royal power. Little went for services, buildings, or supplies.

Expenditures.   When we turn to how the king's revenues were spent (Table 4), we are confronted with a long list of rather traditional budget categories. Louis XIV's expenditures cannot be treated like a modern governmental budget because much of what the king did was hidden behind obscure categories and because many governmental operations were carried out at the expense of the participants: Ambassadors paid part of their own living expenses, military officers equipped themselves and sometimes their regiments, and so forth. Still, it is interesting to try to group these expenses into meaningful categories such as we see in Table 5. Here, in stark outline, are displayed the values of the French crown. Military activities, the traditional preoccupation of the king and nobility, absorbed by far the largest part of the king's revenues. The rest of the money went to life at court, support of the grandees and the king's family, the king's building projects, and debt service. The only activities that would have directly reached the public were improvements in Paris and the building of roads and bridges.

Such a conclusion is overly pessimistic, perhaps, because the king did provide the population with military defense, cultural projects, institutional stability, and the impetus for many projects that were funded by local parties. And, of course, the financial picture was much more complicated than these brief statistics suggest. Still, we can see some striking trends. Taxes were predominantly paid by commoners, while nobles, clergy, and royal officers were markedly undertaxed. Yet the nobles were the prime beneficiaries of the tax revenues. The king was sucking

Table 4. Government Expenditures by Category

	1663	1669	1675	1681	1687	1688
KING'S HOUSEHOLD AND COURT						
Royal household	520,570	545,667	557,377	772,958	563,227	557,662
Food and drink account	1,222,667	1,406,291	1,814,510	1,564,065	1,692,000	1,601,079
Special household expenses	1,144,082	3,166,729	862,238	1,146,974	1,023,287	683,829
Minor household expenses	438,885	411,189	426,895	462,678	353,232	338,764
Stables	369,027	510,540	370,240	823,043	769,843	726,423
Purchase of horses	12,000	12,000	12,000	12,000	12,000	12,000
Alms and offertory	151,741	39,708	82,593	122,070	362,966	315,000
Household policing	61,050	61,050	61,050	61,050	61,050	61,050
Swiss guards	35,909	43,738	49,352	59,538	49,038	50,028
Hunting and falconry	206,563	261,852	297,724	312,174	406,597	335,354
Favors and tips	100,044	146,995	131,281	133,861	226,562	236,889
King's spending money	939,661	874,000	1,637,000	1,073,000	1,991,414	1,996,500
Petty donations and travel	333,049	459,305	648,868	1,293,322	833,961	1,336,393
Total	**5,535,248**	**7,939,064**	**6,951,128**	**7,836,733**	**8,345,177**	**8,250,971**
ROYAL CONSTRUCTION	**1,905,825**	**5,775,866**	**3,695,416**	**6,441,001**	**7,757,438**	**6,985,978**
PENSIONS AND PEOPLE AT COURT						
Household of the queen mother	1,423,955	—	—	—	—	—
Household of the queen	1,052,427	1,035,451	1,144,145	1,231,721	—	—
Household of the Dauphine	—	—	—	1,021,382	1,059,372	1,074,593
Household of Monsieur	861,359	375,359	864,704	1,076,000	1,010,000	1,049,200
Household of Madame	252,000	252,000	252,000	252,000	252,000	252,000
Household of duchess of Montpensier	300,000	252,000	—	—	—	—
Stipends of royal council and officers	1,679,361	2,064,153	1,532,371	2,111,787	2,138,312	2,128,395
Other stipends	1,111,392	194,200	188,550	417,700	211,800	208,000
Stipends of marshals of France	903,038	516,853	559,482	358,390	573,081	550,481
Regular pensions	1,367,500	1,178,784	1,649,310	1,465,075	2,732,179	2,607,515
Total	**8,951,032**	**5,868,800**	**6,190,562**	**7,934,055**	**7,976,744**	**7,870,184**

FOREIGN POLICY						
Secret subsidies abroad, foreign policy	1,886,689	3,037,741	6,388,562	3,545,243	1,334,500	2,710,330
Ambassadors and embassies abroad	406,891	395,550	591,950	816,655	285,266	657,700
Total	**2,293,580**	**3,433,291**	**6,980,512**	**4,361,898**	**1,619,766**	**3,368,030**
PUBLIC WORKS						
The Bastille (royal prison)	112,563	70,518	136,827	200,386	146,517	169,305
Paving of Paris streets	16,997	96,199	60,380	55,197	53,666	53,666
Bridges and roads	152,637	367,108	—	314,450	1,095,811	762,708
The Paris guard	—	—	—	—	116,731	119,723
Wolf hunting	23,993	34,293	34,293	34,293	34,293	34,293
Total	**306,190**	**568,118**	**231,500**	**604,326**	**1,447,018**	**1,139,695**
MILITARY DEFENSE, WARFARE						
Swiss Regiment	551,978	—	100,000	298,000	211,576	260,050
Standard military garrisons	3,175,659	2,738,489	2,219,548	2,430,594	2,304,346	2,280,335
Payments to troop commanders	—	—	584,936	1,057,805	1,202,700	1,311,987
Extraordinary military expenses	9,056,937	15,629,047	48,390,558	31,611,643	35,518,162	44,453,359
Military bread ration	—	—	9,717,399	712,195	—	897,797
Billeting of troops on the move	—	—	6,165,781	1,788,925	1,962,563	2,921,590
King's musketeers, special forces	667,060	634,952	187,080	187,335	185,461	185,448
French and Swiss guards	2,119,064	1,628,958	—	—	—	—
Artillery	644,310	—	13,725	10,166	6,420	31,833
Upkeep of fortifications	995,262	2,687,008	3,379,269	7,190,879	7,101,611	11,993,059
Navy and royal galleys	2,688,370	12,896,497	10,260,746	6,976,543	9,413,307	10,164,940
Total	**19,898,640**	**36,214,951**	**81,019,042**	**52,264,085**	**57,906,146**	**74,500,398**
KING'S SECRET EXPENSES (MOSTLY DEBTS)	6,085,508	4,939,926	2,454,894	3,265,022	6,851,814	3,907,111
DEBT SERVICE, INTEREST	1,569,714	11,531,542	4,337,361	58,292,953	1,166,624	3,110,037
Grand Total	**46,545,737**	**76,271,558**	**111,860,415**	**141,000,073**	**93,070,727**	**109,132,404**

Table 5. Summary of Government Expenditures by Category

	1663	1669	1675	1681	1687	1688
SUMMARY BY CATEGORY						
King's household and court	5,535,248	7,939,064	6,951,128	7,836,733	8,345,177	8,250,971
Royal buildings and construction	1,905,825	5,775,866	3,695,416	6,441,001	7,757,438	6,985,978
Pensions and people at court	8,951,032	5,868,800	6,190,562	7,934,055	7,976,744	7,870,184
Foreign policy	2,293,580	3,433,291	6,980,512	4,361,898	1,619,766	3,368,030
Public works	306,190	568,118	231,500	604,326	1,447,018	1,139,695
Military defense and warfare	19,898,640	36,214,951	81,019,042	52,264,085	57,906,146	74,500,398
King's secret expenses (mostly debts)	6,085,508	4,939,926	2,454,894	3,265,022	6,851,814	3,907,111
Debt service, interest	1,569,714	11,531,542	4,337,361	58,292,953	1,166,624	3,110,037
Total	**46,545,737**	**76,271,558**	**111,860,415**	**141,000,073**	**93,070,727**	**109,132,404**
PERCENTAGE OF TOTAL EXPENDITURES BY CATEGORY*						
King's household and court	11.9	10.4	6.2	5.6	9.0	7.6
Royal buildings and construction	4.1	7.6	3.3	4.6	8.3	6.4
Pensions and people at court	19.2	7.7	5.5	5.6	8.6	7.2
Foreign policy	4.9	4.5	6.2	3.1	1.7	3.1
Public works	0.7	0.7	0.2	0.4	1.6	1.0
Military defense and warfare	42.8	47.5	72.4	37.1	62.2	68.3
King's secret expenses (mostly debts)	13.1	6.5	2.2	2.3	7.4	3.6
Debt service, interest	3.4	15.1	3.9	41.3	1.3	2.8

* Because of rounding, some totals may not add up to 100%.

money from the countryside and lavishing it on armies, his court, and his officers. Along with the high nobles at court, the officers in the army, and the robe nobility (all of whom evaded the basic taille), the financiers — those who lent money to the king or farmed his taxes — also benefited. Remember that one-third of all the tax revenues were being distributed in the provinces, mostly to these people. In addition, the financial backers of the crown included many of the same grandees, ecclesiastics, and robe nobles who were beneficiaries of the tax system in other ways.[3] Louis XIV was managing a vast flow of wealth out of the hands of the agricultural producers and urban merchants and artisans and into the hands of the nobles, officers, and financiers.

This process did not augur well for Colbert's attempts to revive the economy. We can see in the previous documents, however, that he was aware of the problems and working hard to correct them. There was some improvement. The tables show that the *pays d'états* were gradually assuming more of their share relative to the *pays d'élections;* that indirect taxes (which affected everyone) were gaining at the expense of direct taxes; that the costs of debts were declining (which is not to say that the budget was balanced); and that the king's secret expenses were under better control. At the same time, a comparison of expenditures versus net revenues and a look at the increasing cost of war demonstrate that Colbert's budgets were going to be overwhelmed by Louis XIV's vast international ambitions. In addition, the vast overtaxing of agricultural producers hampered agricultural progress, while the attractions of noble exemptions and financial windfalls lured merchants away from capitalistic enterprise.[4]

---

[3] Daniel Dessert, *Argent, pouvoir et société au grand siècle* (Paris: Fayard, 1984).

[4] It should be noted that in 1695, the royal government inaugurated a new tax, the *capitation,* which in theory was a head tax paid by everyone, even the great nobles and the royal family, according to their station in life. This tax did eliminate some inequities by forcing the privileged to pay, but it still excluded the clergy. Furthermore, the principle of unequal treatment continued, since the capitation was an add-on tax that did not change the nature of the taille.

4

Reforming the Provinces:
The Grands Jours d'Auvergne

The instructions drawn up by Louis and his ministers demonstrate an impressive conception of organized administration. But the real issue in an analysis of absolutism is what sort of impact their directives had in the provinces, where their programs might have been buried in a sea of indifference. Chapters 4 and 5 show royal agents interacting with local elites. First we will travel to the backward mountains of the Massif Central, to the Auvergne, south of the Loire River and west of the Rhône. Louis XIV was determined to "see that justice reigned," as he said in his decree of 1665, and to put a stop to violent oppression of the weak by the powerful. He therefore instituted a *Grands Jours,* or special court, consisting of about twenty judges from the Parlement of Paris, including one president, sixteen councillors, and one royal prosecutor, plus a master of requests to act as keeper of the seals. The Paris Parlement was chosen because the Auvergne region lay within its district, even though Paris was more than two hundred miles away.

This move was an important symbolic gesture. By sending his judges to clean up a region where local nobles still terrorized the people and violence was endemic, Louis was signaling his intention to extend his authority over the countryside and chastise backward nobles and corrupt priests and officials alike. By using the Parlement of Paris, which had caused so much trouble during the Fronde, rather than a special commission, he was indicating that his premier court was back under his control and that there would be significant benefits for those who collaborated with him. The arrival of this crowd of stern Parisian judges, with their entourage of families and servants, in the rustic town of Clermont, must have been the social event of the decade for the local population. The Grands Jours sat for four months, issued 692 sentences in criminal cases, and reviewed about a thousand civil cases.[1]

[1]The best modern study of the Grands Jours is Arlette Lebigre, *Les grands jours d'Auvergne: désordres et répression au XVIIe siècle* (Paris: Hachette, 1976). A good analysis in

The account of this court is by Esprit Fléchier, a young priest serving as tutor to the son of Louis-François de Caumartin, the master of requests assigned to the Grands Jours. In later life, Fléchier became bishop of Nîmes, the author of elegant funeral orations, and a spiritual leader in Louis XIV's church. Fléchier found himself at loose ends in Auvergne, so he decided to take notes on this adventure and compile them for his friends in Paris. In reading these excerpts, you should keep in mind the strong bias of the author. He was a Parisian snob writing home about the backwardness of the provincials and aiming to entertain. He was not allowed to attend the court sessions, which were secret, so his information was secondhand, reflecting the gossip that was circulating at the time. Nevertheless, other documents confirm that Fléchier's information is essentially accurate. He may not have been aware of all the details, but he did report on real cases.

Fléchier's account offers us a fresh view of life in the mountains, far from the sparkle of the royal court. It suggests quite a bit about the life of the rural nobles and peasants — the world the king had to reform — but it also provides evidence of the biases of Parisians. In the end, Fléchier's account, which immortalized these events for posterity, played into the hands of the king by transmitting the message Louis wanted everyone to hear: that he was a just and powerful king who restored order and protected his people, and that overweening private citizens who threw their weight around would no longer be tolerated.

Letters Patent for the Establishment of the Grands Jours

PARIS, AUGUST 31, 1665
LOUIS by the grace of God, king of France and of Navarre, to all those who see the present letters, GREETINGS: Because the lawlessness during the foreign and civil wars that have desolated our kingdom for the past thirty years has not only weakened the force of the laws and the rigor of the ordinances but also introduced a great number of abuses, in both the administration of our finances and the distribution of justice, the first

English is Malcolm Greenshields, *An Economy of Violence in Early Modern France: Crime and Justice in the Haute Auvergne, 1587–1664* (University Park: Pennsylvania State University Press, 1994), 209–29.

Esprit Fléchier, *Mémoires de Fléchier sur les Grands-Jours d'Auvergne en 1665,* ed. Adolphe Chéruel (Paris: Hachette, 1856), 316–21.

and principal objective that we have set for ourselves, the one to which we have devoted all of our efforts after the consolidation of our conquests, the establishment of public security, the restoration of our finances, and the reestablishment of commerce, has been to see that justice reigns and to reign by justice in our state, persuaded that there is nothing that we owe our subjects more or for which we are more responsible to God, from whom alone we hold our crown. We are informed that the problem is greatest in the provinces the farthest removed from our court of Parlement; that the laws are scorned there; that the people are exposed to all kinds of violence and oppression; that weak and miserable persons find no assistance from the authority of the law; that gentlemen often abuse their reputation and commit actions unworthy of their birth; and that moreover the officers are too weak to be able to resist these vexations, therefore crimes remain unpunished. To remedy these disorders whose increase over time might diminish our royal authority, weaken the jurisdiction of our sovereign courts, and extinguish that of our lower officers, WE HAVE RESOLVED to set up a jurisdiction, commonly known as a Grands Jours, and to have it sit and function this present year in our city of Clermont for the provinces of lower and upper Auvergne, Bourbonnais, Nivernais, Forez, Beaujolais, Lyonnais, [etc.]. . . .

Excerpts from the Memoirs of Esprit Fléchier

. . . Everyone from Clermont and Montferrand came out to watch as this troop of magistrates coming to render them justice passed by. All the corps of the city were assembled, spread out along the road in the open countryside, waiting for the opportunity to deliver their harangues crammed with references to "the moon and the sun" and "great days [grands jours] and little days." After we had suffered through these unfortunate encounters, we entered the city, where we had to listen to still more speechifiers, who didn't want to waste a single morsel of all their past schooling. Each attempted to establish his reputation by a tedious display of unfortunate eloquence, after which we all retreated, exhausted, into the houses that had been prepared for us. . . .

Saturday and Sunday were spent exploring the city or listening to a thousand compliments delivered by the principal officers from the local

Esprit Fléchier, *Mémoires de Fléchier sur les Grands-Jours d'Auvergne en 1665,* ed. Adolphe Chéruel (Paris: Hachette, 1856), 36–39, 41, 50–51, 138–40, 160, 194–95, 201–2, 210–11, 219–20, 230, 258–59, 261–63, 269–70, 278–79.

courts who had come to humiliate themselves in the presence of the judges from Paris, and by various clerics who came in a group to cite Saint Paul and Saint Augustine, to compare the Grands Jours to the Last Judgment, and to cite every last verse from the Scriptures that might possibly be applied to human justice. A Jesuit at the head of his *collège* and the most venerable Capuchin from his province stood out above the others with their citations of the best passages from the holy fathers and their praise of the Grands Jours, and demonstrated how Saint Augustine and Saint Ambrose had prophesied what was currently happening in Auvergne.[1]

As for Clermont, hardly a city in France is as disagreeable. Its location is inconvenient because it is at the foot of the mountains. The streets are so narrow that the widest is just the size of a carriage; two carriages create a jam capable of causing the damnation of the coachmen, who curse much better here than anywhere else. . . . On the other hand, the city is well populated; and if the women are ugly, one can say that they are certainly fruitful, and while they may not provide much love, they produce a lot of children. . . .

The ladies of the city came to pay their respects to our ladies, not one at a time, but all in a troop. You couldn't receive a visit without your whole room being filled up. There were never enough chairs, and it took a long time to seat this demimonde. There was such a crowd that you would have thought it was an assembly or a conference. I have heard that it was fatiguing to salute so many people at once, and there was awkwardness both before and after so many kisses. Since most of them are unschooled in courtly ceremonies and know only their provincial ways, they go around in large groups so that they can reinforce one another and not stand out. It is amusing to see them enter, one with arms crossed, another with arms lowered like a doll. All their talk is about trifles, and they are happy if they can turn the conversation around to talking about their embroidery. . . .

The opening of the Grands Jours was held on Monday, with a nice speech that M. Talon[2] delivered with marvelous eloquence. He began with a maxim of philosophy: that all things act with more or less force the closer or farther away they are. He explained this principle with

---

[1] Saint Paul, Saint Augustine, and Saint Ambrose were ancient authorities of the Catholic Church. Fléchier is ridiculing the pomposity of the local dignitaries of Clermont. The Jesuits were a religious order associated with the Catholic Reformation who frequently ran *collèges,* or secondary schools, in provincial towns. The Capuchins were another order of monks.

[2] Denis Talon, solicitor general of the Paris Parlement, was the royal prosecutor presiding over the Grands Jours.

examples drawn from nature and concluded that the court, being far removed from this province, could not impose its justice if it did not send judges from time to time with the authorization of the prince. He moved imperceptibly into praise of the king and demonstrated that there had been princes who had fled from the gaze of their people, whose office had been like a mysterious veil covering all their actions, that they had tried to place themselves in the ranks of the gods by having so little interchange with men, and that they had reason to defend their majesty by retreating and hiding their faults out of fear of the contempt and hatred of their people. Our monarch had no such reasons to hide his actions, which were all grand and dazzling; he communicated with his subjects and rendered justice either in person or through the officers he chose to send to his provinces. Talon did a brief summary of the life of the king and demonstrated that all that was lacking was this fine action to repress violence committed in his kingdom and rescue his people from the oppression of the powerful. . . .

When I arrived, I noticed that there was general terror everywhere, throughout the countryside as well as in Clermont. All the nobility was in flight, and there was not a single gentleman who had not examined the dark corners of his life and tried to remedy any wrong he might have done to his dependents to avoid the complaints that might be made. . . .

We had barely arrived when the president and M. Talon jointly decided to arrest the viscount of La Mothe de Canillac, who was well regarded in the province and, in everyone's opinion, the most innocent of all the Canillacs. . . . The judicial process server was ordered to take along the provost of Auvergne and his archers, and not to inform the viscount of his orders until they were executed, because the provost was known to be an intimate friend of the viscount, who had even invited him to dinner that very day. So they went together to the house, where [the viscount] had already gone to bed, and when the process server had read him his orders, the criminal was so surprised that he didn't even know what he was doing, and he thrust into the provost's hands some letters it is said he had received from a mistress, for he was a gallant man. He was taken to the city prison. . . .

On November 28 the du Palais case was decided. It was the first sentence issued in absentia by the court of Grands Jours. The sentence was severe because the offense had been highly criminal. Count du Palais had purchased Feurs, which is an important village in Forez, and when he attempted a little vigorously to make good on his seigneurial rights, M. de Magnieu, who is a well-bred man with some land in the same parish, raised some points of contention between them that did not seem very important at the time but became so after the fact. Pleas were filed in the courts by one and the other, and it looked as if the case was going to be resolved in the usual way. But a certain animosity and bitterness arises between those who plead in court, and hatred and vengeance often complete what justice has begun. . . . A declared enmity grew up between these two gentlemen, with the result that du Palais was accused of planning to assassinate de Magnieu and laying ambushes for him. Because of this assassination attempt, or for other judicial reasons, the latter obtained a decree against the former and sent five process servers to his château at du Palais to serve some papers that were not very pleasant. It is said that du Palais had been forewarned and had summoned some of his friends, and that he had assembled in his house all the brave fellows in the neighborhood. The process servers arrived and executed their mission at the door of the château, following all due procedures, informing these messieurs that they were subject to the laws and ordinances of the courts like everyone else. . . . They withdrew to the nearest village to spend the night, but no one wanted to take them in because they were enemies of M. du Palais, who was either loved or feared. They were no better received in other locales, and although it was getting very late, they were obliged to go and find lodging six leagues away. They had settled in and were sleeping deeply when two groups of men on horseback arrived from du Palais, violently entered the inn, went into a room where three of these agents were sleeping, and, firing more than twenty pistol shots, killed two of them and broke the shoulder of the third, who was forced to drag himself, bleeding profusely, to the room where his companions were staying. Seeing that they were in terrible danger, these jumped to their feet and begged for mercy, expecting to die. Some of the perpetrators, steamed up by the first murders, wanted to finish off [the process servers], but one of the more reasonable [perpetrators], if you can call anything in this episode reasonable, pleaded for [the process servers'] lives. So he allowed them to live but subjected them to extreme punishment. They were taken all the way to du Palais, completely naked, in the rigor of the season; they were given a thousand lashes with a whip on the road; and they were sent back almost as dead as their companions, and forbidden to look behind them on pain of death. . . .

By warrant, du Palais, father and son, were both condemned to have their heads cut off, and some judges even wanted them to be broken alive on the wheel. Their goods were confiscated; the fine was forty thousand livres; the château at du Palais was demolished. Some of those who had participated in the event were condemned to the wheel. Thus Justice had her vengeance, and the people who had previously ignored her orders were made to fear her warrants. . . .

In the course of this affair it became evident that the peasants were becoming emboldened and were more than willing to testify against the nobles when they were not held back by fear. If you didn't speak to them in an honorable way and greet them with civility, they would appeal to the Grands Jours, threaten to get you punished, and protest against your violence. One lady from the countryside complained that all her peasants had purchased gloves and believed that they no longer had to work and that they were the only ones in the kingdom that the king cared about anymore. . . . [The peasants] even persuaded themselves that the king had sent this company to restore their lands to them, regardless of the circumstances under which they had sold them, and they considered everything their ancestors had sold up to three generations ago to be their inheritance. These simple ideas, which made everyone who was not involved laugh, caused unpleasantness for those who were directly concerned, because they were forced to tolerate insolence that they were not accustomed to and ignore slights that they were not used to ignoring. . . .

About the same time, a good village curate was judged, who, out of extraordinary zeal, had gotten carried away and preached against the king and his ministers. He had said quite seriously to his parishioners that France was badly governed; that it was a tyrannical kingdom; that he had read such wonderful things in an old book that spoke about the Roman Republic; that he wanted to live without any subordination and without allowing any imposition of tailles [taxes]; that the people had never been more harassed; and other edifying things like that, which he and his boorish listeners found more pleasing than the Gospel. These little people thought the sermon had been well preached that day and considered it a great truth that they should live without the taille. . . . They believed that the king should live off his [personal] revenue and that there should be no more tax collectors in the world. The most prudent person in the parish had scruples about hearing such a sermon and decided to complain. And since he was a man with good sense, he offered brotherly criticism to his pastor, who, not content with having spoken of the king, wanted to talk about God as well, and having started with stupidity, went on to finish with impiety and blasphemy, attacking the heavens and the earth. He was arrested and condemned to a year's banishment and certain fines. . . .

It wasn't enough to punish the crimes that had been committed; the court had to prevent future offenses. . . . The court ordered (1) that lords with high justice[3] be required to name persons of probity and talent as their judges and see that they perform their functions accurately on pain of an arbitrary fine the first time and being held responsible in civil court for their mistakes in the event of a recurrence; (2) that the judges be required to investigate and try all the crimes in their jurisdiction, whether or not there was a civil plaintiff; (3) that in cases where there was no civil plaintiff they were to prosecute the case for free, without fees;[4] this was also to be the case when the plaintiff was poor and could not pay fees; the same rule was to be observed in civil cases if the plaintiffs were poor; that the lords were required to punish crimes committed in their territory or else be deprived of their judicial rights and the judges to be deprived of their offices; . . . (6) that all lords with high justice were to maintain their prisons in a secure state, with a jailer to guard them and a register duly numbered at the beginning and the end; (7) that these lords were to supply bread to those accused of crimes, to hold judicial hearings to render justice, and to maintain a safe depository for the court records; (8) that the records of the clerks are to be kept in a public depot, at the expense of those who own the office of clerk, in the location where justice is rendered. . . .

After these petty affairs they examined the baron of Senegas (whose trial greatly embarrassed the gentlemen of the Grands Jours both because of the large number of accusations and because of the skill of the defendant), who conducted a spirited defense. He was accused of getting town governments elected through his own private authority and levying various fees and exactions by force in their name. He enlisted foot soldiers and cavalry to collect his extortions at the expense of the royal revenues. He impeded taille collections and interfered with the regularity of their payments in places where he had authority. He levied exactions and particular taxes on the communities, demanded payment in silver or other types of bribes in certain villages, set up a weighing station to skim off a penny per pound, and did a number of other things worthy of being labeled oppression and tyranny. The second group of charges concerned religion. He was accused of having removed a banner and demolished a chapel consecrated to the Virgin, using the materials to fortify one of his own houses. He was also sought for appropriat-

---

[3] Lords with high justice were nobles who had the right to maintain their own seigneurial (private) courts with the capacity to try capital cases committed within their jurisdictions. These regulations required them to act more responsibly by offering some of the safeguards that subjects received in royal courts.

[4] All courts charged fees for their services. In most cases, the plaintiff who brought the case to trial was expected to pay the court costs. This measure required private lords to try without fees the cases of plaintiffs too poor to pay.

ing the tithe belonging to a prior in one of his properties and forbidding his subjects to rent the property out, so that he could control it. The third group of charges included two or three assassinations, several unjust imprisonments, several ransoms exacted with extraordinary violence, a great many usurpations, and various work services unjustly extorted by force. The thing that caused the greatest horror was a degree of inhumanity that warranted exemplary punishment and signaled a very cruel and tyrannical soul. He had had some grievance against a man who was under his jurisdiction, and since he was by nature incapable of patience and overwhelmed with the urge for vengeance, he had him seized and locked up in a very humid wardrobe, where he could neither stand up nor sit down and where he was given a bit of nourishment to prolong his torment, with the result that after he had spent several months in this horrible prison breathing nothing but corrupted air, he was reduced to almost nothing and was pulled out half dead and completely unrecognizable. . . .[5]

The case of M. de Beaufort de Canillac preoccupied the chamber several days later and split the votes of the judges over part of his verdict. This gentleman is from the house of Canillac, which gives a good idea of his nobility but not of his conduct, since there was universal dissoluteness in that whole family. He was accused of several violent extortions and of acts that approached assassination. He had gone into a village where some kind of gathering was being held for a festival or a market, and promenading through the streets, perhaps after attending some kind of debauchery, and seeing a gentleman at a window, he spoke some words of mockery that annoyed the man and caused him to reply in a decidedly impolite manner. Since it is easy to get drawn into this sort of conflict, they soon arrived at insults and got carried away. Overcome with rage, Beaufort went into the house along with some of his friends and drinking companions and attacked his opponent, who defended himself vigorously like a man of courage. But overcome by the number of his opponents, he was killed on the spot. Although this was an extremely black deed, [Beaufort de Canillac] didn't hesitate to be present at the entrance ceremony of the Grands Jours with La Mothe de Canillac and de Pont-du-Château, and it is said that he was sleeping in the same house when the former was arrested. We may guess that he left it

---

[5] Fléchier reported that the judges were split over the death sentence. In the end, they sentenced Senegas to a large fine, razing of his fortified dwellings, and perpetual banishment.

precipitously. He was condemned in absentia to a fine of twenty-five thousand livres, which is more than his entire fortune, and to having his throat cut. The votes were split over the razing of his houses. . . .

There were so many fugitive criminals that no sooner had one trial been completed than another one began. After sentencing M. de Lévy, they took up the affair of the marquis of Salers, which was one of the blackest seen during the Grands Jours. He was a man of breeding, of spirit, some even say of probity, when he followed his own inclination and not that of his wife. He had an enemy about whom he could justly have complained if he hadn't preferred to avenge himself by violence. His passion, inflamed by his impetuous spirit, caused him to assemble certain of his friends and some others to demonstrate that he would not tolerate being insulted. He attacked the person he was seeking, who had taken refuge in a house, and finding it too difficult to break in the doors, [the marquis] instructed his men to climb up onto the highest point of the building, tear off the roof, and enter the room where this unfortunate person was located, warning him that he should prepare to die. Some say that he summoned a priest and gave [the man] time to confess; others say that he didn't have the patience to wait. In any case, they stabbed [the man] a thousand times, gouged out his eyes, and departed with a considerable satisfaction at having avenged themselves and a great deal of remorse for having committed a crime. At the first word of the Grands Jours, this gentleman withdrew like the other guilty parties and ultimately was condemned in absentia to having his throat cut, paying a substantial fine, and having his house razed to the ground. . . .

It would be difficult to recount all the criminal cases that were judged at the end of the Grands Jours. . . . Suffice it to say that assassinations, murders, kidnappings, and oppression were the most common reasons for judgments and that there was such a great number of criminals that one day thirty at a time were hanged in effigy. It was a fine sight to see so many portraits displayed at the place of execution, in each of which a hangman was cutting off a head. These nonbloody executions and these honest representations, which bore only a modicum of infamy, offered a spectacle that was all the more agreeable in that they provided justice without blood being spilled. These pictures remained for a day, and all the people came out of curiosity to see this crowd of criminals in paintings, who died incessantly and yet did not die at all; who were prepared to suffer the final blow without fearing it; and who, in fact, will not stop being naughty, since they are only unhappy in the pictures. This is a way the law has found for defaming those it cannot punish and for punishing the crime when it does not hold the criminal. It would have made a fine tapestry for the walls of the criminal judge. Some said that these effigies could have decorated the sitting room of M. Talon very nicely.

Among those who were found worthy of the ultimate punishment, the marquis of Canillac holds the prize for being considered the greatest and the oldest sinner in the province. He began being wicked more than sixty years ago and has never stopped since. . . . I will not stop here to recount all the irregularities he is accused of. Suffice it to say that he has practiced everything that tyranny could invent with regard to taxes. On his lands they collected Monsieur's taille, Madame's taille, and the children's taille, and his subjects were forced to pay over and above the taille of the king. It is true that he has some rights documented in ancient deeds, which allow a few lords to collect a few taxes on certain occasions, such as when they or their oldest sons get married; but the marquis knew how to extend these rights and collected annually what other people collect only once in a lifetime. To facilitate his plans and prevent grumbling, he housed in some towers twelve rascals, dedicated to all sorts of criminal activity, whom he called his twelve apostles. They catechized those who rebelled against his law with swords and clubs and committed terrible acts of violence whenever they were assigned a cruel mission by their master. He had given them very apostolic names, such as "Without Engagement," "Break Everything," and the like. . . . Taking advantage of the terror aroused by these abominable names, he levied considerable duties on the meat people eat regularly, and if they practiced too much abstention, he shifted the tax onto those who did not eat any. His greatest revenue was from justice: For the slightest offense he had poor unfortunates imprisoned and judged, and forced them to buy their way out of their sentences with cash. He would have liked everyone in his jurisdiction to act like him and often encouraged them to commit evil deeds so that he could make them pay afterward, with great rigor. Indeed, no one has ever done so much, wanted so much, and profited so much from crime as he. He not only made people pay for acts they had committed, but they also had to buy the freedom to commit them, and if you had money to give him, you could be a criminal or become one. . . . He was sentenced to a large fine and the confiscation of his property, and two or three towers that had served as the refuge for his apostles were razed to the ground. . . .

They sentenced Baron de Cusse to death. After having some sort of dispute in the courts with M. de Champestières, the baron had gone to de Champestières's house and assassinated him. The count of Apchier, who is considered one of the principal criminals of the province because of the impositions and violence he imposed on his lands, was found guilty. He is accused of levying tailles, besieging houses, giving the whip to some bourgeois, and even treating women shamefully. This is a man who appears mild and humble, and makes a thousand curtsies when he is in Paris and needs somebody for something, but who reverts to his original arrogance when he is back at home. People criticized the intendant for having held Apchier in his power after the king's declaration for holding the Grands Jours had been issued, yet letting him get away. He may have had orders from the Parlement, or perhaps he did not want to give these gentlemen [of the Grands Jours] something that would enhance their success, since he had not been named as one of the commissioners, even though he was already in the region. M. de La Tour, who was no more innocent than the others and had done some bad business of his own and accompanied the count of Apchier on his criminal expeditions, suffered the same fate and was executed in effigy along with him. . . .

That same day they sentenced the marquis of Malause, the nephew of M. de Turenne,[6] who is one of the principal lords of the upper Auvergne. M. Le Peletier[7] had investigated the fact that he had been in possession of a parish for several years and was using the church's property for his own purposes. Although there would have been no danger in his appearing and it would have been an easy way of getting the penalty reduced, he chose flight, perhaps to avoid the dishonor of being held prisoner, perhaps for more important reasons that are not known. This benefice that was worth a thousand écus of revenue was a great convenience for him and a great support for his affairs, and the expenses were so small that he gave no more than two hundred livres to the [priest] who administered it. Despite whatever consideration these gentlemen might have had for M. de Turenne, they condemned his relative to a sizable payment of alms and a penalty of eighteen thousand livres. That was the philosophy of the gentlemen who dominated in these backward regions: to make personal use of everything that belonged to them. Their small regard for religion, their immense greed for property, the authority they enjoyed among the inhabitants of these mountains, and the remoteness of any kind of justice caused them to take all kinds of liberties.

---

[6] Turenne was one of Louis XIV's greatest generals. He is mentioned again on page 186, when he converts from Protestantism to Catholicism.

[7] Jérôme Le Peletier was one of the judges sent from the Parlement of Paris to hold the Grands Jours.

They oppressed the church after having oppressed the poor, and not content with the inheritances of their neighbors, which they used at their convenience, they usurped the inheritance of the spouse of Jesus Christ and tyrannized the priests after tyrannizing the people. . . .

Fléchier's account focuses on the most spectacular cases of noble and clerical corruption and the most dramatic punishments. To put the Grands Jours in a better perspective, it might be useful to cite the more accurate statistics provided by Arlette Lebigre.[8] *Of the 692 known criminal sentences issued by the court, 87 of the guilty parties were nobles, 4 were clergy, 27 were royal officers, and 574 were commoners. Of the known crimes they committed, the most frequent were murders (107), thefts (37), aggravated violence (34), embezzlement (24), duels (14), and rape (14). There were 370 death sentences issued, of which only 23 were actually carried out. Six nobles were executed, 1 priest, and 16 commoners. The other 347 death sentences were issued in absentia against defendants who had fled, and 94 of these were carried out symbolically, in effigy. Those who fled usually had their property confiscated. Other sentences included banishment (163; 82 in absentia); condemnation to the galleys (42; 21 in absentia), and flogging (21). Thus serious penalties were issued against commoners as well as nobles. Few of the major sentences were carried out in person, but the impact on the population of 23 actual executions and 94 symbolic ones must have been considerable.*

[8]Arlette Lebigre, *Les grands jours d'Auvergne: désordres et répression au XVIIe siècle* (Paris: Hachette, 1976), 133–58.

5

Reforming the Provinces: Interaction with Burgundy

Our examination of the interaction between the royal ministers and the provinces continues with a case study of the province of Burgundy. When ministers like Colbert tried to manage the provinces, they had to reckon with a variety of local authorities. Indeed, there was no substitute for the influence and prestige of powerful regional leaders. Not only did these people have to be won over, but they also had to be reconciled with one another, as each competed for a share of the same influence. One of the effects of absolutism, then, was a proliferation of jealous authorities.

Unlike the backward Auvergne, Burgundy was a rich, influential province with a full range of important institutions, most of them located in its capital city, Dijon. Let's take a minute to review Burgundy's chief institutions. The province had its own sovereign court, the Parlement of Dijon, which was comparable to the Parlement of Paris in the north of France and the Parlement of Aix in Provence. It was a collection of almost one hundred well-connected robe nobles who saw themselves as more than just a court of appeals for the region. In fact, they considered themselves to be the preeminent governing institution in the province. They decided cases in the name of the king, registered and enforced his laws, and defended provincial liberties, while protecting their own social positions. The First President of the Parlement was the top official who presided over the court. As an appointee of the king, he was supposed to keep the other judges in line, but as a man selected from within the court, he was also a defender of its collective interests whenever possible. Dijon also housed the Chambre des Comptes, a smaller sovereign court similar to the Parlement, which judged more specialized financial matters. The judges in these two courts saw themselves as the preeminent authorities for the region, thus they were bound to come into conflict with the other authorities.

The representative of the king in the province was the governor or his substitute, the royal lieutenant. As a prestigious grandee who knew the king personally, the governor was a man accustomed to giving orders. He served as military commander of the province and exercised a kind of executive authority by taking charge of any troops garrisoned in the province and carrying out the king's orders by formally presenting them to local bodies. He also mediated disputes and used his contingent of guards to enforce royal commands. In the 1660s, the governor of Burgundy was the prince of Condé, who had been a leading rebel in the Fronde and whom we encountered in chapter 1 stirring up trouble in Agen and Bordeaux. Like most other frondeurs, he had become a loyal advocate of royal power by the 1660s, but he was still a potentially dangerous figure.

The third pole of authority was the intendant. As we saw in chapter 3, he was a master of requests sent out by the king to reside in the province and report directly to the secretaries of state and the royal council. He was an administrator, whose job it was to collect information and see that the royal administrative agenda was carried out. Unlike the parlementaires and the governor, the intendant was usually an outsider who had little reason to protect local interests. Generally legally trained, he would be imbued with a mission to implement the royal program and thereby further his own career. Intendants had certain delegated judicial and administrative powers, but they were managers of royal programs, not substitutes for other authorities. As intruders and reformers, their efforts brought them into direct conflict with the parlementaires and sometimes the governor, all of whom had considerable pride and prestige invested in the idea that they were the primary monitors of provincial affairs.

Each town in Burgundy had its own municipal government. Dijon, with some twenty thousand inhabitants, was administered by a *viscount mayor* and six *échevins,* elected respectively to two- and four-year terms by a process of co-option from among the leading legal and merchant families. These men thought of themselves as proud upholders of a distinguished municipal tradition. They were in charge of collecting taxes and commanding the urban militia, and they held justice rights in their city comparable to those of a lord in the countryside. They were inferior in status to the parlementaires and the governor, but as far as they were concerned, they were in charge of governing their city, even though it contained the Parlement, the Chambre des Comptes, and the intendant.

Thus a variety of individuals and agencies, each with a slightly different kind of authority, claimed to govern Burgundy. The Parlement, and within it the First President; the governor; the intendant; and the mayor and échevins of Dijon all had jurisdiction in one way or another during times of crisis. All acted in the king's name. All had networks of allies and vested interests in the decisions that were made. No one except the intendant cared very much about the royal agenda, except when pleasing the king became politically necessary. Loyal though they might have been to the crown, the provincial authorities were unlikely to share the broader perspective of the king and his ministers.

LETTERS TO AND FROM BURGUNDY

The following letters to and from Burgundy can be read like a play in which each of the various actors speaks from a slightly different vantage point. Your job is to figure out how they are interacting. Remember, you are eavesdropping on the chief power brokers of French society as they negotiate the limits of their power. Listen to the terms they use and the way they interact. Be mindful of the impact Louis XIV and his orderly government had on provincial leaders who were just coming out of the Fronde. Note how each of these authorities picks up and mimics the political discourse used at court: service, obedience, pleasing the monarch, and avoiding disorder. Watch how these regional leaders are caught between their desire for personal advancement, their need to defend regional or corporate interests, and their wish, usually genuine, to serve the king. Note how jealous these authorities are of one another and especially how important symbolic signs of deference and hierarchy are to them. Everyone is making use of a rare and valuable commodity — the royal authority — which entails the glory of obeying superiors and the power to command subordinates.

The three main protagonists are Nicolas Brulart, Claude Bouchu, and the prince of Condé. Nicolas Brulart, marquis of La Borde, was First President of the Parlement of Dijon from 1657 to 1692. In 1658, he was sent into exile with other parlementaires for opposing royal laws too strenuously. Restored to favor, he returned to Dijon determined to please the king and Cardinal Mazarin. Meanwhile, the prince of Condé, a frondeur, was restored to favor in 1660 and renamed governor of the province after a period of exile in Spain. Claude Bouchu held the post of intendant from 1654 to 1682. He was unusual among intendants in that he came from distinguished origins in the province. His father had been First President of the Parlement of Dijon, and his brother succeeded Brulart in that post. But Bouchu, though socially indistinguishable from

Brulart, was very much an architect of Colbert's reforms — a man impatient with local resistance. Like most intendants, he wanted to wield his royal authority to bring about change and had to be restrained by more cautious voices around the king. All three men wanted to please Louis XIV, while criticizing the others' positions.

In the first letter, Brulart reports to Mazarin on the state of the province and complains about the insubordination in the Parlement, which presents a direct challenge to Brulart's role of managing the company in the name of the king.

Brulart to Mazarin

DIJON, JANUARY 5, 1660

I am obeying your order to provide a report of the state of things in the province and the disposition of people's minds. I will begin, Monseigneur, with the public welcomes I have enjoyed on all sides, based on the common knowledge that Your Eminence is my protector and deigns to place some confidence in me. I feel obliged to thank you for this honor, which I owe to Your Eminence alone, along with my appointment and my reinstatement [in the Parlement].

Everywhere I went in Burgundy, I found transports of joy over the change of governor that is being made. This is because of the esteem with which Monsieur the prince [Condé] is viewed and the expectation on the part of the large number of creatures and servants loyal to him and to Monsieur his father that they would enjoy the advantages of his protection. The lack of affection felt for Monsieur d'Épernon [his predecessor] has made the rejoicing all but universal. . . .

Upon my return, I found more scorn than ever for the senior members of the Parlement, whom the young insult in the haughtiest way during discussion of both private and public cases. Such disorderliness, which is unheard-of in other parlements, will continue to make this Parlement miserable. We must not expect that the king will be properly served as long as things continue to be so topsy-turvy. Just imagine, Monseigneur, for the past four or five years all the councillors from the Chamber of Enquêtes have been entering and serving in the

---

Choix de Lettres inédites écrites par Nicolas Brulart (hereafter referred to as Brulart), ed. M. de Lacuisine (Dijon: Imprimerie Loireau, 1859), 1:121–24.

Grande Chambre, in violation of their own rules and all the most definitive regulations. They outshout and outtalk the dean of the Parlement and myself. They form a majority and decide everything, especially public matters, with the passion of aroused men instead of the voice of experience. A reform bringing this Parlement in line with the Parlement of Paris . . . would be the most important business the king could have in Burgundy. . . .

In the next letter, note how the returned governor, Condé, is behaving himself and how much Brulart already detests Bouchu, the intendant.

Brulart to Mazarin

DIJON, APRIL 20, 1660

I must report what has happened in this province since Monsieur the prince arrived. The Parlement sent a delegation to greet him both in the countryside and at Dijon, observing the procedures followed in 1647 when he came [the first time] to take possession of the governorship. . . . He advised me several times to see that the [welcoming] delegations be modest in their praise of him and avoid talking about the things that happened during his absence [the Fronde]. . . . Yesterday he came to the palace accompanied by the duke of Enghien [Condé's son]. Monsieur the prince spoke vigorously in his speech of his obligations to the king, and from there he went on to Saint Jean de Losne to inspect the state of the fortifications, which are in poor condition. . . .

I must report to Your Eminence that it is very important for the success of royal affairs that you send here [as intendant] a man who is not publicly detested like M. Bouchu. He makes the easiest matters hard to carry out when they are in his hands. I won't say whether he deserves this universal hatred, because most of the things people complain about happened in my absence. For myself I will always get along as I should with those bearing orders from the king. But I can assure Your Eminence that he is so scorned and detested that the result can only be damaging to the king's service. . . .

April 20: Brulart, 1:158–60.

Once every three years, a regional assembly, the Estates of Burgundy, met in Dijon to grant taxes to the king, since Burgundy was one of the pays d'états discussed in chapter 3. The Estates were divided into three houses, or estates: the clergy, the nobility, and the "third," which represented town governments. Here Condé is himself becoming a royal agent, using his extensive provincial contacts to smooth the process of negotiating a tax grant. In this letter, we can see a typical negotiation, including the personal egos that had to be placated. Note the importance of protocol, including placement by rank. Be aware of the interplay between the king's agents, who are going to get what they want, and the provincial deputies, who are bargaining for reductions and concessions. Note how each side tries to manipulate the other.

Condé to Colbert

DIJON, JUNE 18, 1662

. . . I could not open the Estates on the 12th because a number of deputies of the clergy and the third estate had not yet arrived. Also, a dispute arose between the count of Amanzé [the royal lieutenant] and the First President, which forced me to postpone the opening until the next day. It would not have been appropriate to begin until this conflict had been completely settled, since I detected much bitterness between these two gentlemen, to the point of making sharp remarks, and the matter would no doubt have heated up if it hadn't been resolved.

The issue was their rank in marching from the Logis Du Roi, where it is customary to pick up the governor, to the Cordeliers' church, and from there to the assembly hall. At Mass and in the assembly itself there was no dispute over places: The First President normally doesn't attend the Mass because the royal lieutenant has the best seat; on the other hand, the First President has the right to sit at the right hand of the governor in the assembly, and the royal lieutenant sits at his left. Thus the problem was over the order of march from the Logis Du Roi to the Cordeliers', which is normally done on foot with the governor, and from the church to the Cordeliers' chamber, where the meeting is held.

After proposing many solutions, I decided to tell them that, because of my gout, I could not easily walk on foot from my lodging to the Cordeliers', so I would go in my carriage with some of my gentlemen, and

---

June 18: Brulart, 1:229–34.

everyone was to await me at the Cordeliers'. Monsieur the First President would abstain from attending the Mass as usual, and from the Mass to the chamber, one of these gentlemen would march in front of me and the other behind. That would avoid either one giving way to the other, and neither would have the advantage. With that settled, Monsieur d'Amanzé marched in front of me, the First President marched behind me, and everything was resolved, but only provisionally pending receipt of the king's orders. . . .

Getting back to the Estates, the opening was Tuesday the 13th. The morning was spent in speeches and ceremonies and the afternoon in naming deputies [to visit the king]. The next day they began to discuss the free gift.[1] The matter was placed on the floor, and before it was voted, these gentlemen sent a delegation to me to ask whether the sum the king was demanding included everything and whether the gift they gave the king would free them from all taxes, especially the "subsistence" and "winter quarters" [for the troops],[2] since, with peace restored, they hoped the king would free them from this expense.

I replied that they should have known the intentions of His Majesty from the reading of M. Bouchu's commission, and that this was not therefore an issue to be raised; that, getting down to details, I had to report that because the king is obliged to maintain quantities of troops and pay them more regularly than he does during the war, His Majesty is unable to avoid drawing considerable aid from his subjects for the troops' subsistence. It was not like previous peace treaties, because then His Majesty had not made considerable conquests; now he had retained a number of important fortresses that he had to maintain; . . . and finally that it was impossible for the king to give his people all the relief they desired, especially at a time when his domain [royal property] was completely alienated [mortgaged] following a great dissipation of his finances. . . .

Since then the Estates have deliberated every day, persuaded that the extreme misery in this province — caused by the great levies it has suffered, the sterility [of the land] in recent years, and the disorders that have recently occurred — would induce the king to give them some relief. That is why they offered only 500,000 livres for the free gift. Then,

---

[1] The so-called free gift was the sum the Estates granted to the king, which they then collected and delivered in place of a taille collected by the king's own agents. This was one of the privileges of the province.

[2] These were sums levied to pay troops passing through the province. The *subsistence* tax was the cost of food for passing troops, while the *winter quarters* tax was the cost of lodging the troops in private homes during the winter months.

after I had protested this in the appropriate manner, they raised it to 600,000, then 800,000, and finally 900,000 livres. Until then I had stood firm at 1.5 million, but when I saw that they were on the verge of deciding not to give any more . . . and seeing that it was only fear of impotence that was restraining them from making a larger effort, I finally came down to the 1.2 million livres contained in my instructions and invited them to deliberate again, declaring that I could not agree to present any other proposition to the king and that I believed that there was no better way to serve their interests than to obey the king blindly. They agreed with good grace and came this morning to offer me a million. They begged me to leave it at that and not to demand more from them for the free gift; and since I told them they would have to do a little better to satisfy the king completely on this occasion, they again exaggerated their poverty and begged me to inform the king of it, but said that, rather than not please him, they preferred to make a new effort, and they would leave it up to me to declare what they had to do. I told them that I believed His Majesty would have the goodness to be satisfied with 1.05 million livres for the free gift, and they agreed, while pressing me to make the king aware of the extreme need they found themselves in, which I promised to do. So, Monsieur, there is the deed done. . . .

In addition I must tell you that the Chamber of the Clergy and the Chamber of the Nobility acted marvelously in this affair, hardly causing any difficulty with anything that was proposed. True, the Chamber of the Third Estate caused a little more trouble, but this is excusable because they are the ones who bear most of the taxes. When I return, I will bring a list of those who acted best; His Majesty will decide if he considers them worthy of some sort of reward, as has always been the practice, and he will act as he sees fit.

The following exchange reflects Louis XIV's attempt to regulate procedures in the parlements. During the Fronde, the Parlement of Dijon, like most of the others, was the scene of feverish political activity, as the more active councillors demanded reforms and tried to take over the sessions. Brulart is on the king's side in wanting this unruly behavior to cease; in fact, he advocated this reform in his letter on January 5. Note the pretensions of the Parlement and Louis XIV's response.

Brulart to La Vrillière[1]

DIJON, JANUARY 31, 1663
The Parlement is continuing its joint meetings of chambers concerning acceptance of the [procedural] regulations established by His Majesty.[2] I think yesterday was the seventh time they assembled, not counting four other meetings of a great number of presidents and eight or ten councillors, who examined the regulations with me and drew up suggestions concerning what might happen when they are put into effect. None of this is bringing the conclusion of the affair any closer, and people are in such a mischievous mood that everyone is working to make the regulations as useless as possible. If these assemblies go on much longer, it might be necessary to suspend them and command the implementation of the entire set of regulations, to preserve the respect due to orders from the king and in the interest of justice. . . . They believe that they are sovereign legislators. They become blinded by their own interests, not wanting to recognize that parlements, like other subjects, must be submissive to their prince. You wouldn't believe the agony that these false opinions cause me in a company that is only too full of them. . . . I try every possible approach to calm them down. I give in on everything that does not violate the actual text of the regulations, and I frequently remind them that it is not in their power or mine to touch the text. . . .

Louis XIV to Brulart

PARIS, FEBRUARY 13, 1663
Monsieur Brulart, I have seen — in the dispatch that you wrote me on the 4th of this month — what happened in my Court of Parlement of Dijon concerning the recent regulations that were sent, both concerning

---

[1] Louis Phélypeaux de La Vrillière was the secretary of state responsible for corresponding with Burgundy and reporting to the ministers and the king.

[2] During the Fronde, parlementaire agitators developed a tactic whereby political business could be discussed in joint sessions of all the Parlement's chambers. Brulart and the king wanted to keep the various chambers separate and require them to stick to judicial business.

January 31: Brulart, 1:258–61.
February 13: Brulart, 1:269.

the seating of the officers who compose it and the form of the administration of justice. I would have preferred for the remonstrances issued on this subject to have been avoided by a complete and peaceful execution of my orders and by the subsequent adjustment of problems that might have arisen concerning certain points that are subject to interpretation. But since I do not wish such incidents to destroy the unity that must exist in the company, I am instructing my cousin the prince of Condé to settle everything by sensible accommodation and, if he can, to the satisfaction of each person. I thought I should inform you of this by saying to you in this letter that you are to accept whatever he may decide. . . .

Here is our first comment from Bouchu. Remember that he is an intendant bent on reform and also a personal rival of Brulart. Note how the sides are drawn on fiscal reform. Bouchu is trying to clean up the debts of local communities so that they can pay their taxes without ruining themselves. His tone is defensive because he is fighting powerful vested interests.

Bouchu to Colbert

DIJON, FEBRUARY 14, 1663
. . . We are working without respite on examining the debts of the communities, and we are currently dealing with those from Beaune. It is true, Monsieur, that they are excessive and immense, but no one can deny any longer that this investigation is legitimate and that I was completely correct to pursue it, now that they see that it could not be avoided. We have found that in the three communities that have presented their records, there are more than 1.5 million livres of debts — that is, five hundred thousand at Dijon, four hundred thousand or more at Semur, and more than six hundred thousand at Beaune — not counting the unpaid tailles, which I cannot assess very clearly. The misfortunes of war certainly caused part of them, but poor administration for the past thirty years — not to mention the confusion caused by continual disorders, the deaths of many persons who could have given us information and of those who were responsible and could have been punished, the good faith placed by the majority of the creditors in a practice that was vicious but universal and sometimes ordered by the very people who should have opposed it — all these reasons hinder us from achieving the good

results that we would like and reduce us to punishing only the mischief and negligence of the creditors and the magistrates. . . .

There, Monsieur, that is why I have made enemies, since during my seven years assigned to this province I have never stopped exposing all the irregularities I have encountered, which involve the most powerful individuals; but I have been able to prevail only since His Majesty took over the personal direction of his affairs and made you his chief director. . . .

Read carefully Bouchu's excellent description of the problem of vested interest. The desire to settle the debts of the municipalities so that they will be free to pay more taxes to the crown is being blocked by local authorities who want the old system to continue. Bouchu is beside himself with rage, because the authorities in Beaune have obviously been complaining against him. Think about how the sides are lining up on this issue.

Bouchu to Colbert

DIJON, FEBRUARY 17, 1663

The complaints about which you wrote me, from numerous inhabitants of Beaune to the royal council, are simply the results of the inequality and injustice inherent in the tax levy. [This tax] is a product of the freedom mayors and échevins have claimed to impose whatever sums they want. This [abuse] has been practiced in every community in Burgundy, burdening the lesser people to the advantage of the magistrates and the important citizens of each community. When they were supposed to pay ten thousand, the mayor and échevins had no difficulty imposing twenty thousand or more. The self-interest of the magistrates and the important inhabitants lies in the fact that the former can appropriate these sums or use a good part of them for useless expenses such as trips, feasts, presents, and other things of that nature, while the latter, themselves often magistrates, pay little or nothing of these taxes anyway. The magistrates compel the poor to pay, along with those who lack support in each community, while sparing the most powerful; or they get themselves exempted by means of collective payoffs or discharges from the Parlement of Dijon. They also claim exemptions by virtue of holding petty offices in the sovereign courts or in the household of the king, the queen, the late

G. B. Depping (hereafter referred to as Depping), *Correspondance administrative sous le règne de Louis XIV* (Paris: Imprimerie Nationale, 1850), 1:666–72.

Monseigneur the Prince, or the current Monseigneur the Prince. . . . The Parlement of Dijon has always allowed the communities to impose these taxes without obtaining permission letters, although the ordinances firmly prohibit such practices. . . .

I must note in passing, Monsieur, that the same injustice that is practiced in every community through these taxes and surtaxes, in which the weak pay two or three times their assessments while the powerful pay nothing at all or very little, is also practiced by the *élus*[1] [in assessing] the unprotected communities differently from those that are controlled by members of the Parlement, members of the Chambre des Comptes, and important churchmen or gentlemen. . . .

I must also report another great irregularity. When the important inhabitants of Beaune saw that if the royal orders were executed, they would no longer have the exemptions and discharges they had enjoyed in the past, more than fifty of them appealed their assessments. I am sending you the list drawn up by the mayor and échevins. You can see, Monsieur, the expense that these lawsuits will impose on every community if they are allowed to proceed. Before the auditing of debts, the mayor and échevins were perfectly happy to see these lawsuits because they were a pretext for borrowing, taxing, and charging expenses for trips to Dijon. . . . The remedy I found in Bresse was to tax the offices of all these cheaters in each community, to the point where hardly anyone complains. If we did the same here, we would get rid of more than three-quarters of this chicanery; but messieurs the *élus* have neither the knowledge nor the authority, nor the goodwill nor the energy, to carry out such endeavors.

You see, Monsieur, that would require offending all the most powerful persons who are protected by the Parlement and the Chambre des Comptes, for almost all the agents of the province had their origins [in those courts], and these people are so far from seeking justice that they even stipulate in the leases by which they rent out their farms to their tenants that [the lands] will maintain their taille exemptions, and this stipulation is religiously observed. People like that, whose loyalty lies anywhere but to the king and their duty, will never carry through on any project to restore order, and they will force the king either to watch the province being ruined or to [intervene and] alter its situation. . . .

Comic scenes like the following reflect the importance of precedence and hierarchy. They were not funny to the participants, however.

[1] The *élus* were agents of the provincial estates who were responsible for assessing the amount each community would pay toward the taxes approved in the estates.

Brulart to La Vrillière

DIJON, FEBRUARY 21, 1663

... An incident has occurred which merits a report to you: Two wives of presidents [in the Parlement] quarreled over a seat at the sermon, and it came to exchanges of words and blows. One of them, Madame Baillet, wanted to displace the other, Madame Jacob, who was occupying her seat. When the latter claimed the right to keep it because, said she, it was in a spot that belonged to her, one of her valets pulled Madame Baillet by the arm. Right after the service President Baillet; Councillors Legouz, Bouhier, and Ragys; the general prosecutor; and the dean — all brothers and brothers-in-law of Madame Baillet — went in two carriages to President Jacob's house. They entered wearing their robes and demanded that this president turn over his valet for punishment. They claim they acted civilly, but Monsieur Jacob says they uttered insults and threats. When the valet passed by in a courtyard, he was recognized by one of these gentlemen, who ran after him. President Jacob followed and held the man back by his robe, but the man turned around and grabbed Jacob by the collar of his doublet, which he tore. Jacob adds (which is denied) that he was struck by several blows, including one to his face, which appeared swollen. The valet was then pursued by the same man, who broke in the door to the kitchen where [the valet] had taken refuge; [the valet] retreated into another shed, whose door was also broken in. But when the valet picked up several large clubs, the attack ceased. ...

Recall that forest revenues were an item in Louis XIV's budgets.

Colbert to Bouchu

JUNE 5, 1663

I am writing these lines to ask you to send me a list of all the local offices of waters and forests in Burgundy and Bresse — the names of all the forests in each district, explaining for each what it consists of and what kind of trees are planted there.

February 21: Brulart, 1:271–74.
June 5: Pierre Clément (hereafter referred to as Clément), ed., *Lettres, instructions et mémoires de Colbert* (Paris: Imprimerie Impériale, 1867), 4:207.

Please also send me a memorandum on all the alienations [renting out] of forests that have been carried out in the district and the names of the persons who have taken up the leases.

Note how Colbert collects information. Here Bouchu is replying directly to Colbert's call for information about the officers of the province (see page 87). You can see how government is built on personal ties.

Bouchu to Colbert

DIJON, NOVEMBER 13, 1663

To satisfy the orders you did me the honor of issuing in your letter of the 8th of this month, I am sending a list of all the officers in the Parlement with their good and bad qualities.

Presidents

BRULART, First President, is known to you; he seems to me to have common sense, mediocre intelligence, and much presumption.

FYOT, an elderly officer, calm, assiduous, performs his job very well; a respectable man and devoted to the service of the king.

DES BARRES, has common sense, is a good jurist, a little capricious and litigious.

FREMIOT, a quiet man with good sense and a mediocre mind.

JOLY, a gentleman, good jurist, very capable and assiduous at his post, a little odd and melancholy.

BERNARD, a gentleman, good jurist, capable, loves books, quite peculiar.

BAILLET, a young man of mediocre gifts.

Councillors *[a selection]*

DE THÉSUT, the dean [of the company], a man of spirit, reasonably capable, rather firm, seventy-seven years old or older, yet assiduous.

DE GAND, a gentleman, good jurist, capable enough, very pleasant and amenable, devoted to royal service.

November 13: Brulart, 1:315–20.

BERNARDON, a good jurist, the most capable man in the Parlement and the busiest, a quiet man devoted to royal service.

MASSOL, has no ability, negligent in his post, very mediocre character and weak.

DE VILLERES, a gentleman, good jurist, but he resigned his post this week to give it to his son.

LE GOUZ, reasonably good sense, has ordinary capacity; a man of conspiracies, always opposed to the king's affairs, delights in having certain councillors in his pocket or those of his relatives and friends; a crude man, unmanageable.

LE BELIN, mediocre ability, good temperament but rather slippery and unreliable; little devoted to royal service; he was banished in 1658 after the suspension of the Parlement, but Monsieur the duke of Épernon [then governor] vouched for him. . . .

[Other names are omitted.]

What I might add, Monsieur, as a general characteristic, is that Monsieur the prince has almost absolute power over this entire corps and its individual members. In general they are very attached to their interests, and they nurse their resentments for a long time: There are quarrels involving them or their families that never seem to die. . . . I can assure you that I have told the truth to the extent it is known to me, and I have done it without rancor toward those who proclaim themselves to be my enemies and announce very frequently and publicly that, since they cannot be my judge, they will avenge themselves on those close to me whenever they get the chance. . . .

Here is an example of the rivalry between companies of royal officers and their haughty view of their surroundings. You would never know that Dijon even had a municipal government.

Brulart to Chancellor Séguier[1]

DIJON, DECEMBER 16, 1663
This Parlement is no longer able to tolerate the inconvenience of the mud in this city, which makes it as filthy as any village in the kingdom,

[1]The chancellor was the chief of the judicial system.

December 16: Brulart, 2:8–9.

so it has issued a decree of which I am sending you a copy. The same steps have been taken twice before in the past twenty-five years, but the Chambre des Comptes has still decided to block them with the outrageous claim that this order could be issued only in collaboration with them, on the grounds that all inhabitants of the houses of this city, which includes officers in that body, are being required to contribute to a street-cleaning fund, which can be established only with their approval because [sovereign] companies have no authority over one another. But overlooking the fact that one could prove the contrary using many examples, this clearly involves nothing more than a police regulation over which the Parlement holds sovereign jurisdiction. . . . We have done the Chambre des Comptes the honor of allowing one of their members to participate in the collections in each parish. However, since they are very stubborn and enterprising, I thought I should inform you of their attempts to sabotage this decree, which is so important for the whole city, and our company implores you to protect it in this situation, where the officers of the Comptes will not fail to use false pretexts to launch an appeal to the royal council by surprise.

In the next letter, we again see a reflection of one of Colbert's major concerns — reform of the management of France's forests. When owned by the king, forests could be an important source of revenue. In addition, Colbert was interested in sources of masts for the fleet he hoped to build. His investigation and reorganization culminated in a great forest reform ordinance in 1669. But the real issue here is the jurisdictional conflict between Bouchu and the Parlement. Both are supposed to represent the king, yet they fight fiercely with one another.

Bouchu to Colbert

DECEMBER 10, 1664

I wrote you by the last courier about the Parlement of Dijon's attempt to block the implementation of a legal verdict I issued in collaboration with the requisite number of judges and in accordance with all proper procedures stipulated in the forest reform. Their attempt is contrary to the authority of the king. They know perfectly well that for two years I have had

December 10: Brulart, 2:16–18.

the authority to implement [the forest reform] in this city. They tolerated the trial for more than three weeks knowing full well that it concerned the murder by ambush of a forest guard, that [these guards] are indispensable agents for the preservation of our forests, and that [the murder concerned] an officer acting in the line of duty. If this act were to remain unpunished, it would become impossible to find any [guards] and the forests would be abandoned to the whims of anyone.

I thought I should inform you that the audacity of the officers of the Parlement increases day by day, and that while they are triumphing in their latest effort, they are announcing loudly that in the future they will impede the execution of all the king's orders. In effect they intimidate everyone who tries to function here and discourage everyone who has been issued a legal summons — whether for the forest reforms, the auditing of debts, the investigation of titles of nobility, or other things — from cooperating. If this continues, not only will I be obliged to stop where I am, but everything I've done up to this point, which is more than half of the job, will be overturned without hope of recovery. . . .

The next three letters show how the rivalry of Bouchu and the Parlement jeopardized public order. The crowd in Noyers is rioting against excise taxes that they blame on Bouchu and the commission that audited the debt accounts. As we will see in chapter 6, the reaction of the crowd is typical. Note the positions the Parlement takes, and consider which side the king supports.

Bouchu to Colbert

DIJON, JANUARY 25, 1665

. . . This is to inform you of a new outrage undertaken by the Parlement of Dijon against the authority of the king over the auditing of the debts of the province. I issued a decree announcing certain excise taxes in the town of Noyers to raise revenues to pay off that community's debts by order of the king, as I have done in every other town. . . . But when this decree was announced from the pulpit of the parish church of Noyers, many persons stormed into the houses of a man named de Selles and a man named Millot on grounds that they had been present at the verification of debts, pillaged them, abused de Selles' wife, and dragged

January 25: Brulart, 2:32–34.

him through the streets. By some great good fortune de Selles and Millot both avoided being killed and after escaping came to me to complain, whereupon I ordered that the case be investigated. . . .

When Monsieur the First President [Brulart] was informed of this, he assembled the chambers and, with all the fanfare he could muster, summoned de Selles and Millot to appear before the Parlement and forbade them to appeal anywhere else, using threats that would not be tolerated if an individual uttered them. These poor men came to tell me what had happened and added that they had declared to the Parlement, which was pressing them to lodge their complaints, that they did not want to become plaintiffs because of the excessive sums it would cost them if this case was prosecuted at their own expense. They also told me that they did not dare pursue the investigation in accordance with my decree out of fear of incurring the hatred of the Parlement.

There you have it, Monsieur — the effects of the affair I had the honor to write you about at the time of the Parlement's first indignity against the authority of the king in the forest reform. . . . They brag about this on every possible occasion, taking pleasure in discrediting the king's affairs, while seducing and poisoning the minds of the people. They are now doing the same with the excise taxes, saying that they will block them in any way possible, that they won't be used for the payment of communal debts, and that [instead] the king will appropriate them.

Here is Brulart's account of the same affair. Without being disloyal, he defends the Parlement and blames Bouchu for the trouble.

Brulart to La Vrillière

DIJON, JANUARY 25, 1665
You will see in the enclosed document from our registers the general prosecutor's complaint to the Parlement concerning an uprising that occurred at Noyers eight days ago, and you will also see the decree that was issued ordering an investigation. Our commissioner left yesterday with one advocate general to investigate, issue arrest warrants, and restrain the rioters by their presence. And since diligence is necessary and one can never be too hasty in taking care of disorders that harm the royal

January 25: Brulart, 2:28–29.

authority and threaten the public safety, the Parlement thought it should apply His Majesty's sovereign justice to stop the course of this violence. I have no doubt that you will keep [His Majesty] informed while you await my report on what actually happened, as seen in the evidence that the commissioners will gather. But it is important to tell you that other towns in this province are also stirred up and that, among others, Beaune and Châtillon are aroused to the point where it is to be feared that they might have trouble from an uprising of the populace, who are extremely angry at the most distinguished and important inhabitants. It is certain that this growing problem is the result of the auditing of the debts of communities, and this is why the Parlement has not interposed its authority as it would otherwise have done.[1] But when the problem reaches the point of sedition, gatherings of crowds, and public pillaging of houses, the company believes that it is pleasing the king and doing its duty by causing these disorders to cease and reestablishing the calm. . . .

Here is the king's response to Brulart.

La Vrillière to Brulart

PARIS, FEBRUARY 3, 1665

I have received your letter of the 25th of the past month and reported it to the king, who, after considering the effects that the uprising in Noyers might have, thought it appropriate to give orders to M. Bouchu to do an investigation and then send it to the royal council. He commanded me to tell you that his intention is that your company suspend everything concerning this matter in order to let the intendant act and that later we will study the whole affair and decide on the appropriate solution.

The next letter is a good example of the intendants carrying out Colbert's passion for improving waterways that we saw in his memorandum on page 89. Note the complexity of the issues and the local rights that need to be compensated.

---

[1] Brulart means that Bouchu is stirring up all this trouble with his investigation into community debts, but he is being tactful because he knows that Bouchu is carrying out Colbert's policy.

February 3: Brulart, 2:34–35.

Bouchu to Colbert

PORT DIGOIN, OCTOBER 30, 1665

I am sending the report of my study of the Deune and Bourbince Rivers and the ponds of Longpendu, Montchanin, and others in the area, according to the king's orders to investigate the possibility of transnavigating from the Loire to the Saône River and thus connecting the seas [Atlantic to Mediterranean]. I was accompanied by M. Bourguignot, *élu* of the third estate [an official of the Estates of Burgundy], and M. Rogoley, named as clerk by His Majesty, along with M. de Francine-Grandmaison, intendant of waters and fountains of France, and M. Chamoy, engineer and architect of the king.

We could not have proceeded with more care and effort, having worked seventeen days from morning to night with such great desire to perform our duty well that we slept only in small villages and abandoned houses on the edge of the rivers. Every one of us did his job to the full, and everywhere we went, I was careful to consult anyone else, gentlemen or others, who might contribute to our success. I would venture to suggest that however difficult it was for you to make any decision on the basis of previous reports, with their lack of precision and excess of pretension, this report will enable you to know the facts as if you had been there yourself. . . .

[Pages of details are omitted.]

The Bourbince River, which flows from the Longpendu Pond and half a league from there is reinforced by two large streams, runs ten leagues from its origin to the Loire, which it flows into at La Mothe Saint Jean near Port Digoin, two thousand *toises* [a measure of length] above the Arroux River. It passes through underbrush and mostly uncultivated land, with a few meadows and much unproductive soil. . . . There are twenty one mills on this river; nineteen would be preserved, one would be moved, and one would be destroyed. I have indicated in the margin the rent for each, and I would try to arrange as good a deal as possible to indemnify the owners, which should not be too expensive. The materials for the bridges which would number six; for the locks, which would number forty; for the five dikes; and for the roadways are [readily avail-

---

October 30: Depping (1855), 4:46–51.

able]. There are ten ponds that must be tapped and for which we must indemnify the owners; I have written in the margin the rent on each of them. . . .

Here is a good example of the difficulty of tax reform, given the social pressure to protect and extend local privileges.

Bouchu to Colbert

DIJON, MARCH 21, 1666

The cathedral chapter of Autun has sent a canon [priest] to me bringing two decrees of the royal council dated the 18th of last month. In one His Majesty discharges the priests and religious houses of paying excise taxes [on commodities entering the city], while the other, issued at the request of the syndic of the diocese, summons the mayor and échevins of Autun before the royal council but in the meantime discharges them from paying excise taxes and other city fees. If these two decrees are enforced in Burgundy, all the work we have done to free the cities from the terrible burdens they were under and to place the inhabitants in a position to be able to pay their taille and still survive, and all the trouble this has cost us, will have been in vain. The cities will be plunged back into greater confusion than ever, since this is the only way they have of paying their debts, which come to six million. These excises were granted on condition that they be levied indiscriminately on churchmen, gentlemen, officers in the sovereign courts, and other privileged persons. If all these persons were exempted, the taxes would not be worth half as much, because rich people make up the more respectable part of the king's subjects in the province, not to mention the frauds that would be committed in their names. If these decrees are upheld, no doubt all the other ecclesiastics in Burgundy will acquire the same rights; the gentlemen will follow their example and get the same, which it would only be just to grant them, and once the ecclesiastics and gentlemen have it, the officers of the sovereign courts, who have the clout to bring it about, will follow. . . .

Local people were not as enthusiastic as Colbert and his agents about economic reform.

March 21: Depping, 1:679–81.

Bouchu to Colbert

... Attached is a report I drew up after the bidding on the work to make the passage from the Saône to the Loire navigable had been announced on six successive Sundays in the cities of Dijon, Châlons, and Lyon. You will see that no entrepreneur has come forward to undertake these works, nor has anyone contacted the lieutenant generals of Lyon and Châlons, to whom I sent our decrees, nor have they contacted me on the day I indicated. Assuredly, Monsieur, there is no one in these provinces intelligent enough or rich enough for such enterprises, and for such a grand project we must expect to find them only in Paris. I await your orders on this affair. ...

In the next letter, we see the impact of Colbert's enormous interest in promoting manufacturing enterprises by granting exclusive privileges to entrepreneurs who would set up manufactories where artisans were concentrated under one roof and assigned to the production of some new commodity, according to the strict standards established by Colbert himself. These efforts, though impressive, often failed because they could not compete with cheaper foreign products or were not adequately supported by traditional local producers. Note how Bouchu, in the king's name, manipulates the municipal elections of Auxerre, a small city where he wants to set up manufactories. Note also the implicit resistance of local manufacturers to these plans and the patronizing way Bouchu handles the young female workers.

Bouchu to Colbert

AUXERRE, NOVEMBER 4, 1667
... I arrived here Monday and found people so divided and agitated against one another that I have never seen anything like it. There was no one, from the bishop on down, who had not taken sides; you heard of nothing but plots and threats, and I don't doubt that it would have come

April 21: Depping, 4:51.
November 4: Depping 1:683–84. Depping III, 814–16.

to blows and caused a dangerous uprising with no one there to stop them. I have used these four days to reconcile them as much as possible, and with such success that the meeting held today by order of the king to name a mayor and other officers was completely calm. There had never been such a numerous assembly, and there was not a single inhabitant who did not attend. And since I understood from your letter that you wanted Billard, president in the local court, to become mayor, I have arranged things so that although he did not receive a plurality of votes in the assembly held on October 2, he received all the votes [today], even those from the officers of the *élection* and the *prévôté* [local courts], and some from people in the présidial [court] who are his sworn enemies. . . .

As regards the manufactories, I had a long conference with Madame de La Petitière. She complained to me that many of the girls who were working at French lace are now making Parisian lace in their houses on their own behalf, and not in the house of manufacture on behalf of the entrepreneurs. I had with me the mayor and échevins, and I asked them in her presence why these faults were occurring; they told me that they lacked the jurisdiction that would allow them to make [the girls] go and work in the house of manufacture. She also complained that Camuset is diverting some girls into manufacturing stockings, and the mayor and échevins reported in turn that these girls complain that they earn too little. In order to find out about this, I summoned the agent of the entrepreneurs. He brought me their handiwork and showed me what the girls could earn, which I think can reach six, seven, eight, or ten sous per day. Thus they are out of line to complain. As they become more skilled with time, they could earn even more. As for the complaints made by Madame de La Petitière . . . in order to prohibit the girls from making Parisian lace and require them to go to work in the house of manufacture for the entrepreneurs, someone would have to have the jurisdiction to compel them; for good as the regulations are, they stay unenforced unless someone takes charge of them. . . . If you don't want to give the responsibility for matters concerning the manufacture to the *prévôt* [a local judge], you could assign it to the mayor and échevins or to the presidial court; but if you want to know my opinion, I believe that a single person would do it much better than a whole company, because if there is the slightest violation, the entrepreneurs will know whom to turn to for justice, and the responsible party will have to answer for his actions; and besides one could choose a capable man. . . .

[Bouchu volunteers himself.]

After I met with Madame de La Petitière, she asked me to go into the room where the girls were working to appeal to them to work with care, which I did. I found thirty of them, and after having urged them to do a good job, in order to moderate my scolding a bit, I gave them two louis d'or [gold coins] so that they all could eat together, and they promised me they would work with greater diligence than in the past. . . .

Louis XIV also was preoccupied with establishing "hospitals," which were really poorhouses, throughout the realm. In the next three letters, watch how Bouchu intervenes to institute a royal policy and how local rivalries again impede his success. Note the Parlement's response and the alternative proposal offered by the city as a way of getting control of the reforms imposed on them.

Bouchu to Colbert

DIJON, JUNE 23, 1669

I had the honor to write to you eight days ago that I had summoned Joly, mayor of this city, to discuss implementing the decree of the royal council establishing a general hospital and the means proposed by the king for the nourishment and maintenance of the poor. He asked me to let him show the decree to the Chamber of the Poor, composed of several officers from the Parlement, the Chambre des Comptes, the Trésoriers de France,[1] and the mayor and échevins. Having done this, he informed me that the officers from the Parlement, the Comptes, and the Trésoriers de France had resolved not to attend the general assembly that was to be held in my presence by order of the decree. . . . Yesterday when I went to city hall at 1:00 P.M. I found the ecclesiastics represented there by their deputies and a large gathering of magistrates, city officers, and inhabitants; but messieurs from the Parlement, the Comptes, and the Trésoriers de France stuck to their word and did not attend. Nevertheless I proceeded to the complete implementation of the decree, and I will do myself the honor of sending you a copy of the full report with my rec-

---

[1] The Trésoriers de France were another company of royal financial officers who functioned in Dijon.

---

ommendation after I have looked into this matter further, with respect to possible sites and the revenues of the hospital, which I will study through their accounts. . . .

The Viscount Mayor and Échevins of Dijon to Colbert

JULY 14, 1669

Since the general assembly held in city hall by order of His Majesty in the presence of Monsieur Bouchu, intendant of this province, has determined that locking up the poor, who are very numerous here, is necessary and the assembly has examined the means to finance their support, we assume that Monsieur Bouchu will have drawn up and sent you his report. At this time we turn to you, Monseigneur, and beg humbly for your protection in obtaining permission from the king to lock up all the poor in our own hospital, which is large, spacious, and one of the loveliest in France, and to keep them occupied with manual labor as they do in Paris. For their support [we request] the right to continue indefinitely the excise tax of forty sous per *esmine* of wheat milled by the bakers and pastry cooks, raising five thousand livres per year, as we have done for more than seventy years — that is, after the city's debts have been paid off.[1] In addition we request permission to levy a permanent tax of six livres on all wine entering the city from outside our bailliage. However, wine originating on the estates of the inhabitants of this city (regardless of where they lie in the province) will be exempt. This tax will prevail from the day we receive the letters [patent] His Majesty pleases to grant us; and his letters should also stipulate that the hospital will be run in the traditional manner by a president and two councillors from the Parlement, two officers from the Comptes, a trésorier de France, the viscount mayor, and all the échevins of this city, with the right to correct the poor and administer corporal punishment and the power to set up pillory and shackles. . . . We have hopes of great success with all of the above. If you are willing to intervene for us with His Majesty to obtain these things on behalf of the poor, they will unceasingly recognize this great benefit by offering their prayers to God for your prosperity. . . .

---

[1] This tax had been diverted (by Bouchu) to pay off municipal debts, but the city would like to continue collecting it and use it for their hospital.

July 14: Depping, 1:808–9

Bouchu to Colbert

DIJON, JULY 14, 1669

You will find enclosed my report and recommendation concerning the establishment of a general hospital in this city, which, although it is urgently necessary, will never be possible unless you give it your special protection because of the opposition of the Parlement, which opposes on every possible occasion all the good one would like to accomplish. They are so totally carried away with their sovereignty that they believe they alone can initiate action and that the orders coming from the royal council are usurpations, although I've done what I could to disabuse them of this idea; and thanks to your aid and protection I've established many good procedures and fully reestablished the authority of the king against all those who do not acknowledge it. But I can assure you that I have not yet been able to suppress their desire for their former grandeur, and they do not fail to say frequently that they are waiting for better times. . . .

But intendants also had to be kept under control, and Colbert often sent out letters like the following.

Colbert to Bouchu

PARIS, DECEMBER 19, 1670

In reply to your letter of the 11th, I can assure you that His Majesty's intention was never that you should take on affairs other than those in your jurisdiction, or that on pretext that the judges are performing their functions badly or that you can handle things more promptly, you should establish an extraordinary tribunal unheard-of in any province. Therefore do not ask me anymore whether you should send back to the regular judges matters that are not in your competence, because you never should have taken up or monopolized them in the first place.

July 14: Brulart, 2:101–2.
December 19: Clément, 6:31–32.

These Burgundian letters suggest something of the nature of the interactive relationship between the ministers at court and the various authorities throughout France. If we remember that France had about thirty such provinces, each with slightly different circumstances and a different cast of players, we can better understand the strengths and the limitations of Louis XIV's government.

MEETING THE PEOPLE OF DIJON

The letters in the previous section convey an impression of absolutism through the eyes of administrators, confident of their stations in life and sure of their superior right to rule in the name of the king. Here and there, they give us a glimpse of the rest of the population — as oppressed tenants in Auvergne, as rioters against a new excise tax in Beaune, and as weavers in a shop in Auxerre. For these and most other people, life under absolutism meant family, shop, fields, conviviality, and hardship.

The following documents show us a level of city life below the realm of the Parlement and intendant in Dijon, often in the very years when Brulart and Bouchu were writing their letters about government. They are from a series of records kept by the city council concerning disturbances and investigations in response to citizen complaints.

The viscount mayor and six échevins of Dijon considered themselves to be proud leaders of their community. But to Brulart and his colleagues, they were lowly commoners. Listen to how Brulart describes them in a letter to Louvois about military defense.

Brulart to Louvois

DIJON, JUNE 1673

I am obliged to inform you that the mayor is not functioning as he should. He is nothing more than a simple bourgeois and, as a result, has very little authority in this city, which is densely populated with privileged persons. The king has issued regulations stating that the First President must command in the absence of the royal lieutenant. This command is, properly speaking, nothing more than a method of communicating with the mayor so that we can act in a coordinated fashion

June: Brulart, 2:167–68.

concerning everything whose execution is assigned to him. . . . All the
échevins and militia officers in the city are plain bourgeois without any
eminence, which explains why people whose standing is, by nature,
above that sort of person, obey them very poorly. . . .

Here is evidence that the ordinary citizens were not always complacent. A
monitory *was a call for information about the perpetrators of a crime that*
was to be read from the pulpit during Mass by the priests of the seven parish
churches of Dijon. Lanturelu *refers to a major riot that took place in 1630*
and was still remembered in 1668.

Request by the City Council of Dijon for a Monitory, November 21, 1668

[Information is requested concerning] certain criminals, male and female inhabitants of this city, with evil intentions toward the king's service and the public peace, who, in order to sabotage the good rule of
their magistrates, incited the people to an uprising, saying that they
needed to make a *lanturelu.* They carried handbills from door to door to
enlist individuals in their conspiracy and urged women to start the agitation. These women went as far as to threaten tax collectors and attack
Claude Picard, an elder of the parish of Saint Nicolas, who was helping
assess the taxes. . . . The women threw mud on him publicly [and] said
that he was an evil man and that they would burn down his house, forcing him to flee from them . . . and making the people believe that their
magistrates had unilaterally, for no reason, increased the taille rate by
more than one-half, which is pure slander.

The following documents are either requests that came in from inhabitants
or responses to such requests in the form of legal documents drawn up by the
city syndic, a lawyer who acted on behalf of the city government, or his sub-
stitute. When a complaint of some infraction came in, the syndic would in-
vestigate it, then write up a blow-by-blow description of what had happened.
Note that these people are deeply imbued with communal values and tra-
ditional routines. They believe that manufacturing should be done by mas-

Archives municipales de Dijon (hereafter referred to as AM Dijon), I 119.

ter guildsmen, that entertainment and public morality should be regulated, and that sales should take place in open markets at set times and places. This is the traditional, regulated world that Colbert was trying to modify. As you observe the lives of these ordinary people with familiar problems, you also will catch a glimpse of gendered assumptions about the roles of men and women.

Extract from the Deliberations of the City Council, April 7, 1671

Concerning the request presented to the Chamber by Jean Girard, a native of Picardy, the Council of Dijon permits the aforenamed Girard to present Italian marionettes, dangerous leaping [acrobatics], and other gentle distractions that he puts on; and during a period acceptable to the Chamber, he is permitted to have the drum beaten and to post his bills to announce the place where he intends to present the said puppets and dangerous leaps, on condition nevertheless that he not demand more than two sous from those who want to partake of this entertainment.

Petition about Drunken Husbands, April 8, 1672

To Messieurs the viscount mayor and échevins of Dijon, We, Anne Violet, wife of André Perreau, roofer of Dijon, and Jeanne Bavard, wife of Denis Bizot, sergeant in Dijon and elsewhere, complain to the council that a man named DuMey living in Château Lane entertains numerous people in his house night and day, where his cabaret is causing the ruin of their families and bringing disorder to their houses. The wine and the tobacco make them lose their judgment, and when they return home at two or three in the morning, they beat and abuse their wives and children so badly that they are left as if dead on the spot. In addition they exhaust all their resources and reduce their families to begging, making them unable to pay the taxes of the city. The petitioners have gone [to

April 7: AM Dijon, I 123.
April 8: AM Dijon, I 130.

the cabaret] several times, both day and night, to drag away their hus-
bands, but they have been mistreated by DuMey and his wife. When
they threatened that they would complain to the council, [DuMey and
his wife] responded that they couldn't care less and that there were other
[authorities] in the city [who would protect them]. These actions, accompanied by public scandal, blasphemy, and cursing of the name of
God, deserve exemplary punishment. . . . There is a brigade of fifteen or
twenty inhabitants who never leave the place day or night, especially on
holidays and on Sundays, when they ignore the divine service. The petitioners have already complained to the city syndic, but they got no relief,
so they had to turn to the council. . . .

Illegal Vending, June 30, 1673

Gaspard Desvarennes, substitute for Nicolas Guenichot, syndic of the
city of Dijon: Today about 5:00 A.M. having proceeded to the rue Saint
Nicolas with Pierre Dupond, master pastry cook and sworn inspector of
the fish that are publicly displayed for sale to the inhabitants in front of
the large gate, I encountered some women named Reyne, wife of Piochon; Dame Françoise; Dame Jacquette and Dame Barbe, who did not
want to tell me their last names, waiting for men and women from the
[surrounding] villages to bring in fish. They intercept them in front of
the large gate and induce them to go into their rooms and bargain over
the fish. In the presence of Dupond I saw the above-named persons stop
an old woman, who told me she was from Orgeux but wouldn't give her
name, and Piochon and her companions were buying four large pike
from her. Having caught them in the middle of their bargaining, I informed them that they were acting illegally by intercepting the fish before it was displayed in the [public] fish market, and furthermore that it
was not yet the appointed hour for sales. I issued them a summons to appear today in the council chamber of the city in front of the mayor and
échevins, to be prosecuted on the basis of the present report. . . .

Illegal Production, September 11, 1673

Gaspard Desvarennes, substitute for Nicolas Guenichot, syndic of the city of Dijon: Upon hearing from master coopers Nicolas de Saint Didier, Michel Renat, and Claude Baubis that Vincent Doudey, winegrower of Dijon, is constructing new barrels to the disadvantage of the plaintiffs and all the other master coopers without having been admitted into their guild by messieurs the viscount mayor and échevins, and furthermore that he is not employed by master coopers [in the guild] but by private individuals, which is a great disadvantage [to the coopers], I proceeded to the residence of Vincent Doudey accompanied by Claude Boyault, sergeant at city hall, and the above-named sworn masters; I asked him whether he had been certified as master by the council and if he had papers of reception; he replied that he had not been and that he was working for Jean Le Franc and other individuals whose names he didn't mention. The master coopers then inspected seven completed barrels that were sitting nearby, noting that they were built out of red wood and white wood, which would completely ruin any wine placed in them. Therefore I, Desvarennes, had the barrels marked with wax and deposited with Catherine Poussot, widow of Philippe Blondelle, who voluntarily agreed to take custody of them and deliver them when ordered to do so, and by virtue of my authority I issued a summons to Doudey to appear next Friday in the council chamber of city hall before the viscount mayor and échevins to hear the verdict rendered on these barrels and the judgment concerning this confiscation.

Homelessness, September 2, 1674

Étienne Sigault, syndic of Dijon: Today, Sunday, at 8:00 A.M. I was informed that a poor beggar had died during the night on the pavement of the rue Saint Nicolas in front of the house of the widow of Pierre Sirot, bourgeois. I proceeded to the spot and found a dead man laid out on the pavement with his arms crossed, elderly and about sixty years of age. Around him were several persons — men, women, and children. I inquired who he was, and no one could inform me, but several people

September 11: AM Dijon, I 110.
September 2: AM Dijon, I 110.

assured me that he was a poor man who had begged for his livelihood for a long time in Dijon; he had been sick with fever, and he had slept for a long time in the Maison Saint André [presumably a home for paupers] in that street; but yesterday he had gone out and stood in front of the widow's house near the courtyard where Claude Bergeret, merchant, lives and sells wine, and he asked them to give him some. Bergeret told me he had gone up to the poor man and given him a little wine out of charity, and after that he lay down in front of the widow's door. He didn't know if he had spent the whole night there, but when morning arrived he was stiff and dead, and Bergeret told me he had learned that his name was Colin Lagrange. I instructed Jean Liottier, city sergeant, who was accompanying me, to fetch Surgeons Fabar and Fleury to inspect the cadaver. They arrived and, after taking the oath [to tell the truth], reported finding no wound or contusion on his body and that it appeared that Lagrange died from the vehemence of his fever, being old and weak. After that I had Lagrange washed by two poor women after Lady Sirot had charitably donated a shroud, and then Lagrange was buried, with the help of charitable donations, in the cemetery of the Saint Nicolas church near the wall.

Illegitimate Births, April 27, 1675

Jean Thibert, substitute for Étienne Sigault, syndic of Dijon: Today I responded to numerous complaints about the abandonment of children in the middle of the streets. In order to prevent the inconvenience this might cause, and in accordance with a command from the mayor, I went to the Notre Dame parish, accompanied by two sergeants, to the house of François Dorgueil and asked to speak to his wife. She emerged from a group in front of the house and came up to me. I asked her name and status, and she replied she was Michelle Carreau, wife of Dorgueil. I asked her to open the door of the house, and we went up a wooden staircase, which descended into a courtyard where there is a tiny garden, to an upstairs room; there we found a bed with two young girls lying on it, with their infants at their sides. I administered Carreau the oath to tell the truth and asked them their maiden names and by whom they had been made pregnant. They said they were Claudine Marey and Jeanne Charley. Marey was pregnant by a worker named Jean Bernier, who claimed to be head butler of Monsieur Du Houssas; she had given birth eight days ago and had been living in Carreau's house for two months, and her child had been baptized in the Notre Dame church by the vicar under the name of the father. Jeanne Charley was from Dijon and had been made pregnant [in the hospital] by René Laroche, baker from the rue de la Charrue; she had given birth two months ago. Their declarations were confirmed by Carreau. Speaking to her, I said that she was to take care of the two babies and see that they were not exposed in the streets like many others, for fear of the accidents that might occur; that she should not let them out of the house without knowing what would become of them; and that she would be held personally responsible if she failed to declare their status to the council when commanded to do so. Carreau promised to do this and to inform the syndic if other pregnant girls arrived so that the preservation of their babies could be ensured. Carreau also told me that she delivers babies for young girls, that that is her profession: matron.

Here is more evidence of popular insubordination. The growers of the grapes that went into Burgundian wine, who lived in Dijon in large numbers, were exercising what they considered to be their customary right to gather firewood in certain forests outside the city. Note how they respond, when challenged, and how the crowd of onlookers eggs them on.

A Riot by Winegrowers, January 1684

Minutes of the city council, early February. Several days ago three hundred to four hundred winegrowers organized an uprising and, marching to a drum, flags flying, without permission, went out of the city on pretext of going to the forest, from which they returned armed, arrayed in ranks, commanded and led by sergeants chosen from among themselves. Yesterday it was decided to arrest them when they returned from the woods. The syndic of the city went to the Guillaume gate accompanied by three échevins; the winegrowers entered, drum beating, and the officials tried to arrest a few of them. But the winegrowers formed into a sort of battalion and attacked their magistrates, shouting, "Harlan!" and waving swords and clubs. The magistrates, especially the city syndic, barely escaped. A crowd of two hundred persons watched, but when they were commanded to help the authorities, some refused, while

---

January: AM Dijon, I 100. This is a summary of the deliberation rather than a verbatim translation.

others were insolent enough to speak scornfully, saying loudly that they should burn down the houses of the authorities. Many winegrowers, and especially their wives, then threatened to set fire to the houses of the magistrates. It is necessary to teach these people to respect their magistrates.

Arrests were made, and the archives contain long interrogations of witnesses, which add further details about this incident. After the arrests, the following petition, written in an awkward popular style, was issued on behalf of the prisoners. The winegrowers, now humbled, had to apologize to save their friends and families. Notice, however, their reason for the original mobilization and where they place the blame.

Petition to the Mayor and Échevins from the Protesters

You are humbly requested by some poor winegrowers and all your most faithful servants from the population of the poor to have pity and compassion on the unfortunate, miserable souls who are in prison in this city for assembling at the sound of the drum to go to the woods, which they should not have done. They did not intend to offend you; they did it only to muster some strength against those who wanted to stop them from cutting and loading wood, and to protect themselves from people who wanted to mistreat and assassinate them. This was the reason, messieurs, for their assemblies and no other evil purpose. Messieurs, a few bad words may have escaped from the serpentine tongues of a few evil women, which you might rightly want to investigate and prosecute to prevent the use of such language; but we are counting on your kindness, messieurs, not to allow this poor populace to suffer for its bad language, and then we will all be in your debt to pray the Lord for your prosperity and health.

Debauchery of Youth, March 28, 1688

Nicolas Guenichot, lawyer in the Parlement, syndic of the Estates of the province and of this city of Dijon: Today I was informed of complaints coming from all sides that, in violation of the commandments of the church and numerous decrees of the council, which prohibit innkeepers and cabaret owners from receiving young men and heirs of respectable families in their establishments to encourage their debauches and libertine activities, especially during the night, several innkeepers are holding open house in their cabarets and allowing young men to spend whole nights in debauchery while they gorge themselves with wine. They are committing a further criminal offense by giving them meat to eat during the holy period of Lent, to the scandal of the whole city. I paid visits to several of these lodgings accompanied by [names of five sergeants of the city], and when I had entered the cabaret of Nicolas Jacob, who lives on the rue du Potet, I went to an upper room, which has a door onto a staircase that leads down to the courtyard. There I found a table with five or six debauched young men sitting around it eating meat, and when I appeared, they almost all fled carrying platters still filled with fowl and other meats, but they didn't succeed in hiding everything. I grabbed on to one of the platters on the table, which contained whole heads of woodcock and a dish of sauce, and since these young libertines were still on the stairway fleeing with their platters, I ordered [Sergeants] Marchand and Rousseau to pursue them. They did so, and Marchand managed to grab a platter that held almost a whole woodcock carved up. During these revelries the debauched eaters of meat, drunk on wine, failed to excuse themselves and repent to God for their bad behavior; instead one was so insolent as to sit down at the table in our presence and continue his forbidden meal, and when we would not tolerate this, he had the temerity in his drunkenness to place his hand on his sword and give the appearance of wanting to draw it; while another, his comrade, even drunker than he was, tried to grab a platter containing the remains of woodcock made into a stew, which I had ordered to be transported to my house for presentation to the council. And because the crime of Jacob merits exemplary punishment, I drew up the present report and had him served with a warrant to appear next Wednesday, last day of the present month of March, in the council chamber of the city, to be judged on the basis of the conclusions that I will draw up against him, in testimony of which in front of witnesses I have signed.

6

Social Unrest: The Revolts of 1675

Louis XIV was noted for establishing a regime of order, and we have seen its effects in Burgundy and elsewhere. It is worth remembering that the Sun King was presiding over a delicate balance of social forces and that one reason regional elites supported him was that they needed his prestige, and sometimes his troops, to maintain their social positions. It is less well-known that there were serious popular uprisings during Louis's reign, in the county of Benauge near Bordeaux in 1661, in Boulonnais in 1662, in Vivarais not far from Auvergne in 1670, in the Cévennes mountains in 1702 and 1710, and in Quercy in 1707. There were smaller riots in many major cities at various points in the reign.

The most striking phenomenon was the wave of revolts that swept western France in 1675. These were protests against a series of new indirect taxes created by Colbert to help finance the Dutch War (remember Colbert's problem with Louis XIV's budgets). Tax farmers were empowered through contracts to collect new fees for legal transactions; to sell stamped paper that would be required for official documents; to collect a new tax on tobacco, then becoming common; and to collect a tax on pewter, which required putting an official mark on every item. (Pewter was the material used for dishes by people of modest means.) Thus it looked to the common people as if greedy tax farmers were intruding on their everyday lives by taxing their dishes, their ability to relax with tobacco, their marriages and wills — in short their lives. What Colbert intended as a sensible approach to the budget (remember how much revenue came from indirect taxes), the common people saw as an outrageous gabelle, the term they used for an unfair, burdensome tax.

Rioting started in Bordeaux in March and spread up the coast to Bergerac, Rennes, Nantes, and points in between. In June the peasants of Brittany began to rise up, attacking not just the new taxes and their agents but also their lords and even the church. These documents give us vivid eyewitness accounts of some of these events. As you read them, remember that they were written by financiers (and a bishop), who were appalled at what was happening and took the most negative view of the rioters. These crowds were, on occasion, cruel and violent, but their primary motive was protest, not random violence. Notice how focused these revolts are: There is almost always a reason why the crowd does what it does. Notice the people's organization and their demands. Think about these episodes as evidence of some of the social tensions underlying Louis XIV's rule. Letters describing similar events in many places, with tax offices pillaged and tax collectors in flight, poured in to Colbert. For a few weeks, it must have seemed to him as if his whole system was crumbling. This chapter includes just a few of these documents, chosen to give the flavor of these protests and the terrified response of the tax farmers.[1]

The Bordeaux revolt was one of the most serious uprisings of the seventeenth century. Following is one account of the events.

Eyewitness Account by Ferrant, Agent of the King's Tax Receiver Le Maigre

BORDEAUX, MARCH 30, 1675

I have taken refuge with my wife in the Château Trompette [the citadel of Bordeaux]. This is the biggest rebellion in Bordeaux since the days of Constable Montmorency [1548]. It was carried out by the lowest kind of people, along with women and children, but their conduct and language suggest that they had some advice from higher up.

Things seemed calm, and the tax farmer was starting to visit the pewter makers to mark their wares. A few small problems seemed to have been resolved, and he had requested an escort of some city archers and a jurat.[1] They had already finished marking in the shop of a pewterer named Taudin in the rue Neuve. They went on to a boutique in the rue du Loup, which is where the clamor started. As you know, that street is filled with artisans. They saw the markers marking, and when the jurat

[1] This phenomenon is more fully explored in William Beik, *Urban Protest in Seventeenth-Century France: The Culture of Retribution* (Cambridge: Cambridge University Press, 1997), chapter 7.

[1] The jurats were the city councillors of Bordeaux. In another city, they might have been called échevins.

Bibliothèque Nationale de France (hereafter B.N.) Mélanges Colbert 171, fols. 126–94. This is a summary of the document rather than a word-for-word translation.

entered a shop where the marking had already been resisted, women started to shout out that this was a gabelle. Hearing the noise, the rabble came running up from a nearby market. They attacked the authorities with rocks and tried to seize the two men who were marking. The jurat tried to calm people down, and when this failed, he changed his style and said he was going to escort the markers to city hall [for security]. A reinforcement of archers arrived, and they set out with difficulty. Captain Calle had to fire a shot, which wounded a barrel maker, who then died in the rue d'Arnaud Miquau. Chains went up in all the streets, with cries of "Beat up all the *gabelleurs*" and "Long live the king without any gabelle." That was Wednesday at 3:00 to 4:00 P.M. News of the uprising reached the Saint Michel quarter, shops closed, and the rabble formed troops that ran through the streets armed with clubs, swords, knives, scissors, and shotguns. Near the La Grave gate they encountered a poor bourgeois who was suspected of being a *gabelleur*. They massacred him without even questioning him and dragged his body around the city by the feet, to the beat of a drum. They went down the Grande Rue du Fossé and the rue des Tanneurs, passing in front of the windows of [First] President Daulède [from the Parlement], then back down the rue Sainte Catherine up to Saint Maixant, then down the rue Margaux. I was in my room, and this happened so fast that all I could do was close my door. When they went by, they put a mark on my door and knocked, but, thank God, they didn't stop. They went along the rue Castillone, then to the Place Puypaulin in front of the intendant's door, where they gave this poor cadaver [the dragged body] a hundred blows, then straight to the house of M. Viney. Poor Viney just had time to jump into the carriage of the count of Montaigu [commander of royal forces in the Château], who took him to the Château. His wife didn't even have time to climb in, but she ran off in the other direction. I heard they were pillaging M. Viney and the office of the domaine [a tax office], where the secretary of the intendant lived. They did all this in less than two hours, with indescribable cries and growls of rage. Meanwhile one group went to the shop of the pewterer Taudin and pillaged all his dishes and furniture. They go about this with such rage that they don't even try to profit from it. They took two storerooms' worth of [pewter] dishes, loaded them on carts, and dumped them in the river. At Viney's house they were busy all night long, burning everything and tearing down the building.

Night was falling. All the officers of the city were greatly embarrassed and in complete disarray. The respectable bourgeois were in shock, each wary of his neighbor, not daring to speak, each locked up in his house. Montaigu retired to the Château and put the garrison on alert, but it is too small to do much good. Two companies did go out about 8:00

P.M. and battled their way down the rue du Chapeau Rouge. The crowd, intent on pillage, was insolently waiting for them, not flinching. Although the rebels were in confusion and without discipline, one of them had the effrontery to fire a shot from a musket at the person at the head of the two companies, who was badly wounded. Nevertheless, the troops attacked the pillaged houses, firing and charging with swords, arresting four to eight rioters and killing seven or eight more, while others were wounded and fled. Meanwhile it poured rain, and the troops withdrew to the Château.

I'm sure the crowd entered the rue Margaux intending to pillage my office, and thank God I wasn't there. I spent Wednesday night and Thursday at my brother-in-law's, receiving regular reports. I could only get to the Château Trompette on Thursday evening. All night long on Wednesday, all you could hear in the street were cries of "Long live the king without the gabelle," and even the children were singing the same tune.

Thursday morning the marshal [the duke of Albret, governor of the province] was worse [he was sick], so Montaigu went to the Palais de Justice [seat of the Parlement] accompanied by an escort. . . . He found it filled with scum shouting, "Long live the king without the gabelle," and demanding the release of the prisoners, along with the abolition of the marking of pewter, the tax on tobacco, the five sous per *boisseau* of wheat,[2] the tax on legal acts, the stamped paper tax, and the five sous on lambs slaughtered by butchers; otherwise they would sack everything.

The Parlement had intended to issue sanctions, but they decided it was not wise until the crowd was disarmed, so they issued a decree forbidding public gatherings and sent parlementaires into every quarter to calm the population. When the court adjourned, several of the judges were followed right up to their houses by crowds threatening them out of concern for the [fate of the] prisoners.

That afternoon they encountered poor M. Tarneau, councillor in the Parlement, in the street on his way home; they demanded the prisoners; he didn't reply the way they would have liked; he started to go in his door; they fired a shot and he fell. His wife ran out and started to lift him up, but they massacred him with punches and swords and gave him a thousand blows after he was dead. She also took some blows but was not killed. President Lalanne and Councillors Marboutin and Dandrault were taken prisoner,[3] and they sent a scoundrel with two hundred to three hundred rebels to inform Montaigu that if the prisoners were not

[2] A *boisseau* was a measure of the volume of grain, whose magnitude varied from place to place. Five sous per *boisseau* was a tax on wheat.
[3] These hostages were all judges from the Parlement.

released, the lives [of the hostages] were at stake. They also asked for Calle, who had shot the barrel maker. The prisoners were released, but they were not given Calle.

On Friday the marshal [Albret] felt better and wanted to go and talk to the mutineers, who were barricaded in the Saint Michel quarter. He went, accompanied by 100 to 120 nobles and 100 men from the garrison. There he found the rebels ranged in orderly battle formation in the cemetery of Sainte Croix and along the boulevard, some 800 men. At twenty paces from them a ruffian dressed all in rags stepped out of their ranks, saber raised high, and approached up to three paces from the head of the marshal's horse. The marshal (using the familiar form of address): "Very well, my friend, whom are you angry at? Are you intending to speak to me?" At which this miserable person, without flinching, replied, "Yes, I am the deputy of these people of Saint Miquau to inform you that they are loyal servants of the king but that they want no more gabelles, nor tax on pewter, nor tobacco, nor stamp tax, nor tax on legal acts, nor five sous per *boisseau* of wheat, nor tax on arbitration." The marshal (very softly): "Very well, my friend, since you assure me that the people of Saint Michel are loyal servants of the king, I am here to assure them that I would like to take them under my protection, provided that they disarm themselves and return to their duty; and I promise that I will intercede for them before the king." Very well, replied the ruffian, "in that case give us a decree of Parlement to that effect, and we will be satisfied, provided you also obtain an amnesty for everything we have just done, without which we declare to you that we are going to spare nothing and that we are resolved to perish rather than suffer any more." The marshal agreed and went straight to the Parlement, with all these armed people following along, and the decree was issued. Since then they have disbanded, but it's certain that if the courier [from the king] does not bring back the expected amnesty, they will take up arms again.

The Mayor and Consuls of Bergerac to de Sève, Intendant of Bordeaux

MAY 3, 1675

We must report on a major uprising that occurred this afternoon. A large number of women carried off all the stamped paper and without any dis-

May 3: B.N. Clairambault 796, 63.

orderliness threw it in a brook that runs across the city and passes the office. . . . One group then stormed into the building, where the office of the tax on legal transactions is housed. We rushed there diligently, and believing we could limit the damage, we had the registers of the tax given over to this mutinous troop. Just when it seemed that there was nothing more to fear, the son of the clerk unfortunately mistreated one of the women, and her cries attracted many other people coming from outside. They took over the avenues leading to the building in spite of our efforts, and soon had removed all the registers and furnishings from the office, throwing everything out the windows. Those who were not participating in the pillage gathered everything up in the street and burned it up at a spot outside the city. . . .

La Case, Tax Collector from Quimper [Brittany], to Colbert

JUNE 24, 1675
Monsieur:
We have been forced to withdraw all our agents from the districts of this bishopric, as I wrote you previously. . . . We held out in this city hoping that things would calm down, but after suffering insults and attacks on numerous occasions, today we have abandoned our office to protect ourselves from the rage of the people and taken cover in the private houses of our friends. The peasants have entered the city four thousand strong. Along with the artisans, they refuse to tolerate the presence of any financial agents. If we manage to save our lives today, the director of the *grands devoirs* [a tax] and I are determined to leave tonight for a secret location, not in Brest as you suggest, which is impossible because the peasants hold all the roads in that direction, but in Port Louis, where the danger is not as great. Address your letters to M. Adrapé, attorney in the Parlement, who will know where I am.

A proper gentleman has just been brought here who was practically beaten up by the peasants while he was coming out of High Mass, and they cut off the arm of the priest who said the Mass. Madame his wife and all their children came here on foot. Their house has been completely pillaged, and in another parish the local lord was so badly treated that he died from it. . . .

June 24: B.N. Clairambault 796, 163.

Dallier, Tax Farmer from Nantes, to Colbert

JUNE 25, 1675

... They have beaten up a process server right in the court hearing in Châteaulin because he was bringing the decree reestablishing the tax. They chased out the judges and mistreated the criminal prosecutor, pillaged our stamped paper bureau, and razed the house of La Garanne, who was running the tax farms. They haven't stopped there. They forced our agents to desert the bishoprics of Cornouaille and Léon by their threats, as well as all the other tax farms; they search messengers and pillage any stamped paper they find on them, guard the roads, and examine everyone who passes by, so that our roaming agents do not dare go into their country offices. . . .

The Bishop of Saint Malo to Colbert

JULY 23, 1675

Monsieur,

I haven't written you since I left Rennes with the duke of Chaulnes [governor of Brittany], when he went to Port Louis and I accompanied him as far as Ploërmel, because I knew he had kept you sufficiently informed of why he had to leave Rennes and move toward lower Brittany, where the disorders of the peasants are still continuing; but since this problem has spread to many more places . . . I now feel obliged to report what has happened these past days. . . .

Rennes sets the example for the rest of the province, and you will be aware of what happened there last Wednesday at midday, when the stamped paper [office] was pillaged for a second time. This effort did not fail to revive the boldness of these miserable peasants in lower Brittany. While Chaulnes was in Port Louis trying every possible means to get the parishes around Port Louis, Hennebon, Quimperlé, and Quimper-Corentin to lay down their arms and return to their duty . . . I was surprised to learn, upon arriving here last Sunday, that the duchess of Rohan and M. and Madame de Couesquen, who were in a small town

June 25: B.N. Clairambault 796, 165.
Jean Lemoine, *La révolte dite du Papier Timbré ou des Bonnets Rouges en Bretagne en 1675* (Paris: Champion, 1898), 194–200.

twenty paces from here called Josselin, belonging to Madame de Rohan, who has an old castle there, were hesitant to go as far as Pontivy, which is another small town six leagues from here and the principal seat of her duchy. She was originally intending to spend some time there, but she was warned that on the preceding days the peasants of certain parishes near Pontivy were threatening to burn and pillage the house of one of the local farmers, named Lapierre, and several others yesterday and Sunday because the rabble were calling them extortionists. And they stood by their word, for on Sunday at midday an angry mass of them stormed into Pontivy, two thousand strong, threw themselves at Lapierre's house, broke in the door, pillaged all the furniture, took all the wine from the cellars (up to 440 *muids'*[1] worth), rolled the barrels out into the streets, tapped them, and drank them all, except for a few that they transported out of town to divide among themselves. After they were quite drunk, they returned to the house, smashed all the furnishings, and demolished part of the building. The poor bourgeois of the city (which has no walls) didn't dare to repulse them or oppose their violence, so each bourgeois collected whatever he could in the way of furniture and papers and carted them away, fearing more pillage. But these scoundrels, not satisfied, threatened that evening to come again the next day and give the same treatment to many other houses. And that is exactly what they made a point of doing yesterday morning when, after going back into Lapierre's house and ripping out the joists, the rafters, and the roofing, they went off to pillage another house that had also housed the stamped paper. But this one belonged to the brother of the city syndic, and the bourgeois were a bit less in shock than they had been the day before. So a man named Lavoir, who was in Madame de Rohan's château with the *seneschal*[2] of the city, and a number of bourgeois decided to make a sortie from the château with what they could gather up of rifles and muskets and fire on these rabble, most of whom had no firearms and who were out in smaller numbers than the day before. They did this so expertly that they killed fifteen or sixteen and wounded a quantity of others. The rest of these peasants took fright and retired to the countryside, still threatening to return today to visit them when they had greater numbers. But frenzy usually only grabs them during festivals when they get drunk and create disorder, so there is every likelihood that if they try anything more, it will be on Thursday and Friday, which are holidays, not on these two workdays.

[1] A *muid* was a liquid measure that varied from place to place. This is a large quantity of wine.

[2] The *seneschal* was a noble who headed the regional royal court of the *sénéchaussée*.

This Lapierre, who is also *fermier* [agent-tenant] of Madame de Ro-han, took refuge with her in the château of Josselin and left this morn-ing to find Monsieur the duke of Chaulnes. . . . Madame de Rohan is stay-ing here in her château all this week to see what will happen, since we have both been advised that these peasants from lower Brittany would like to come all the way here to continue their pillaging, and that they are loudly threatening to set fire to this abbey because they claim I am also an extortionist and they have been led to believe that I endorsed the gabelle when I was in Rennes with Monsieur the duke of Chaulnes.

I think you know, Monsieur, that this gabelle is their great monster, along with the stamped paper. The [tax] agents in all the little towns around here no longer dare use [stamped paper], and most of them have abandoned their houses or been expelled by the owners for fear that they will be burned down. Almost all the nobles of lower Brittany and the surrounding districts are leaving their country houses and taking refuge in the principal cities, and bringing along what they can of their most precious furnishings and all their papers to keep them from being pil-laged or burned, which is what was done at the château of Kergoët, one of the best fortified of lower Brittany. And what is even worse in all this is that private hatreds and individual vendettas are getting drawn in, to the point where all you have to do to get a crowd to assault your enemy is shout "there goes an extortionist" in front of them.

There you have the current state of things, which I have not thought it appropriate to describe to anyone else, since it is not wise to spread news of this kind any further than necessary. But, truly, it is high time to find a solution. If this much insolence and rebellion can be carried out with impunity, it will set the whole province ablaze. Happily, the towns are still doing their duty. But they are all trembling at the news of these gatherings of peasants and the cruelty they have inflicted on individuals in the larger villages and the countryside, and even more [at their atti-tude] toward the nobility and even the church. They no longer seem to respect the church the way they did in the past, and they are forcing all the gentlemen and ecclesiastics to sign papers stating that they will no longer claim rents or tithes from them. I beg you, Monsieur, to take note of just how far the blindness of these miserable people has gone, and how much they deserve the punishment that is coming to them. . . .

Both Bordeaux and the various regions of Brittany suffered a fierce royal repression when troops became available. The Parlement of Bordeaux was exiled from the city for fifteen years for not handling public order more ef-

fectively, and the bells of the churches in the rebel quarters were removed. Bordeaux was subjected to enormous fines, and all the taxes that had been suspended were restored. Similar punishments awaited Rennes, Nantes, and the Breton peasants. It took several months for order to be restored, but Louis XIV was not going to let his reputation be tarnished by disobedience. Despite some hints of complicity by local elites, these rebellions had mostly been spontaneous uprisings by crowds of ordinary people. Social discontent had not vanished since the Fronde, but it had become more manageable because there were no elite rebels like the prince of Condé. Those people — from the robe, the nobility, the church, and especially the circles of financiers (the groups that benefited most from Louis XIV's rule) — had been seriously threatened, and they were grateful to a king who could protect their interests.

7

Absolutism and the Churches

We cannot understand French absolute monarchy without examining its religious dimension. The king's power was closely intertwined with the church, in both practice and theory. Louis XIV controlled the nomination of French bishops and archbishops, and a great many abbots and abbesses of monasteries, subject to confirmation by the pope. In this way, he had access to immense wealth and vast revenues, which he used for patronage purposes. These high churchmen were regional authorities in their own right, with influence comparable to that of governors or parlementaires. They aided the crown in governing, but they also could lobby corporatively for their own interests. The church was an organized body whose members, down to the last priest, had special legal privileges, including exemption from regular royal taxes and an Assembly of the Clergy that met every ten years to tax itself, grant subsidies to the crown, and negotiate grievances. Like other corporate bodies, the church was well under control during Louis's personal reign, but it was a formidable institution.

Spiritually, the king was enveloped in Catholic pageantry and empowered by the divine right theory of monarchy. Tradition traced the sacred character of the monarchy back to a miracle that had occurred at the conversion of the Merovingian king Clovis around 496, and the king's combined consecration and crowning ceremony dated back to Louis the Pious in 816. When the king was crowned, he was given Communion in two kinds, like a priest, and anointed with sacred oils, after which he performed the ritual of curing thousands of people infected with the disease called scrofula by laying his hands on them.

This view of royalty as sacred obviously strengthened the image of Louis XIV, but it also created problems. The institutional French church, often called the Gallican church, had claims of self-regulation and autonomy from the papacy, which enabled the king to act as their protector against the pope in Rome. But a reform movement within the church called Jansenism threatened to preempt the king's religious authority by adopting a superior moral position and criticizing the worldliness of the king's leadership. Another problem Louis faced was how to deal with France's Protestant population, the Huguenots, as French Calvinists were called. They represented a troubling minority with a special legal status. In this chapter, we will examine each of these issues — the theory of divine right, conflicts with Jansenists and the pope, and the problem of the Huguenots. These issues will take us beyond the scope of most of this volume into the later years of Louis's reign, since it was then that the king's religious intolerance reached its height.

DIVINE RIGHT MONARCHY

Divine right is the theory that the king ruled with the direct mandate of God. This position was argued most forcefully by Bishop Bossuet, a famous preacher who was appointed tutor to Louis XIV's oldest son, the Dauphin, in 1670, for whom Bossuet wrote *Politics Drawn from the Very Words of Holy Scripture*. This treatise is a four-hundred-page work divided into books, articles, and propositions, each of which is demonstrated by means of quotations from the Bible, especially the Old Testament.

The following excerpt contains a few key passages from the heart of Bossuet's treatise. Bossuet argues that royal power, stemming directly from God (and thus not from the pope or the church) must be unlimited to ensure a civil society. There is no right of resistance and no institutional check on royal authority. Bossuet stresses, however, that the king is responsible to God for his people and must observe the laws. This doctrine gave the initiative to the crown, but by stressing the importance of the law, it acknowledged the legitimacy of the existing social structure, including the functions of corporate bodies and the legal privileges of individuals. Thus the practical outcome of Bossuet's argument was not to create a twentieth-century-style dictator, but to intensify the aura of sacredness and legitimacy of a hardworking, interventionist monarch.

Bossuet's Vision in Politics Drawn from the Very Words of Holy Scripture

There are four characteristics or qualities essential to royal authority:

First, royal authority is sacred;
Secondly, it is paternal;
Thirdly, it is absolute;
Fourthly, it is subject to reason. . . .

First, royal authority is sacred.

God establishes kings as his ministers, and reigns through them over the peoples.

The person of kings is sacred . . . and to attempt anything against them is a sacrilege. God anoints them through his prophets, with a sacred unction, as he anoints the pontiffs and their altars. But even without the external application of this unction, they are sacred through their charge, as being the representatives of divine majesty, deputized by his providence for the execution of his plans. . . . The title of "Christ" is given to kings; and everywhere one sees them called Christs or the Lord's anointed. . . .

One must obey the prince by reason of religion and conscience. . . . There is thus something religious in the respect one gives to the prince. The service of God and respect for kings are inseparable things, and St. Peter places these two duties together: "Fear God, Honor the King." God, moreover, has put something divine into kings. "I have said, You are Gods, and all of you the sons of the most High." It is God himself whom David makes speak in this way. . . . [This holds true] even if the king should be an infidel, from the respect one should have for the ordination of God. . . .

Secondly, royal authority is paternal and its proper character is goodness.

. . . We have seen that kings hold the place of God, who is the true Father of the human race. We have also seen that the first idea of power that there was among men is that of paternal power; and that kings were fashioned on the model of fathers. Moreover, all the world agrees that obedience, which is due to public power, is only found (in the Decalogue) in the precept which obliges one to honor his parents. From

Jacques-Benigne Bossuet, *Politics Drawn from the Very Words of Holy Scripture,* trans. and ed. Patrick Riley (Cambridge: Cambridge University Press, 1990), selected pages.

all of this it appears that the name "king" is a father's name, and that goodness is the most natural quality in kings. . . .

The prince is not born for himself but for the public.

The prince must provide for the needs of the people.

Among the people, those for whom the prince must provide most are the weak.

[Note that when using the word paternal, *Bossuet also meant "patriar-chal." In his eyes, the gendered monarchy, in which fathers ruled wives and children, and kings (not queens) ruled subjects, was part of God's plan. In an earlier section, he states,*

The people of God, moreover, did not admit to the [royal] succession the sex which is born to obey; and the dignity of reigning houses seems to be insufficiently sustained in the person of a woman, who after all is obliged to recognize a master when she marries. Where women succeed, kingdoms pass not only out of reigning houses, but out of the whole nation. . . . Thus France, where the succession is regulated according to these maxims, can glory in having the best state-constitution that is possible, and the most in conformity to that which God himself has established.]

Thirdly, royal authority is absolute.   In order to make this term [absolute] odious and insupportable many [writers] pretend to confuse absolute government and arbitrary government. But nothing is more distinct, as we shall make clear when we speak of justice.

The prince need account to no one for what he ordains . . . . Without this absolute authority, he can neither do good nor suppress evil: his power must be such that no one can hope to escape him; and, in the end, the sole defense of individuals against the public power, must be their innocence. . . .

There is no co-active force against the prince. . . . One calls co-active force a power to constrain and to execute what is legitimately ordained. To the prince alone belongs legitimate command; to him alone belongs co-active force as well. . . . In the state only the prince should be armed: otherwise everything is in confusion, and the state falls back into anarchy. . . . It is thus that, for the good of the state, one places all force in one alone. Place any power outside, and you divide the state, ruin the public peace, and create two masters, contrary to this oracle of Scripture: "No man can serve two masters.". . .

Nonetheless kings are not freed from the laws. . . . It must be remarked that this law comprehends not only religion, but also the law of the kingdom, to which the prince is subject as much as anyone else — or rather more than the others, through the righteousness of his will. . . . Thus kings are subject, like the others, to the equity of the laws; both because they must be just, and because they owe to the people the example of justice-keeping; but they are not subject to the penalties of the laws. . . .

The people must fear the prince; but the prince must only fear doing evil.

Fourthly, royal authority is subject to reason.   All men are created capable of understanding. But principally you upon whom reposes an entire nation, you who should be the soul and intelligence of a state, in whom must be found the first reason for all its movements: the less it is necessary for you to justify yourself to others, the more you must have justification and intelligence within yourself.

The prince must know the law. . . . Let him know then the depths of the law, by which he must govern. And if he cannot descend into all the individual ordinances which public affairs generate every day, let him at least know the great principles of justice, in order never to be taken by surprise. It was Deuteronomy[1] (the foundation of the law) which God obliged him to study and know.

How serious is the life of the prince! He must ceaselessly meditate on the law. Thus there is nothing among men which is more serious and more grave, than the office of royalty. . . .

The view of royalty as holy set a high standard to live up to and left the king vulnerable to criticism. Bossuet himself, who often preached at court, worried about the habits of the king, most notably his double adultery with Madame de Montespan. In May 1675, as the king was planning to leave for the military front, Bossuet wrote Louis the following letter. Note how he tries to distract the king with his military pursuits.

Bossuet Chides Louis XIV about the State of His Soul

Sire, the day of Pentecost is fast approaching, when Your Majesty intends to take Communion. Although I have no doubt that you have thought seriously about what you have promised to God, you commanded me to remind you of it, and the time has come when I feel

---

[1] Deuteronomy is a book of the Bible.

Quoted in Jacques Truchet, *Politique de Bossuet* (Paris: Armand Colin, 1966), 137–39.

obliged to do so. Consider, Sire, that you cannot be truly converted if you do not work to remove from your heart not only sin but the cause that leads you to it. True conversion is not content with striking down the fruits of death. It goes all the way to the roots, which would infallibly grow again if they were not pulled up. I confess, this is not the work of a day, but the longer and more difficult it is, the more one must work at it. Your Majesty would not feel assured of a rebel fortress as long as the instigator of the rebellion was living there in good repute. Similarly your heart will never belong peacefully to God as long as this violent love, which has separated you from Him for so long, still rules.

It is that heart, Sire, which God is asking for. Your Majesty has read the words with which He commands us to give it totally over to Him. You promised me you would read and reread them often. I am sending you, Sire, more words from this same Lord, which are no less insistent and which I beg Your Majesty to preserve with the first ones. I have given them to Madame de Montespan, and they have made her shed many tears. And Sire, there is surely no better reason for crying than the feeling that the heart belongs to another creature when God would like to have it. How hard it is to withdraw from such an unhappy and unfortunate arrangement! Still, it must be done, Sire, or there is no hope of salvation. Jesus Christ will give you the strength just as he has given you the desire. . . .

I hope, Sire, that having so many grand things to occupy your days will gradually heal you. Everyone is talking about the beauty of your troops and of what they will be capable of doing under such a fine leader. As for me, Sire, during this time I am contemplating a much more important war and a victory much more difficult to win that God is proposing to you. . . .

Louis was unable to stay away from Montespan when he returned from Flanders. The "change of heart" that Bossuet was hoping for had to wait for the later days of Madame de Maintenon. But our fascination with the king's affairs should not distract us from the larger point that a king whose reputation was closely tied to divine inspiration ran the risk of disappointing expectations and causing disillusionment, especially if he developed a reputation for immorality or things did not go his way. He also left himself open to satire, as we see in Joseph Werner's painting of Louis and Montespan at a decadent feast in 1670 (see Figure 6).[1] Some historians

---

[1] Peter Burke, *The Fabrication of Louis XIV* (New Haven, Conn.: Yale University Press, 1992), has an excellent discussion of the undermining of the image of Louis XIV, 135–49.

Figure 6. *This painting by the Swiss artist Joseph Werner, ca. 1670, illustrates how the king's image could be turned to negative purposes. It portrays Louis XIV as a lecherous satyr with the hoof of a goat, entertaining his mistress Madame de Montespan at a decadent banquet.*
Schweizerisches Institut fur Kunstwissenschaft, Zurich.

call this process of disillusionment desacralization. *In retrospect, they see Louis XIV setting the monarchy up for a fall later in the eighteenth century, when Louis XV and Louis XVI were unable to measure up to the glittering standard he had set for them.*

DEALING WITH THE GALLICAN CHURCH AND THE POPE

The king's alliance with the church also produced practical difficulties. On the one hand, his stewardship of the Gallican church was bound to bring him into conflict with the pope, who also claimed to be chosen by God to lead the Catholic Church. On the other hand, the king could be subject to challenge from Jansenists within the church, whose mystical piety and special calling led them to become spiritual leaders.

Jansenism was a Catholic movement based on the writings of Cornelius Jansen, a bishop from the Netherlands (1585–1638), and Jean Duvergier de Hauranne, abbot of Saint Cyran (1581–1643). Influenced by the writings of Saint Augustine, the Jansenists stressed the sinfulness of humankind and the difficulty of obtaining salvation from an all-powerful God. Without abandoning the Catholic doctrine of good works, they were almost like Calvinists in stressing the need for God's grace and the uselessness of excessive formalities, such as the frequent taking of Holy Communion without proper purification of the soul. Jansenism, which became associated with a convent of nuns at Port Royal outside Paris, was embraced by men and women from the milieu of well-to-do lawyers, officers, and churchmen, many of whom were related to judges in the Parlement of Paris and officials in the king's government. They founded schools and advocated lives of pious service. Major philosophical and literary figures, such as Antoine Arnauld, Blaise Pascal, and Jean Racine, joined their ranks. Thus they had a formidable influence on upper-class French society. If the Jansenists began to attract a following, they could provide a moral authority that rivaled the king's, and inadvertently challenge his position.

In reality, the problems of Gallicanism and Jansenism tended to be intertwined, and their story is quite complex. The king's championing of Gallicanism against the pope can be illustrated by the affair of the *régale*. This was the king's right to appropriate the revenues of a bishopric or archbishopric when it was vacant — that is, from the time the incumbent died until the registration of the papers of the new nominee. It also entailed the king's right to fill any subordinate church posts that would normally have been filled by the holder of the vacant position. In 1673, at the height of his power, Louis XIV issued a declaration asserting his right to the régale in every diocese in the kingdom and requiring all the bishops to acknowledge this fact. Most of them cooperated, but two, Nicolas Pavillon, bishop of Alet, and François-Étienne Caulet, bishop of Pamiers, both of whom had Jansenist leanings, refused to comply as a matter of conscience. They appealed their cases to Pope Innocent XI, who was no friend of Louis XIV. The pope's letter to Louis illustrates the dimensions of the conflict. He is "pulling rank" on the king and asserting his superior authority.

Pope Innocent XI to Louis XIV, December 29, 1679

We have already told Your Majesty clearly and repeatedly, in two earlier brevets, that your declaration of 1673 extending the régale to dioceses never before subject to it is harmful to the liberties of the Church, contrary to divine and human law, and in stark contrast to the practice of your predecessors. . . . You must recognize in our letters the just grief and misery of all the bishops, and moreover you must recognize the will of God, who speaks to you through us and warns you to revoke your edict and everything which has harmed the rights and liberty of the Church. If you do not do this, we are very much afraid that you will suffer divine vengeance, as we have said before, and which we now declare for the third time, although with regret, because of the tenderness which we feel for you. But we cannot resist the will of God, which urges us to tell you this.

When Bishop Caulet died in 1680, there was a struggle over the nomination of his successor. We take up the story by looking at the memoirs of Nicolas Foucault, intendant of the district that included the bishopric of Pamiers. Foucault's report is decidedly one-sided, but it allows you to imagine what the friends of Caulet were saying and doing and how dangerous such a holy crusade might become for the state. Note the way the intendant functions, in a manner similar to Bouchu in Burgundy. Watch the clash of royal orders and episcopal excommunications.

Quoted in David L. Smith, ed. *Louis XIV* (Cambridge: Cambridge University Press, 1992), 61.

Memoirs of the Intendant Foucault on the Resistance over the Régale, 1679–1680

On February 15, 1679, I reported to M. de Châteauneuf [Louis XIV's secretary of state] that the bishop of Pamiers had been distributing copies in Latin and French of the papal brief concerning the régale to the priests in his diocese.

On May 3, 1679, I received an *arrêt* [decree] of the royal council ordering me to seize the revenues of the bishop of Pamiers, and I proposed that they be reserved for the regular operating expenses of the diocese and the surplus for supporting newly converted Protestants.

On August 13, 1679 . . . I received orders to seize the revenues of the cathedral chapter of Pamiers and deposit them with M. Anceau, tax collector of the district of Comminges.

When the bishop of Pamiers issued several ordinances concerning the régale, the Parlement of Paris agreed to consider an appeal against these ordinances.

On September 20, 1679, I sent Châteauneuf a copy of my investigation of a curate and two vicars accused of saying in their sermons that those installed through the régale were excommunicated. They had visited the houses of parishioners and forbidden them to pay anything to those collecting the tithe if it went to any *régalistes*.

In February 1680 the bishop of Pamiers issued an ordinance excommunicating everyone holding a position through the régale in his diocese, and then another ordering fasts, processions, and prayers to appease the wrath of God on his diocese. There is venom in the motives behind this ordinance, which I sent to M. de Châteauneuf.

On April 4 the bishop of Pamiers, wearing his pontifical robes, mounted to the pulpit in his cathedral and personally renewed the excommunications he had already issued against everyone holding positions by virtue of the régale, including their collectors, subcollectors, and those who execute the orders of His Majesty, including the ones I had issued. . . .[1]

---

[1]Bishop Caulet excommunicated everyone who obeyed the king's orders concerning the régale and everyone holding church office by virtue of the régale. This included Foucault himself.

F. Baudry, ed., *Mémoires de Nicolas-Joseph Foucault* (Paris: Imprimerie Impériale, 1862), 57–61.

On April [blank] I received the king's order to arrest M. Laborde, agent of the bishopric of Pamiers, but he remained in hiding. . . .

In May 1680 I received orders to expel from the city the Ursuline nuns, who had been established in Pamiers by the bishop.

On June 8, 1680, I had two *arrêts* of the Parlement of Paris presented to the bishop of Pamiers, one suppressing the pamphlet he had published against the régale, and the other taking up the case of the bishop's excommunication ordinance as abusive. Nevertheless, on the 17th the bishop excommunicated eight *régalistes* for taking possession of their benefices. . . .

At the beginning of August 1680 the bishop fell dangerously ill and died on the 7th.

On August 21, 1680, I informed Châteauneuf that . . . M. Aubarède, self-styled archdeacon and vicar general . . . had mounted the pulpit in Notre Dame du Camp in Pamiers on August 18 and renewed the excommunications of the late bishop, even though the decrees of the Parlement of Paris had been delivered to him. I added that this undertaking by a priest, without authority or legitimacy, deserved to be punished . . . [and] that the Parlement should decree against this fake vicar general and investigate the facts to stop the schemes of this supposed vicar general and the canons who elected him. But the best solution would be to name a bishop to this church whose purity of doctrine and legitimate authority could restore calm in every conscience and make everyone return to his duty. Aubarède and the people in his cabale have used all sorts of deceptions to confuse the people with supposed miracles and preached that, instead of praying for the soul of the departed bishop, they should invoke him like a saint. And, in fact, the people threw themselves on the corpse and ripped off its clothes, which were torn apart and carried off like relics. They even threw stones at the *régalistes*. . . .

The king was ultimately successful in installing a new bishop in Pamiers and repressing this saintly agitation, but the battle was not over. In 1681 the pope declared this nomination illicit and threatened anyone who supported it (which included most of the French church hierarchy) with excommunication. This move outraged the Gallican church and caused Louis XIV to summon a special Assembly of the Clergy in 1682. Under the leadership of Bishop Bossuet, this assembly drew up the Four Gallican Articles quoted below. Note how the bishops carefully define the boundary between papal and royal jurisdiction. The French church hierarchy is taking the side of the crown against the pope.

Declaration of the Clergy of France, 1682

Many persons are attempting to overturn the decrees of the Gallican church, whose liberties, based on the holy canons of the church and the tradition of the church fathers, our ancestors supported so zealously. There are also those who, using these liberties as a pretext, do not hesitate to question the primacy of Saint Peter and the Roman pontiffs, his successors instituted by Jesus Christ, to whom all Christians owe obedience. . . .

It is with the aim of remedying such inconveniences that we, archbishops and bishops assembled in Paris by order of the king, along with the other deputies representing the Gallican church, have thought it appropriate, after serious deliberation, to establish and declare:

1. That Saint Peter and his successors, vicars of Jesus Christ [the popes], and the entire church have received their power from God alone in spiritual matters that concern salvation, but not in temporal and civil matters. . . . We declare as a result that kings and sovereigns are not subjected by the order of God to any ecclesiastical authority in temporal matters; that they cannot be deposed either directly or indirectly by authority of the head of the church; that their subjects cannot be released from their duty of submission and obedience or absolved from their oath of fidelity; and that this doctrine, necessary for the public peace and equally advantageous for the church and for the state, must be inviolably followed because it is in conformity with the Word of God, with the tradition of the Holy Fathers, and with the examples of the saints.

2. That the plentitude of power retained by the Apostolic Holy See and the successors of Saint Peter, vicars of Jesus Christ, in spiritual matters is such that the decrees of the Holy Ecumenical Council of Constance . . . retain all their force and virtue *[the Council of Constance had placed church councils above the pope]* . . . and that the church of France does not condone the opinions of those who attack these decrees or who weaken them by saying that their authority is not well established. . . .

3. That consequently the exercise of the apostolic power must be regulated according to the canons created by the Holy Spirit and consecrated by general respect; that the rules, customs, and constitutions received in this kingdom must be maintained; and that the limits set by our fathers remain unbreachable . . .[1]

[1]This provision affirms the authority of the Gallican church.

Léon Mention, *Documents relatifs aux rapports du clergé avec la royauté de 1682 à 1705* (Paris: Alphonse Picard, 1893), 27–31.

4. That although the pope has the principal role in questions of faith and his decrees concern all churches and every church in particular, his judgment is not irreversible unless it receives the consent of the church.

Pleased, Louis XIV ordered that these articles be taught throughout France. Pope Innocent XI retaliated by refusing to consecrate any priests who had attended the 1682 Assembly of the Clergy. This move created a standoff because church posts could not be filled without the pope's consecration. Between 1682 and 1693, bishopric after bishopric fell vacant. Innocent XI excommunicated Louis XIV, and Louis XIV occupied the papal city of Avignon with troops. In 1693 a new, more conciliatory pope recognized the royal appointees, and the king withdrew his requirement that the Four Articles be taught. The issue of the régale was quietly dropped, but the king continued to exercise all the powers he had originally claimed.

DEALING WITH THE JANSENISTS

The issue of doctrinal control within the church was especially acute with respect to the Jansenists. Their devotion to the contemplative life and their attacks on the more ceremonial and superficial aspects of Catholicism brought them in conflict with the Jesuits, a militant religious order known for its more pragmatic support of the king and the state. When the conflict between the Jansenists and the Jesuits became a major source of division within the French church, Louis sided with the Jesuits, who provided his personal confessors[1] and had few reservations about supporting his policies. The Jansenists, by contrast, had been among the king's prominent opponents during the Fronde. This taint of political opposition, plus the fact that the Jansenists had beliefs that were not easily abandoned made them seem subversive. In 1653 the pope had condemned the writings of Cornelius Jansen, and in 1657 the Assembly of the Clergy had followed suit. In 1661 Louis XIV required priests to sign an anti-Jansenist "formulary" that the bishops had drawn up. But the popularity of the movement grew among influential elites, aided by the publication of Blaise Pascal's *Provincial Letters,* which wittily at-

---

[1] The confessor was a priest and spiritual adviser assigned to hear the king's confession and absolve him of sin. Because of this intimate relationship, the royal confessor could significantly influence the monarch.

tacked the Jesuits. In 1679, just at the time he was fighting the pope over the régale, Louis began a new attempt at repression that lasted until the end of his reign.

In his later years, Louis became increasingly involved in stomping out Jansenism. Ironically, to quash a new Jansenist theological work — Pasquier Quesnel's *Moral Reflections on the New Testament,* published in 1693 — Louis was thrown into the arms of the pope, whose support he needed to get the work condemned. When Louis promulgated two papal bulls condemning Quesnel in 1705 and 1713, he antagonized the parlements and the ecclesiastical establishment by implicitly allowing the pope to dictate to the French church. He had come full circle from allying with the French church against the pope and the Jansenists to allying with the pope against the Jansenists and the French church. In the process, he had antagonized many influential people, who began to question the king's religious role, and thus absolutism, providing a foundation for the resurgence of Jansenism as an opposition movement in the eighteenth century.

A sense of the moral influence of the Jansenists can be gained from the next selection, drawn from a partisan account of the final closing of the Jansenist convent of Port Royal in 1709. Narratives like this were intended to project a belief in the holiness that supporters attributed to the Jansenists and to make the king's policy appear despotic.

Suppression of the Abbey of Port Royal des Champs by d'Argenson, Paris Lieutenant of Police, 1709

[D'Argenson] gathered his officers and archers, acquired twelve carriages and a litter, and gave all the necessary orders for this expedition. The whole company was to arrive at Port Royal des Champs on Sunday, October 28, Feast of Saint Simon and Saint Jude. But the weather was abominable and the rain continuous, as if the skies were protesting against this enterprise. So he had to postpone the expedition until the next day. . . . The guards, archers, and officers passed the night in the woods of Port Royal and built great fires while waiting for daybreak. Meanwhile the condemned virgins, unaware of what was brewing against

Quoted in Charles Augustin Sainte-Beuve, *Port Royal,* ed. René-Louis Doyon and Charles Marchesné (Paris: La Connaissance, 1928), 6:194–201. The origin of this account is not indicated by Sainte-Beuve, who was a nineteenth-century literary critic and historian.

them, passed the night at the feet of Jesus Christ, their spouse, adoring him in their usual manner. . . .

When the nuns were leaving the choir about 7:30 A.M., two officers on horseback entered the courtyard, and d'Argenson arrived, accompanied by a commissioner in a carriage with four horses. . . . The mother prioress was notified that d'Argenson wanted to speak to her. She had him taken to the great parlor, where, after mutual salutations, he told her that he had royal orders to enter the convent and peruse the archives. . . .

At the end of prayers, the mother prioress confidently rejoined d'Argenson, who ordered her to assemble the community in the chapter hall. The chapter bell was immediately rung, and the nuns arrived. The mother prioress placed d'Argenson in the seat of the abbess and positioned herself next to him, with all the sisters in their usual places and the commissioner and the two officers sitting next to d'Argenson. He asked whether there were any other nuns. He was told that there was one very elderly sister who was sick and paralyzed. "If she cannot come on her own, let her be carried in, for it is necessary that everyone be here," [he said]. Six sisters brought her on a mattress and a stretcher. . . . This good mother, named Euphrasie Robert, was eighty-six years old and was the sister of M. Robert, councillor in the Grande Chambre [of the Parlement]. D'Argenson asked for the other nuns. The mother prioress replied that this was the whole community; there was nobody else except the lay sisters, who never attended chapter meetings and had never been included in their affairs. D'Argenson replied, "They must come, too, for they are also involved in this." They were brought in, seven of them, who, along with the fifteen nuns, made twenty-two persons in all. It was then that d'Argenson ordered the chapter door closed and guarded and spoke this way:

"Ladies, I have come here to announce a sacrifice that you must make today. Although I am devastated to be the one charged with orders from the king concerning you, they must be faithfully executed, and when you leave this chamber you are never to see each other again. I am announcing your complete dispersal prescribed by His Majesty's orders. You have only three hours to prepare yourselves." . . . The mother prioress came forward and said in a confident voice, "My lord, we are ready to obey; half an hour is more than enough time to say our final farewells and pick up a breviary, a Bible, and our constitutions." Then d'Argenson told the mother prioress and the whole community, "My ladies, the orders I have received to disperse you into different convents do not specify a particular house for each of you. Since it is left to me to fill in the places as I see fit, I will allow you to confer among yourselves as to which

houses suit you. You, Madame Prioress, where would you like to go?"
She replied, "Monsieur, since our community is to be separated and dis-
persed, I am indifferent as to where I will be, for I expect to find God
wherever I am; but since you ask my advice, it seems best for the weak-
est to be placed in the houses that are closest so that they will be less in-
convenienced by the trip."

D'Argenson began to read the first lettre de cachet[2] which ordered
Mother Saint Anastasie Du Mesnil to depart immediately for Blois with
Sister Françoise Agnès de Saint Marthe, to two different houses. They
received their orders with respect and promised to fulfill them. All the
others displayed the same submission with a firmness and constancy
that greatly surprised d'Argenson and those in his company. It was then
that they realized that these virtuous daughters sought only the Lord
and were assured of finding Him anywhere. . . . When d'Argenson had
finished reading His Majesty's orders, these holy daughters reas-
sembled like a small flock without a pastor, saying adieu to one another
until eternity, embracing tenderly and kneeling before one another to
humbly ask forgiveness, animated by a lively faith and a firm hope. . . .
D'Argenson was touched by this ceremony, and his eyes appeared
moist. . . .

[The next] day, October 30, a priest sent by Father Le Tellier [the
king's Jesuit confessor] arrived with orders to inspect the books, manuscripts, images, and paintings. He did his job thoroughly, opening all
the packets and letting nothing leave without his permission. He
strongly condemned the *New Testament* by Father Quesnel, banned [sev-
eral other books], and seized all the manuscripts, including the short
statements of piety, mostly drawn from Holy Scripture, that the sisters
had placed in their books. The portraits of M. Arnauld, Saint Cyran, and
Mother Agnès horrified him. He tore up several of them and shrugged
his shoulders concerning the others. That day was spent regulating the
affairs of the servants and sending them away. On Thursday, eve of the
festival of All Saints, d'Argenson stationed a garrison of twelve archers
and two officers [in the convent] . . . and made many packets out of
the items found in each cell, which he had moved to a large room that
was locked and sealed with his seal. He did the same with the library,
after having all the books that had been found in the cells put there.
While he worked, the officers were stuffing themselves down below
and consuming all the fowl, not remembering the vigil of All Saints, or

---

[2]A lettre de cachet was a direct command from the king ordering the arrest or exile of
someone.

Figure 7. *An artist's rendition of the expulsion of the nuns from Port Royal in 1709 by d'Argenson.*
This type of image was increasingly used against Louis XIV by his enemies.
Bibliothèque nationale, Paris. Photo B.N.

perhaps imagining that their assignment exempted them from fasting and abstinence.

On Friday morning, All Saints' Day, d'Argenson left to report to the king about carrying out his orders and told him that he had been surprised at the constancy of these nuns and especially by their perfect obedience. The king replied that he was satisfied with their obedience but angry that they did not belong to his religion. . . .

———

DEALING WITH THE HUGUENOTS

A final consequence of the king's sacred authority was the necessity for religious uniformity. If Louis XIV was God's representative on earth, then surely it was his duty, as he promised in his coronation oath, to extirpate heresy. Indeed, if church institutions were an integral part of the royal system of government, then non-Catholics who avoided them might appear to be politically subversive. Even worse, in a state where every ceremony was infused with rich Catholic symbolism, the presence of dissidents might seem insulting to God, and thus be viewed by the community as a threat and a betrayal.

The Huguenots (French Protestants) had fought during the religious wars of the sixteenth century to achieve a legitimate place in French society. At their height, they may have numbered about 10 percent of the total population of France, but they were strategically concentrated in certain provinces and enjoyed strong support from powerful noble families there. It was this elite involvement, along with dedicated popular support, that made compromise necessary. In 1598 Henry IV issued the Edict of Nantes, which concluded a generation of religious wars by according the Huguenots a distinctive legal status. This edict allowed them to maintain churches in places where they were already established (but not in Paris), keep their institutional structure consisting of local consistories and regional and national synods, run schools and charitable organizations, have their cases tried in bipartite courts where half the judges were Protestants and half Catholics, bequeath property, and so forth. But what was intended by the crown as a temporary measure dragged on for more than eighty years, as royal minorities and foreign wars, armed Protestant rebellions under Louis XIII, and the difficulties of the Fronde made it necessary to continue conciliating the Huguenots.

By the 1660s, the Catholic majority considered these rights, which had come to look like a permanent entitlement to the Huguenots, to be a procedural nightmare and a doctrinal insult. Petitions poured in to the king from individuals, organizations, and church lobbyists protesting every sort of Protestant accommodation: use of places of worship and cemeteries, residence of ministers, upkeep of hospitals and schools, right to maintain church towers or bells, nature of representation, and questions of precedence. In response, the various governmental bodies whittled down the rights of Protestants. Edicts restricted their member-ship in guilds and companies of royal officers, disadvantaged Protestant creditors, forbade conversions to Calvinism and relapses from Catho-licism to Calvinism, favored Catholic priests in hospitals and at death-beds, Catholicized city governments, and ultimately closed down Hu-guenot worship in more and more localities. Thus Louis XIV's ultimate revocation of the Edict of Nantes in 1685, while viewed as an act of despo-tism by European Protestants, was also the final fulfillment of a long-standing groundswell of Catholic demand.

We are going to examine this repression as it unfolded in Languedoc, the southern province where Calvinism was strongest. The official Cath-olic term for the Huguenots was R.P.R., which stood for "the supposedly reformed religion" in French. The terms *Protestant, Calvinist, Huguenot, and R.P.R.* are used here interchangeably. Huguenot places of worship were called temples because the term "church" *(église)* referred exclu-sively to Catholic churches. What emerges from these documents is the sorry plight of many Protestants who faced the moral dilemma of whether to be faithful to their beliefs or their king. As we can see, they did not passively await their fate, but their options were limited, given their dwindling numbers, the lack of support from personages at court, and the immense authority of Louis XIV when he was doing what the majority of his people wanted. Protestants were faced with a combina-tion of legal harassment and bribery, and Catholic strategy focused es-pecially on their ministers as community leaders, who, unlike Catholic priests, were married and had families to look after. The Huguenots' re-sponses, besides converting, included legal appeals, plans (largely illu-sory) for insurrections, and emigration. These documents also show what an important role the intendant could play in engineering this sort of harassment process.

The first text is a report concerning the joint work of one Catholic and one Protestant commissioner named by the king to investigate complaints about the implementation of the Edict of Nantes in Languedoc — the sort of com-plaints that were coming in to the king from Catholics. Their disagreement suggests how different these issues looked from the perspectives of the two re-ligions and how the Calvinists were being increasingly harassed as early as 1663.

Commission for the Execution of the Edict of Nantes, 1663

The commission held three sessions in Nîmes and Pezenas and judged the affairs of the three dioceses of Nîmes, Uzès, and Mende. Every community that has public Protestant worship has been summoned to present proof that it already existed in the years specified by the Edict. There has been such widespread Protestant usurpation that if the cases where there was disagreement [over the legality of Protestant worship] were all decided in favor of the Catholics, almost two hundred localities would lose their worship and two hundred temples would be demolished. Protestant worship was confirmed in ninety-four other localities. The commissioners disagreed on the following points:

1. All communities shall have a single clerk who must be Catholic.
2. All unique positions shall be held by a Catholic; tax collectors cannot collect Protestant taxes that go to ministers and Protestant expenses.
3. Protestants are forbidden to ring any church bells from Holy Thursday through Holy Saturday.
4. In localities with Protestant worship, Protestant schools can only teach reading, writing, and arithmetic.
5. Every community is to have a political council that is at least half Catholic.
6. In localities where the number of Catholics is too small to constitute half of the political council, the [Catholic] priests are to have entrance to the council with the right to speak first.
7. Since the smaller temple in Nîmes was built on the site of the former *collège* [secondary school], the Catholic commissioner argues that it should be given back to the Jesuits. The Protestant opposes this.
8. Endorsement of the Catholic claims that the Protestants can maintain only primary schools in Nîmes because they have no letters patent verified in the sovereign court approving the *collège*.

Prince Henri de Latour d'Auvergne, viscount of Turenne, was from one of France's most important noble families and had been one of Louis XIV's leading generals. When he converted from Protestantism to Catholicism in 1668, even Saint Maurice commented on it in his court memoirs.

Paul Gachon (hereafter referred to as Gachon), *Quelques préliminaires de la révocation de l'édit de Nantes en Languedoc (1661–1685)* (Toulouse: Privat, 1899), xix–xxiii.

Commentary by Saint Maurice, November 23, 1668

The conversion of M. de Turenne has produced advantageous results for his family since the king has made the duke of Albret, his nephew, a cardinal. . . . The Protestants are discovering that they no longer have any protectors. The king has abolished the Chambers of the Edict[1] of the Parlements of Paris and Rouen where their law cases were tried; there is talk of demolishing the temple of Charenton [in a suburb of Paris] and of forbidding any temple within six leagues of Paris. They have appealed with petitions and loud voices, but they have received no satisfaction, and I have been told that when they informed His Majesty that they expected no less from him than a continuation of the protection for their privileges that they received from his grandfather and father, he replied that Henry IV feared them but did not love them, and that while he [Louis] did not love them, he feared them even less. They are greatly depressed and humiliated because they have no protector, no captain, no fortified places, and no money.

The following exchange gives us a rare look at daily friction between Protestants and Catholics in a local setting. Note that as early as 1678, Protestants were talking about emigrating if the king's position hardened.

Verbal Abuse, Protestants to Catholics [Summary], 1678

The intendant d'Aguesseau receives complaints from the syndic of the Catholic clergy of Nîmes that on Sunday, May 8, when the priest of Saint Hippolyte [a town in the mountains near Nîmes] was on his way to visit a sick person, carrying the Holy Sacrament under a canopy and accompanied by a procession of Catholics carrying lighted candles, Protestants coming out of their temple collected in the street and jeered at the Catholics as they went by. The intendant ordered an investigation by a

---

[1] Chambers of the Edict were special chambers in some parlements where cases involving Protestants were decided by a committee of judges, half of whom were Protestants, the other half Catholics.

November 23: Marquis de Saint Maurice, *Lettres sur la Cour de Louis XIV, 1667–1672,* ed. Jean Lemoine (Paris: Calmann-Lévy, 1910), 1:257–59.
1678: Archives Départementales du Gard G450.

Catholic judge, whose report contained the following charges against the Huguenots. People had said that they should throw the priests off the bridge; that the papists must be truly blind to carry candles in broad daylight. A priest who called out to let him through was pushed into the mud; a woman's voice shouted, "Poor blind people, you can't see anything even at high noon." When the sergeant who marched in front of the procession told the crowd to remove their hats to honor the Holy Sacrament, some walked away and others left their hats on. A priest struck a young boy who had insolently refused to remove his hat. The wife of the minister Malet was seen at a window making grimaces and scornful gestures. Someone said, "The priests are as stupid as dogs," to general laughter. People were later heard saying that if the priest had tried to make them take off their hats, as he did to the boy that he struck, they would have run him through with their sword or waited until night with arms to kill him, and if this continued, they would get rid of him. Another group said that if the king pushed them too far on account of their religion, they would leave and go to England to join with others and form an army of more than fifty thousand men. This testimony was sent to the royal council, which issued arrest warrants for those named and instructed d'Aguesseau to try them before the presidial court of Nîmes.

The royal authorities were hardly neutral and were constantly inventing new pressures, as the following selection shows.

Memoir by the Intendant d'Aguesseau on How to Convert the Pastors and Huguenots of Languedoc, 1679

The surest method [of conversion] is to use the king's authority to stimulate the bishops' enthusiasm for instructing and preaching, which they do not do nearly often enough, especially in the distant provinces. . . . The people want to be instructed, and it is a general complaint among the newly converted that they don't find in our religion the same instruction that they had in theirs. . . .

As for the ministers, there are two earthly objectives that should be added to those God has left in the hands of the church: first, to cause them pain, inconvenience, and difficulty even maintaining their position if they remain ministers; and second, to make them see the considerable advantages enjoyed by those who change religion.

[The following list summarizes a few of the most interesting points.]

1. Enforce the rules stating that the Huguenots have to send an accounting of their tax collections to the royal council. This will consume them in expenses and make it hard to pay their ministers. . . .

3. The taxes they collect to pay their debts and the salaries of their ministers are assessed on the land, like royal taxes; turn them into levies on individuals. . . . Collecting from individuals will lead to a flurry of lawsuits that will make it harder to collect money for the ministers, and the poor will convert if they are charged too heavily.

4. Make the ministers pay more taxes by cutting back on their exemptions, declaring that their salaries are exempt, but not their property.

5. End the practice by which Huguenots are exempted from paying taxes used for the building of Catholic churches. . . . This will cause them to be doubly taxed, and many will convert to avoid paying their religious tax. . . .

7. In addition to reducing the number of ministers and making it more difficult for them to subsist, see that the ministers are aware of the advantages they will enjoy when they convert. The Assembly of the Clergy should set up a fund of 300,000 livres a year to pay the pensions of ministers who convert. When Protestant ministers die, the congregation supports their wives for a year. So pay the wives three years from the same fund. Ministers can set up their sons in the ministry. Make up for this by giving their oldest son, or the son of their choice, a pension for life. And provide 500 livres for each daughter they want to marry. . . .

10. Royal edicts require ministers to maintain certain rules of conduct. Use this as a pretext to make them swear an oath before the Catholic commissioner that they will abide by all the rules on pain of being deprived of the ministry. This will restrain them from invectives against the Catholic Church, and when they are unable to resist, they can be deprived of their posts, and there will hardly be a year when several will not be removed this way. . . .

Verbal Abuse: Catholics to Protestants [Summary], 1680

The Protestants of Montpellier appeal to the royal lieutenant that their ministers are repeatedly being insulted at baptisms by Catholics. Two ministers report that they were bothered in the street by taunts of "There goes the minister!" and that when they are proceeding down the street to a baptism, their party is stopped by priests who insist on talking to the children who are being baptized.

Letter of the Intendant d'Aguesseau to Secretary of State Châteauneuf, Toulouse, September 29, 1682

Monsieur:
In this province, many legacies have been left by Protestants for the poor of their religion. These legacies are permitted by the Edict of Nantes. But since there is hardly a community that does not have a small hospital where the poor and the sick, both Catholic and Protestant, are housed, it appears that the king might justly issue a declaration attaching all these legacies to these hospitals. This would create a fund that would be taken from the Huguenots, who use it to maintain the poor of their religion, and it might result in some conversions. . . .

The following account was written in the mid-eighteenth century by a Catholic historian on the basis of actual documents.

Demolition of the Main Protestant Temple in Montpellier, 1682

The occasion was provided by a royal declaration of July 6, 1680, which prohibited Catholics from turning Calvinist and prohibited any ministers from receiving them [in their temples], on penalty of suspension and

1680: Archives Nationales TT 256B, fol. 56.
September 29: Gachon, c–ci.
1682: Charles d'Aigrefeuille, *Histoire de la ville de Montpellier,* new ed., ed. M. de La Pijardière (Montpellier: Coulet, 1877), 2:188–90.

Protestant worship being banned in any temple where a Catholic had been received. Well, it so happened that a young lady, Isabeau Paulet, daughter of a former minister from Uzès, who was then councillor in the presidial court of Montpellier, abjured Calvinism in the convent of the Daughters of the Visitation at the château of Teirargues belonging to Mademoiselle des Portes. Two years later, she returned to Montpellier, where, at the urging of her mother, she went to a Protestant sermon and was given Communion by Bourdieu the elder, the town minister. When this was known, the matter was brought before the Parlement of Toulouse, which, in a decree of November 16, sentenced Paulet to make legal amends, suspended the minister Bourdieu from his functions, and ordered the temple of Montpellier to be demolished. To evade this ruling, the consistory appealed to the royal council and sent a deputation, consisting of four ministers and many others from the consistory, to see M. de Noailles [military commander of Languedoc]. They asked Noailles to allow them to continue to worship until orders were received from the royal council. When he refused, two gentlemen in the deputation asked him imprudently whether he didn't know that there were 1.8 million Huguenot families in France. To which Noailles replied, looking at an officer of his guards, that while he waited to learn the fate of those 1.8 million Huguenot families, he would escort these gentlemen to prison. . . .

That very evening M. de Noailles and M. d'Aguesseau, the intendant, wrote to inform the king of what had happened, and the consistory similarly dispatched a special courier ten days later. But M. de Noailles's courier had such a head start that he soon arrived back with an explicit order to demolish the temple within twenty-four hours. "And you would please me," added the king in his letter to the duke of Noailles, "if you would do it in twelve."

Noailles sent to ask the consistory whether their courier had returned yet and what orders he had brought. When they replied that they had had no response, he showed them his orders and asked them whether they would like to demolish the temple themselves so that they could make use of the materials. Their consternation was so great that they could barely open their mouths to beg him to exempt them from this task. He told them, "With pleasure," and within the hour he had summoned the consuls and ordered them to get fifty or sixty masons and march straight to the temple. When they had done this, he went there himself, accompanied by his guards and his entire household, went inside, and shouted loudly to the masons, "Courage, my friends, long live the king! Fear nothing, work hard, let's get going." When this signal had been given, they began by destroying the altar. Then, climbing up on the roof, they soon had it completely uncovered, since it was made of simple planks. . . .

This temple had been built in 1585 in January, as you could see from a date on the great arch that spanned the temple. . . . But what was most noticed was that Friday, December 3, Feast of Saint Barbara, was the date when the Huguenots of Montpellier were preparing to defend the city against the siege by King Louis XIII in 1621. They began to tear down all the churches in the city, and the next day, the 4th, they finished destroying them. Thus, sixty one years later, the worship of the Calvinists was abolished on the same day as they had abolished that of the Catholics. And to make matters worse, they learned that the courier they had sent to Paris had been arrested and taken to the Bastille, where he was held for ten or twelve days.

Report of the Intendant d'Aguesseau on the Situation in Montpellier and Languedoc, July 18, 1683

Since the demolition of the temple of Montpellier, the Huguenots of this city and the surrounding region are assembling in the countryside at the home of the wife of President de Vignoles and the home of the marquis of Chayla at Saint Jean de Vedas, which is one league from Montpellier. The lord of that village has demolished the interior of his house to create a room that can hold three thousand people, and in the assemblies held there, they take a sort of oath of union never to abandon the cause of God.

The minister Bourdieu the younger has been allowed to go to Montpellier from time to time to see his family and his property, in order for us to have the opportunity to negotiate about his conversion. But he has not listened to any offers made to him because he is expecting to be given a post at the next synod, so it is time to send him away. . . .

If His Majesty does not want to prohibit the synods from meeting completely, the most useful policy for the [Catholic] faith would be to order that a Catholic commissioner be present. But to get the maximum benefit from this, it is extremely important that His Majesty choose a very able man and that he be given secret instructions to get the principal leaders of the consistory to quarrel among themselves, since they

July 18: Gachon, cx–cxiii.

are already jealous of one another over its governance. He should let them get into disputes over the issues that divide them and try to win them over individually with offers of temporal advantages. . . .

Nîmes and Uzès are the centers of heresy in Languedoc. True religion is oppressed there by the Huguenots, who are very numerous and have made themselves the masters. Those two consistories, especially Nîmes, are animating all the rest of the province and have sent emissaries everywhere to dissuade those who are thinking of converting. They encourage them to borrow as much as they can and then flee to foreign countries, where they promise them great assistance. The consistory of Nîmes has taken up a collection that they say is just for charity, which is said to come to thirty thousand livres. . . .

The Parlement of Toulouse has issued an *arrêt* [decree] forbidding ministers to admit boys younger than fourteen and girls under twelve into their temples if their fathers are Catholic. This order has been presented to the consistories of Languedoc, but it has had no effect because the ministers recognize only orders coming from the royal council.

His Majesty has ordered Protestant attorneys and solicitors to resign their positions. The Huguenots are using incredible effort and unbelievable tricks to attract business for them as arbitrators and expert consultants, and in this way they are eluding the orders of His Majesty. . . .

The following list contains a few of the approximately 130 names of Protestants who went into exile before the final blow fell. They were mostly men; half were married with families, the others "young men." The fact that the intendant had such a list shows how carefully he watched the Huguenots. This list also offers a glimpse into many family tragedies.

D'Aguesseau's List of Protestants Who Have Left Languedoc in Violation of the Royal Orders, August 3, 1685

Bourdieu, formerly a minister in Montpellier, married and has one child, is in England with his son and grandson. His wife is in Montpellier.

Gautier, former minister in Montpellier, has property in Gallargues, has a wife and two children, is now in Brandenburg, and his wife is in Montpellier.

August 3: Gachon, cxxiii–cxlv.

Espessil, young man, merchant, has a house at Mauguio, has been in Holland for four years.

Étienne Lauvas, bookseller, not married, left no property, has been in Holland for three years with his mother and sister.

Claude Cavalier, glove maker, married, is outside the kingdom. We don't know where, but his wife is in Montpellier.

Lady Condeot, sister-in-law of Philippe Dumont, bourgeois; they are in Orange [papal territory, thus not part of the kingdom].

Pierre and Jean Anco, brothers, young men, pastry cooks, are in London.

Louis Sabre, young man from a good family, unmarried, went to Paris with his uncle, now is in England.

Lisse, tailor from La Salle, is in Geneva.

David Roquette, silk merchant, young man, unmarried, is in Amsterdam along with his brother Samuel, who deserted [the army] and joined him.

Paul Chomil, merchant, owns a vineyard and some land near Annonay; don't know where he is; he left when his wife converted, but she died recently.

Pierre Baille, married with four children; they're all in Amsterdam.

Here is the official edict of Revocation, which was responsible for dispersing French Protestants all over Europe, carrying with them atrocity stories about the despotism of the king. Note the specific terms.

Revocation of the Edict of Nantes, Fontainebleau, October 25, 1685

Louis, by the Grace of God, King of France and Navarre; to all present and to come, greetings. King Henry the Great, our grandfather of glorious memory, wishing to avoid having the peace he had established for his subjects disturbed because of the R.P.R. after all the losses his people had endured during the civil and foreign wars, issued an edict at Nantes in the month of April 1598, which established the way adherents to that religion were to be treated, the places where they could worship, and special judges to administer justice to them, and included specific

François Isambert, et al., *Recueil général des anciennes lois françaises* (Paris: Plon, 1822), 19:530–34.

articles regulating everything he thought was needed to maintain peace in his kingdom and diminish the aversion each religion had for the other, so that he would be better able to accomplish his chosen task of reuniting in the church those who had so easily distanced themselves from it. The intentions of the king, our grandfather, could not be realized because of his premature death, and the execution of the said edict was interrupted during the minority of the late king, our honored lord and father of glorious memory, by new schemes on the part of those of the R.P.R. . . .

Now that God has finally allowed our peoples to enjoy a perfect calm and we ourselves are not occupied with protecting them from our enemies, we have been able to profit from this truce [of 1684 with foreign powers], which we ourselves facilitated in order to be able to give our complete attention to successfully achieving the plans of the kings, our grandfather and father, which we have supported since our accession to the throne. We now see, with proper acknowledgment to God, that our efforts have achieved the goal we had sought, and the better and greater part of our subjects of the R.P.R. have embraced the Catholic Church. Because of all this, the regime of the Edict of Nantes and everything that was ordered on behalf of those belonging to the R.P.R. has become obsolete. Therefore we decided that there was nothing better we could do to erase from memory the troubles, the confusion, and the evils that the growth of this false religion had caused in our kingdom and that gave rise to the said Edict and to so many other edicts and declarations that preceded it, or resulted from it, than to revoke entirely the said Edict of Nantes and the detailed articles attached to it and everything that has been done since on behalf of the said R.P.R.

1. We therefore for these reasons and in full knowledge, power, and royal authority, by means of the present perpetual and irrevocable edict, do suppress and revoke the Edict of the king, our grandfather, issued at Nantes in April 1598. . . . As a result, we desire and it is our pleasure that all the temples of the R.P.R. situated in our kingdom, country, lands and all seigneuries within our obedience be immediately demolished. . . . *[A summary of the rest of the terms follows.]*
2. Our subjects of the R.P.R. are not to assemble for worship in any place or house for any reason.
3. Noble lords are not to hold worship services in their houses or fiefs of any sort on pain of confiscation of goods and property.
4. Ministers of the R.P.R. who have not converted are to leave the kingdom within fifteen days and are not to preach or perform any functions in the meantime, or they will be sent to the galleys.

5. Ministers who convert, and their widows after their death, are to enjoy the same exemptions from taxes and troop lodgings that they had as ministers, and they will receive a pension a third larger than the salary they received as ministers, and their widows will receive half of this sum after their death.

6. Converted ministers can become lawyers or doctors of law without the usual three years of study and for half the fees usually charged by the universities.

7. Special schools for the children of the R.P.R. are prohibited.

8. Children of R.P.R. parents are to be baptized by the chief priests of their parishes and raised as Catholics, and local judges are to oversee this.

9. If Protestants who left the kingdom before this edict was issued return within four months, they can regain their property and resume their lives. If, however, they do not return within four months, their goods will be confiscated.

10. All subjects belonging to the R.P.R. and their wives and children, are forbidden to leave the country or to send out their property and effects. The penalty for men is the galleys and for women confiscation of their persons and property.

11. The declarations already issued concerning those who relapse are to be executed in full.

And, in addition, those who adhere to the R.P.R., while waiting until it pleases God to enlighten them like the others, may continue to live in the cities and communities of our realm, continue their commerce, and enjoy their property without being bothered or hindered because of the R.P.R., on condition, however, of not practicing their religion or assembling for prayers or worship or for any other pretext, with the penalties stated above.

Giving Protestants the right to hold on to their beliefs if they didn't practice them was hypocritical in the extreme, considering the circumstances. In fact, before the revocation was issued, Louis XIV sent companies of dragoons[1] to terrorize Protestant households by lodging in their houses and committing many atrocities until the residents converted. The twentieth-century historian Louis Dermigny describes the process in Languedoc.

---

[1]Dragoons were a type of cavalry who fought as mounted infantry, arriving on horseback but fighting on foot. They carried rifles called fusils.

Royal Dragoons in Languedoc, 1685

September–October 1685 was for Languedoc the harvest of souls. The converting troops were led, drum beating, by the new intendant Basville, just arrived from Poitou, where he had perfected the method, assisted by Noailles, military commander of the province. Scarcely had he taken up his functions in Montpellier when he summoned the leaders of the Protestants and invited them to abjure, as Castres and Millau had done before them. The next day, when eight companies of troops had reinforced those camping at the gates, the leaders capitulated. In three days there were thousands of abjurations. Then it was the turn of Nîmes, the isolation of which had already begun, with Lunel and Sommières giving in to the threat of dragoons on the 29th, Marsillargues and Aimargues on the 30th, Bernis and Codognan on October 1. On the 3rd, in a city [Nîmes] surrounded by 8,000 men, the members of the consistory, who had been summoned before Basville, Noailles, and Cardinal Bonzi, tried in vain to negotiate. Harassed day and night by certain weak souls, they finally resigned themselves to abandoning their beliefs, and on the 4th Bishop Séguier received 4,000 Huguenots in his cathedral and issued a general absolution. Then the contagion of the example of Nîmes spread like a trail of gunpowder. . . . Several days later Basville announced, "Every parish has been cleaned." And on October 18 the king could sign the revocation edict without scruples because, as the bishop of Mende wrote, "The inhabitants of the R.P.R. have all by the grace of God been converted to the faith of the Catholic, Apostolic and Roman Church."

List of Property Belonging to Protestants Who Have Fled from the Diocese of Montpellier [Summary], 1686

Lists eighty-one names of émigrés for this one diocese (there were twenty-two dioceses in Languedoc) and, for many of them, the houses, farms, vineyards, merchandise, or just furnishings they left behind, valued at 617,000 livres. The individuals include Jean Durant, lawyer; the baron of Temelac; Vivens, captain of cavalry; Madronnet, captain of in-

---

1685: Philippe Wolff, ed., *Histoire du Languedoc* (Toulouse: Privat, 1967), 359–60.
1686: Archives Nationales TT 256B, fols. 1214–1339.

fantry; Jean Boissonnade, solicitor in the Cour des Aides; Laurent and Louis Galdy, brothers; David Barbut and his two children; Dauphine Peyre, wife of Barbut; Antoine and Jean Sabatier, father and son, merchants; David Brousson, perfumer; Pierre Artaud, merchant of stockings; David Roumie, spice merchant; François Feuillade, master surgeon, and his wife; Dame Rose de Ranchin, widow; Étienne Bessan, cobbler; Abraham Soubatier, master cutler; Tiphène Soubatier, his daughter; Marguerite Pageze, widow; Antoine Blanc, master tailor; Bonnet, master cooper; Jean Servan, merchant-furrier; Isaye Paravisol, embroiderer; René Bertrand, minister, his wife and two children; Jacques Breguier, merchant of wool, and his wife; David Eusache, apothecary; André Vingille, baker; Pierre Rigaud, bookseller, and his two daughters; Antoine Servel, master plasterer, and his wife. . . .

EPILOGUE

Louis XIV's need to protect his relationship with the French church against meddling by the pope, Jansenist criticism, and Protestant heresy followed from the ideological arguments for absolutism, but the repression that resulted damaged his reputation long after the fact. Here are the comments of the Princess Palatine after the death of the Sun King:

The Princess Palatine Remembers Louis XIV

OCTOBER 21, 1719
The old trollop [Madame de Maintenon] and Father La Chaise [Louis XIV's Jesuit confessor] persuaded the king that all the sins he had committed with the Montespan would be forgiven if he persecuted and expelled the Huguenots and that by doing this he would get to heaven. The poor king believed every word, for never in his life had he read one word of the Bible, and this was the origin of the persecution which we had seen. . . .

MAY 8, 1722
So great a fear of Hell had been inspired in the king that he believed all those who had not been taught by the Jesuits were damned, and feared

---

Quoted in H. G. Judge, ed. *Louis XIV* (New York: Barnes & Noble, 1967), 61–62.

that he, too, would be damned if he had anything to do with them. If you wished to ruin someone you had only to say, "He is a Huguenot," or "He is a Jansenist," and then it was all over for him. My son[1] wished to take into his service a gentleman whose mother was an avowed Jansenist. The Jesuits, in order to turn the king against my son, told him that the Prince wished to take a Jansenist into his service. The king caused my son to be summoned and asked him, "Now then, my nephew, what do you think you are doing in taking a Jansenist into your service?" "What, me?" replied my son, "I have no such idea." The king said, "You are taking so and so, whose mother is one." My son began to laugh and replied, "I can assure Your Majesty that he is certainly not a Jansenist; indeed, there is reason to fear that he does not believe in God." "Oh," said the king, "if that is the only difficulty and you can assure me that he is not a Jansenist, you may take him."

[1] Her son was Philippe d'Orléans, the regent of France, whom we encountered as a boy on page 72.

8

The King and His Image

One of Louis XIV's greatest successes was to leave in his wake the image of grandeur and order that we still remember today. Even the chapters of this book reflect what Louis wanted us to think about: the life at Versailles, the Grands Jours d'Auvergne, Colbert's economic reordering, the glories of an orthodox Catholicism (Bossuet), and the less glorious extirpation of Protestantism — all were aspects of royal rule that the king consciously planned and left documents or monuments to commemorate. In his memoirs written for his son, Louis recalled that when he came to personal power, "disorder reigned everywhere." This was something of an exaggeration, but it is the idea that has come down to us along with the sense that Louis ended the disorder. This favorable impression was already being received and transmitted by the memoir writers whose accounts we read in chapter 2. It was painted on the ceiling of the Hall of Mirrors at Versailles by Le Brun, where we see a Roman Louis sitting on a throne, "assuming personal power," amid glorious portrayals of the campaigns of the Dutch War. To be sure, "grand" can easily become "grandiose," and all this glory could easily turn sour, as it did for many people in the second half of the reign, when the king grew old and the country suffered from too much warfare. I have tried, in this book, to provide a more balanced view by stressing the realities of provincial life, the necessity for compromise with regional elites, the king's oppressive moves against religious dissidents, and the stifling nature of the court. But the king's message always breaks through.

It is interesting to note that Louis's reputation was planned from the start. Charles Perrault (1628–1703), the author of a book of fairy tales and a leading figure in Louis XIV's early cultural projects, describes the process in his memoirs. Perrault wrote these memoirs at the very end of his life, so there may be some hindsight included in his recollections of the early days of the reign.

Charles Perrault on Colbert's Plans to Glorify the King

At the end of 1662, when Monsieur Colbert had predicted or knew already that the king would make him Superintendent of Buildings, he began to prepare himself for carrying out this duty, which he considered much more important than it appeared to be in the hands of Monsieur de Ratabon [his predecessor]. He imagined that he would have to work not only on finishing the Louvre, a project begun so many times and always left incomplete, but also on raising many monuments to the glory of the king, such as triumphal arches, obelisks, pyramids, and mausoleums. Nothing was too grand or magnificent for him to propose.

He thought also that it would be necessary to strike a large number of medals, to consecrate for posterity the memory of the great deeds which the king had already achieved and which he foresaw would be followed by deeds even greater and more noteworthy.[1] All these exploits would be commemorated, along with the princely entertainments such as feasts, masquerades, carousels, and other similar diversions. So that these events might be described and illustrated with wit and understanding, and then circulated in foreign countries, where the way in which they are handled does nearly as much honor to the king as the deeds themselves, Monsieur Colbert decided to bring together several men of letters and keep them by his side. Their role would be to advise him on these matters and to form a kind of small council to deal with everything concerned with literature.

One of the first men to be consulted for this "Little Academy" was Jean Chapelain, a poet and member of the French Academy (for writers, founded in 1635 by Cardinal Richelieu). We can see from Chapelain's letter to Colbert that they were thinking along the same lines.

---

[1] The medals were large ceremonial coins struck to commemorate special occasions and engraved with inscriptions in Latin and depictions in bas-relief of the event in question. Colbert organized the Little Academy described in this letter so that scholars could meet informally to create inscriptions and designs for the king's medals.

Charles Perrault, *Memoirs of My Life,* ed. and trans. Jeanne Morgan Zarucchi (Columbia: University of Missouri Press, 1989), 41–42, 89.

Sir, the plan that you have paid me the honor of communicating is great, noble, and completely worthy of the grandeur of the king and of the grandeur of your zeal for His Majesty's service and glory. I have examined it a hundred times, and each time I was more satisfied than the last. Therefore, in my opinion, there is no question whether the idea should be implemented, and the only thing to consider is how it is to be done.

As for the plan concerning the medals, it is an invention that the Greeks and Romans used to eternalize the memory of the heroic actions of their princes, their captains, and their emperors, because of the permanence of the metals they were made of, especially those in gold and silver. I highly approve of your using them as one of the means to perpetuate the king's [memory], since this is a method used throughout the centuries for a similar end, and it is very much in keeping with the royal dignity. . . .

As for poetry, Monsieur, you could not have come up with anything more appropriate to your goal. Of all things durable, it is without doubt the one that best withstands the injuries of time, when a talented hand is involved. All the most famous tombs, portraits, and statues have foundered upon this reef. Even the most exquisite prose works have reached us only in mutilated and crippled form, and only the poetic ones, beginning with Homer, or at least the best of them, have come down to us. So whatever your efforts produce in this genre that is really good at celebrating the king's virtues will infallibly make them immortal. . . .

I come to history, Monsieur, which you have very correctly judged to be one of the principal means of preserving the splendor of the king's enterprises and the details of his miracles. But history is one of those fruits that are good only when kept for late in the season. If it does not explain the motives behind the things that are recounted, if it is not accompanied by prudent reflections and documents, it becomes nothing more than a simple narrative without force and dignity. Consequently, using histories is something that cannot be done during the reign of the prince who is their subject, without exposing the secrets of the government to the public. . . . I believe that putting history to work for His Majesty, in the

Ph. Tamizey de Larroque, ed., *Lettres de Jean Chapelain* (Paris: Imprimerie Nationale, 1883), 2:272–77.

manner in which it should be written, should be done only if the work is to be kept hidden until possible disadvantages can no longer prejudice his affairs or those of his allies. . . .

But in order not to leave the king without the praises he deserves both in prose and in verse, I am of the opinion that the best pens should be employed to deal with these miracles in oratorical fashion by means of laudatory speeches similar to those of Pliny the Younger about Trajan, which many more persons are capable of doing and for which fewer qualifications are required. . . .

There are indeed, Monsieur, other laudable ways of spreading and maintaining His Majesty's glory, of which even the ancients have left us illustrious examples, which still attract the eyes of the world, such as the pyramids, columns, equestrian statues, colossi, triumphal arches, marble and bronze busts, bas-reliefs. These historical monuments, to which we might add our rich tapestry workshops, our fresco paintings, and our engravings, though less durable, are still preserved for a long time. But since these sorts of works belong to art forms other than those of the muses concerning which you asked my opinion, I shall simply mention them to you, so that you may judge whether they should join your other sublime ideas.

[Here is the "advertising campaign" for the king, steeped in awareness of the styles of the ancients. Tapestries, paintings, architecture, and statuary were all enlisted in the transmission of the king's message. As Perrault describes, Louis XIV soon established an Academy of Sciences to patronize scientists; built an observatory, which still stands in Paris; drew up plans for the remodeling of the Louvre; and began work on the Palace of Versailles. Many medals were struck glorifying the king, with inscriptions designed by the Little Academy. Soon the king began to demand victory arches to commemorate his victories like a Roman emperor.]

After the conquests of Flanders and Franche-Comté [1668], Monsieur Colbert proposed the raising of an Arch of Triumph to the glory of the king. Monsieur Le Brun [the painter] and Monsieur Le Vau [the architect] drew up designs for this, and as I had also made one that I sent to Monsieur Colbert and that I called a mere sketch, he wrote in the margin of my letter that that sketch had pleased him more than the designs that he had been given. It was upon this sketch that my brother [Claude, the architect] based the design that has been executed to scale, as may be seen at the Saint Antoine Gate [in Paris].

Figure 8. *Victory arch by François Dorbay erected in Montpellier in 1693 in honor of Louis XIV, one of many such monuments built all over France.*
Its panels celebrate the king's military successes, the construction of the Canal du Midi, and the revocation of the Edict of Nantes.
Photo by the author.

This was the first permanent triumphal arch erected in Europe since an-cient times. Many more followed. In addition to four more in Paris, dedi-cated to Ludovico Magno, "Louis the Great," arches were eventually erected in Tours, Besançon, Montpellier (see Figure 8), and Lille, with others planned for La Rochelle, Marseilles, and Metz. To these were eventually added equestrian statues of Louis XIV in Paris, Arles, Caen, Dijon, Lyon, Montpellier, Pau, Poitiers, and Troyes. In the 1680s, towns and provinces rushed to compete with one another in joining this bandwagon, to please the king and share in his glory. Listen to the Estates of Languedoc, which were triumphant in 1686 after their long-expressed dream of the revocation of the Edict of Nantes had been fulfilled. (The revocation was in fact cele-brated on the victory arch in Montpellier.)

Report to the Estates of Languedoc on the Equestrian Statue of the King, October 30, 1686

Cardinal Bonsy, president of the Estates, recalled that last year the Estates passed a resolution to have an equestrian statue erected in honor of the king. At that time they had wanted to make sure they employed the best craftsmen in the kingdom to carry out this project. He had therefore thought that the best possible course of action was to follow the example of the provinces of Burgundy and Brittany, which had done something similar. . . . On this basis he had made an agreement with Masseline and Hartrelle, sculptors from the Royal Academy, that they would draw up a contract with Joubert, the syndic general of the Estates. By this contract the price for the equestrian statue (see Figure 9) is set at 90,000 livres payable in the city of Paris, namely 10,000 livres next November and the remaining 80,000 over four years until the statue is complete and in a condition to be transported. . . . Now [he said] the assembly needed to vote on the ratification of the contract, if they thought it appropriate, and give orders to have a marble pedestal brought to the city of Montpellier where the statue was to be erected.

The plan was ratified and executed.

THE KING'S OWN WORDS

In 1670 Louis XIV put the finishing touches on a written account of the early years of his reign designed to advise his eldest son, the Dauphin, of the secrets of effective rule. He commented directly on the very events that we have been studying, so we have an opportunity to find out what the king himself thought about his performance. We must approach these memoirs, like all sources, critically. On the one hand, they were conceived as a private testament never intended for publication. The king thus had a reason to be sincere, and the memoirs do contain striking glimpses of his thoughts on what it meant to be Louis XIV. On the other hand, these memoirs were largely written by other people. As early as 1663, when, as we have seen, Colbert was consciously thinking

Ernest Roschach, ed., *Histoire générale de Languedoc par dom Claude Devic et Dom J. Vaissete* (Toulouse: Privat, 1876), 14:1349–51.

REPRESENTATION DE LA STATUE DE SA
MAJESTÉ
Eslevée dans la place de LOUIS LE GRAND le 13 Aouſt.
1699.
Sur les desſins de Monsieur Manſart Sur-Intendant des Baſtimens du Roy,
Executé par Mr. Girardon et fondue par Keler sous la direction de Monsr. de
Coste Architecte ordinaire du Roy.

Figure 9. *Colossal equestrian statue of Louis XIV by Girardon, erected in the Place Louis le Grand [Place Vendôme] in Paris in 1699.*
Bibliothèque Nationale, Paris. Photo B.N.

205

about ways of enhancing the king's image, he started keeping historical notes on the events of the years 1661–1664. Colbert compiled these notes in 1665, in the form of memoirs written in the king's voice. In 1666 Louis began jotting down his own notes. These were more formally transcribed by a man named Périgny, who became the Dauphin's tutor. Louis and Périgny then collaborated on multiple revisions of these various texts, and there were further rewritings in 1670 by another historian, Paul Pellisson, before the text reached its final state.[1]

Although the memoirs are thus a composite work built on a foundation laid by Colbert, they contain observations by the king himself, who oversaw and approved the entire project. They give us the thoughts of the king, but these thoughts are already framed by the points of view that were so deliberately established from the start: the disorder at the beginning of the reign, the assumption of personal rule, the need to restore obedience. The memoirs speak from the perspective of 1670, when the king had fully established his reputation and was looking back over his successes.

The following passages were chosen to illustrate Louis's domestic concerns and his thoughts on the processes of government that we have been studying, although most of the memoirs are devoted to issues of diplomacy and warfare. Think about the connection between these thoughts and the other documents you have read in this book. What kind of a man was Louis, and how did he view his task? What was his attitude toward his subjects? Try to find glimpses of the king's personality, his momentary timidity, and his opinions about kingship. Consider whether he was a victim of his own illusions and whether he lived up to his own expectations. On the basis of the other evidence you have seen, think about what may have been left out of this account.

Excerpts from Louis XIV's Mémoires for the Instruction of the Dauphin

My son, many excellent reasons have prompted me to go to a considerable effort in the midst of my greatest occupations in order to leave you these memoirs of my reign and of my principal actions. I have never

---

[1] This background is provided by Paul Sonnino in his introduction to Louis XIV's, *Mémoires for the Instruction of the Dauphin.*

Louis XIV, *Mémoires for the Instruction of the Dauphin,* trans. and ed. Paul Sonnino (New York: Free Press, 1970), 21, 22, 23–26, 28–33, 35, 37–38, 40–44, 53–58, 68, 78.

believed that kings, feeling as they do all the paternal affections and attachments in themselves, were dispensed from the common and natural obligation of fathers to instruct their children by example and by counsel. . . .

I have considered, moreover, what I have so often experienced myself: the crowd of people who will press around you, each with his own design; the difficulty that you will have in obtaining sincere advice from them; the entire assurance that you will be able to take in that of a father who will have had no interest but your own, nor any passion except for your greatness. . . .

Even from childhood, the very name of do-nothing kings and of mayors of the palace[2] distressed me when it was uttered in my presence. But one must remember the circumstances [of my childhood]: terrible disorders [the Fronde] throughout the kingdom both before and after my majority; a foreign war in which these domestic troubles had caused France to lose a thousand advantages [the war against Spain]; a prince of my blood and of great reputation [Condé] leading the enemy; the state swarming with conspiracies; the parlements still in possession and enjoyment of usurped authority; at my court, very little disinterested loyalty, so that those of my subjects who appeared to be the most submissive were as burdensome and as dangerous for me as the most rebellious; a minister [Mazarin] reinstated in spite of so many factions, very able and very skillful, who loved me and whom I loved, who had rendered me some great services, but whose ideas and manners were naturally quite different from mine, [and] whom I could, nonetheless, neither contradict nor discredit without perhaps reviving against him, through the false impression of a disgrace, the same storms that had been quieted with such great difficulty; I myself still rather young, major in terms of when kings reach their majority, which the laws of the state have advanced in order to avoid greater misfortunes, but not in terms of when private individuals begin to conduct their affairs freely, conscious merely of the immensity of the burden without having been able to test my own strength, wanting more than anything, even more than life itself, to acquire a great reputation if I could do so, but realizing at the same time that my first moves would either lay its foundations or would destroy my hopes for it forever, so that I was almost equally pressed and restrained in my aspirations by the same desire for glory. . . .

Disorder reigned everywhere. My court, in general, was still quite far removed from the sentiments in which I hope that you will find it. People

---

[2]The mayors of the palace were the men who ran the monarchy behind the scenes in Merovingian times.

of quality, accustomed to continual bargaining with a minister who did not mind it, and who had sometimes found it necessary, were always inventing an imaginary right to whatever was to their fancy; no governor of a stronghold who was not difficult to govern; no request that was not mingled with some reproach over the past, or with some veiled threat of future dissatisfaction. Graces [favors] exacted and torn rather than awaited, and extorted in consequence of each other, no longer really obligated anyone, merely serving to offend those to whom they were refused.

The finances, which move and activate the whole great body of the monarchy, were so exhausted that there hardly seemed to be any recourse left. Many of the most necessary and imperative expenses for my household and for my own person were either shamefully postponed or were supported solely through credit, to be made up for later. Affluence prevailed, meanwhile, among the financiers who, on the one hand, covered their irregularities by all kinds of artifices while they uncovered them, on the other, by insolent and brazen luxury, as if they were afraid to leave me ignorant of them.[3]

The Church, aside from its usual troubles, after long disputes over scholastic matters that were admittedly unnecessary for salvation — differences mounting each day with the excitement and the obstinacy of tempers and even mingling constantly with new human interest — was finally threatened openly with a schism [Jansenism] by people all the more dangerous since they could have been very useful, of great merit had they been less convinced of it. It was no longer merely a question of some individual theologians in hiding, but of bishops established in their see, capable of drawing the populace after them, of high reputation, of piety indeed worthy of reverence as long as it were accompanied by submission to the opinions of the Church, by mildness, by moderation, and by charity. . . .

The least of the defects in the order of the nobility was the infinite number of usurpers in its midst, without any title or having a title acquired by purchase rather than by service. The tyranny that it exercised over its vassals and over its neighbors in some of my provinces could neither be tolerated nor could it be suppressed without examples of severity and of rigor. The fury of duels, somewhat mitigated since my strict

---

[3]This paragraph bears a striking resemblance to the complaints expressed in the Mazarinade on page 30. It reminds us that the king was consciously repairing the bad reputation left by his mother and Cardinal Mazarin during the Fronde.

and inflexible enforcement of the latest regulations, already showed through the well-advanced recovery from such a deep-rooted evil that none was beyond remedy.

Justice, which was responsible for reforming all the rest, seemed itself to me as the most difficult to reform. An infinite number of things contributed to this: offices filled by chance and by money rather than by choice and by merit; lack of experience among the judges, even less learning; the ordinances of my predecessors on age and on service circumvented almost everywhere. . . . Even my council, instead of regulating the other jurisdictions, all too often confused them through an incredible number of conflicting decisions all given in my name as if coming from me, which made the disorder even more shameful.

All these evils, or rather, their consequences and their effects, fell primarily upon the lower class, burdened, moreover, with taxes and pressed by extreme poverty in many areas, disturbed in others by their own idleness since the peace, and especially in need of relief and of employment. . . .

All was calm everywhere. Not the slightest hint of any movement within the kingdom that could interrupt or oppose my plans. There was peace with my neighbors, apparently for as long as I would want it myself, owing to the circumstances in which they found themselves. . . .

It would undoubtedly have been a waste of such perfect and such rare tranquillity not to put it to good use, although my youth and the pleasure of leading my armies would have made me wish for a few more external affairs. . . .

Two things were necessary for me, undoubtedly: a great deal of work on my part; a careful choice of the persons who were to support me and relieve me in it.

As to work, my son, it may be that you will begin to read these memoirs at an age when it is far more customary to fear it than to enjoy it, delighted to have escaped from subjection to teachers and to masters, and to have no more set hours nor long and fixed concentration.

Here I shall not merely tell you that this is nonetheless how one reigns, why one reigns, and that there is ingratitude and temerity toward God as well as injustice and tyranny toward men in wanting one without the other, that these demands of royalty which may sometimes seem harsh and unpleasant to you from such a lofty post would appear delightful and pleasant to you if it were a question of attaining them! . . .

I made it a rule to work regularly twice a day for two to three hours at a time with various persons, aside from the hours that I worked alone or that I might devote extraordinarily to extraordinary affairs if any arose, there being no moment when it was not permitted to discuss with me anything that was pressing, except for foreign envoys, who sometimes use the familiarity that they are permitted in order to obtain something or to pry, and who must not be heard without preparation.

I cannot tell you what fruits I immediately gathered from this decision. I could almost feel my spirits and my courage rising. I was a different person. I discovered something new about myself and joyfully wondered how I could have ignored it for so long. That first shyness, which always comes with good sense and which was especially disturbing when I had to speak at some length in public, vanished in less than no time. I knew then that I was king, and born for it. I experienced, finally, an indescribable delight that you will simply have to discover for yourself. . . . The function of kings consists primarily of using good sense, which always comes naturally and easily. . . . Everything that is most necessary to this effort is at the same time pleasant. For it consists, in short, my son, of keeping an eye on the whole earth, of constantly learning the news of all the provinces and of all the nations, the secret of all the courts, the dispositions and the weaknesses of all the foreign princes and of all their ministers; of being informed of an infinite number of things that we are presumed to ignore; of seeing around us what is hidden from us with the greatest care; of discovering the most remote ideas and the most hidden interests of our courtiers coming to us through conflicting interests; and I don't know, finally, what other pleasures we would not abandon for this one, for the sake of curiosity alone. . . .

I commanded the four secretaries of state not to sign anything at all any longer without discussing it with me, the superintendent likewise, and for nothing to be transacted at the finances without being registered in a little book that was to remain with me, where I could always see at a glance, briefly summarized, the current balance and the expenditures made or pending. . . .

I announced that all requests for graces [favors] of any type had to be made directly to me, and I granted to all my subjects without distinction the privilege of appealing to me at any time, in person or by petitions. The petitions were initially very numerous, which did not discourage me, however. The disorder into which my affairs had fallen produced many of them; the idle or unjustified hopes which were raised by this novelty hardly stimulated a lesser number. I was given a great many [petitions] about lawsuits, which I saw no reason for withdrawing arbitrarily from the ordinary jurisdictions for trial before me. But even in these apparently useless things I discovered much that was useful. I learned thereby many details about the condition of my people. They saw that I was concerned about them, and nothing did so much to win me their hearts. . . .

As to the persons who were to support me in my work, I resolved above all not to have a prime minister, and if you and all your successors take my advice, my son, the name will forever be abolished in France, there being nothing more shameful than to see on the one hand all the functions and on the other the mere title of king.

For this purpose, it was absolutely necessary to divide my confidence and the execution of my orders without entirely entrusting it to anyone, assigning these various persons to various functions in keeping with their various talents, which is perhaps the first and foremost talent of princes. . . .

And as for this art of knowing men, which will be so important to you not merely on this but also on every other occasion of your life, I shall tell you, my son, that it can be learned but that it cannot be taught.

Indeed, it is only reasonable to attribute a great deal to a general and established reputation, because the public is impartial and is difficult to deceive over a long period. It is wise to listen to everyone, and not to believe entirely those around us, except for the good that they are compelled to admit in their enemies and for the bad that they try to excuse in their friends; still wiser is it to test of oneself in little things those whom one wants to employ in greater ones. But the summary of these precepts for properly identifying the talents, the inclinations, and the potential of each one is to work at it and to take pleasure in it. For, in general, from the smallest things to the greatest, you will never master a single one unless you derive pleasure and enjoyment from them. . . .

I could undoubtedly have cast my eyes on persons of higher standing, but on none with greater qualifications than these three ministers [Le Tellier, Fouquet, and Lionne], and this small number, as I have already told you, seemed better to me than a larger one.

But to be perfectly honest with you, it was not in my interest to select individuals of greater eminence. It was above all necessary to establish my own reputation and to make the public realize by the very rank of those whom I selected, that it was not my intention to share my authority with them. It was important for they themselves not to conceive any greater hopes than I would please to give them, which is difficult for persons of high birth: and even with all these precautions, it took the world a rather long time to get to know me.

Many were convinced that before long some one around me would gain control over my mind and over my affairs. Most regarded my diligence as enthusiasm that must soon slacken, and those who wanted to judge it more favorably waited to decide later. . . .

I have believed it necessary to indicate this [seizure of personal power] to you, my son, lest from excessively good intentions in your early youth and from the very ardor that these mémoires will perhaps inspire in you, you might confuse two entirely different things; I mean ruling personally and not listening to any counsel, which would be an extreme as dangerous as that of being governed.

The most able private individuals procure the advice of other able persons about their petty interests. What then of kings who hold the public interest in their hands and whose decisions make for the misery or well-being of the whole earth? None [no decisions] should ever be reached of such importance without [our] having summoned, if it were possible, all the enlightenment, wisdom, and good sense of our subjects.

Necessity limits us to a small number of persons chosen from among the rest, and these, at least, must not be ignored. You will discover furthermore, my son, as I soon did, that in discussing our affairs we not merely learn a great deal from others but also from ourselves. . . .

But when, on important occasions, they have reported to us on all the sides and on all the conflicting arguments, on all that is done elsewhere in such and such a case, it is for us, my son, to decide what must actually be done. And as to this decision, I shall venture to tell you that if few lack neither sense nor courage, another never makes it as well as we. For decision requires the spirit of a master, and it is infinitely easier to be oneself than to imitate someone else. . . .

It was necessary for a thousand reasons, including the urgently needed reform of justice, to diminish the excessive authority of the principal courts, which, under the pretext that their judgments were without appeal, or as they say, sovereign and of the last instance, had gradually assumed the name of sovereign courts and considered themselves as so many separate and independent sovereignties. I announced that I would not tolerate their schemes any longer and to set an example, the Court of Excises of Paris having been the first to depart slightly from its duty, I exiled some of its officials, believing that a strong dose of this remedy initially would dispense me from having to use it often later, which has succeeded for me. . . .

I prohibited them all in general, by this decision, from ever rendering any [decisions] contrary to those of my council under any pretext whatsoever, whether of their jurisdiction or of the right of private individuals, and I ordered them, whenever they might believe that either one of them had been disturbed, to complain about it to me and to have recourse to my authority, that which I had entrusted to them being only for rendering justice to my subjects and not for procuring it for themselves, which is a part of sovereignty so essentially royal and so proper to the king alone that it cannot be transmitted to anyone else. . . .

In all these things, my son, and in some others that you will see subsequently which have undoubtedly humiliated my judicial officials, I don't want you to attribute to me, as those who know me less well may have done, motives of fear, hatred, and vengeance for what had transpired during the Fronde, when it cannot be denied that these courts often forgot themselves to the point of amazing excesses.

But in the first place, this resentment which appears initially so just might not perhaps fare so well on closer scrutiny. They have returned by themselves and without constraint to their duty. The good servants have recalled the bad. Why impute to the entire body the faults of a few, rather than the services which have prevailed in the end? . . .

But I know, my son, and can sincerely assure you that I feel neither aversion nor bitterness toward my judicial officials. On the contrary, if age is venerable in men, it appears all the more so to me in these ancient bodies. I am convinced that nowhere else in the state is the work perhaps greater or the rewards smaller. I hold them in the highest affection and regard, and you, my son, who from all appearances will find them even farther removed from their former wild claims, you must be all the more careful to practice what I do myself every day, namely, to display your esteem for them on occasion, to get to know the leading and the most capable individuals among them, to show that you know them — for it is wonderful for a prince to demonstrate that he is informed of everything and that services rendered in his absence are not wasted — to consider them and their families in the distribution of positions and of benefices if they should want to attach themselves to your personal service, to accustom them, finally, through good treatment and kind words to visit you sometimes; whereas in the last century it was part of their integrity not to approach the Louvre, and this not from any malicious intent, but from the false notion that they were defending a supposed interest of the people opposed to that of the prince, without considering that these two interests are but one, that the tranquillity of subjects lies only in obedience, that there is always greater evil in popular control than in enduring even the bad rule of kings, of whom God alone is the judge, that what they seem to do sometimes against the common law is based on reason of state, which is the first of all laws by common consent, yet the most unknown and the most obscure to all those who do not rule.

The smallest motives were important in these beginnings, which showed to France what would be the spirit of my reign and of my conduct from then on. I was disturbed by the customary manner of dealing with the prince, or rather with the minister, almost always putting conditions on what should have been awaited either from my justice or from my kindness. The Assembly of the Clergy, which had been lasting for a long time in Paris, was as usual postponing its separation, which I had desired of it, until the issuance of certain edicts for which it had been pressing. I made it clear to it that nothing would be gained by such means. It separated, and it was only then that the edicts were issued. . . .

As to the governors of strongholds, who so often abused their [authority], I first deprived them of the tax funds that had been given over to them during the war. . . . In the second place, I slowly but surely changed almost all the garrisons, replacing the troops dependent on them with others who recognized only me, and what would have seemed inconceivable a few months previously was executed without the slightest commotion, everyone awaiting and indeed receiving more legitimate rewards from me by doing his duty. . . .

[A long section follows on the state of the various powers of Europe.]

It is usual for mature minds, which have received their first disposition for piety at an early age, to turn directly toward God in the midst of good fortune, although, as a major consequence of our weakness, a long sequence of successes, which we then regard as being naturally and properly due us, will customarily make us forget Him. I confess that in these beginnings, seeing my reputation growing each day, everything succeeding for me and becoming easy for me, I was as deeply struck as I have ever been by the desire to serve Him and to please Him. . . .

I revived, by a new ordinance, the rigor of the old edicts against swearing and blasphemy and wanted some examples to be made immediately; and I can say in this regard that my cares and the aversion that I have displayed toward this scandalous disorder have not been useless, my court being, God be thanked, more exempt from it than it long has been under the kings my predecessors. . . .

I dedicated myself to destroying Jansenism and to breaking up the communities where this spirit of novelty was developing, well-intentioned, perhaps, but which seemed to want to ignore the dangerous consequences that it could have. . . .

And as to my great number of subjects of the supposedly reformed religion [Huguenots], which was an evil that I had always regarded, and still regard, with sorrow, I devised at that time the plan of my entire policy toward them, which I have no grounds for regretting, since God has blessed it and still blesses it every day with a great number of conversions.

It seemed to me, my son, that those who wanted to employ violent remedies did not know the nature of this disease, caused in part by the excitement of tempers, which must be allowed to pass and to die gradually instead of rekindling it with equally strong contradictions, always useless, moreover, when the corruption is not limited to a clearly defined number, but spread throughout the state.

As far as I have been able to understand, the ignorance of the clergy in previous centuries, their luxury, their debaucheries, the bad examples that they set, those that they were obliged to tolerate for that very reason, the excesses, finally, that they condoned in the conduct of individuals contrary to the public rules and sentiments of the Church gave rise, more than anything else, to those grave wounds that it has received from schism and from heresy [the Protestant Reformation]. The new reformers obviously spoke the truth on many matters of fact and of this nature, which they decried with both justice and bitterness. They were presumptuous in regard to belief, and people cannot possibly distinguish a well-disguised error when it lies hidden, moreover, among many evident truths. It all began with some minor differences which I have learned that the Protestants of Germany and the Huguenots of France hardly consider any more today. These produced greater ones, primarily because too much pressure was put upon a violent and bold man [Martin Luther] who, seeing no other honorable retreat for himself, pushed ahead into the fray and, abandoning himself to his own reasoning, took the liberty of examining everything that he had accepted, promised the world an easy and shortened path to salvation, a means very suitable for flattering human reasoning and for drawing the populace. Love of novelty seduced many of them. The interests of various princes mingled in this quarrel. . . .

From this general knowledge, I believed, my son, that the best means to reduce gradually the number of Huguenots in my kingdom was, in the first place, not to press them at all by any new rigor against them, to implement what they had obtained from my predecessors but to grant them nothing further, and even to restrict its execution within the narrowest limits that justice and propriety would permit. . . .

But as to the graces [favors] that depended solely on me, I resolved, and I have rather scrupulously observed it since, not to grant them any, and this out of kindness rather than out of bitterness, so as to oblige them thereby to consider from time to time, by themselves and without constraint, if they had some good reason for depriving themselves voluntarily of the advantages that they could share with all my other subjects.

However, to profit from their greater willingness to be disabused of their errors, I also resolved to attract, even to reward, those who might be receptive; to do all I could to inspire the bishops to work at their instruction and to eliminate the scandals that sometimes separated them from us; to place, finally, in these highest posts and in all those to which I appoint for any reason whatsoever, only persons of piety, of dedication, of learning, capable of repairing, by an entirely different conduct, the disorders that their predecessors had primarily produced in the Church. . . .

I assumed all these cares out of true gratitude for the blessings that I was receiving every day, but I also noticed at the same time that they were very useful to me in preserving the affection of the people, very pleased to see that I was not too occupied to continue my pious devotions with the same regularity in which the Queen my mother had raised me, and particularly edified that year when I performed the stations of a jubilee on foot with my entire household,[4] something that I did not even think worthy of note.

And to tell you the truth, my son, we are lacking not merely in justice but also in prudence when we are lacking in veneration for Him whose lieutenants we are. Our submission to Him is the rule and the example for that which is due to us. Armies, councils, all human industry would be feeble means for maintaining us on the throne if everyone believed he had as much right to it as we and did not revere a superior power, of which ours is a part. The public respects that we pay to this invisible power could indeed justly be considered the first and most important part of our entire policy if they did not require a more noble and more disinterested motive.

Watch out, my son, I implore you, not to approach religion with only this idea of self-interest, very bad when it stands alone, but which, moreover, would not succeed for you because artifice always comes out and does not long produce the same effects as truth. All the advantages that our post gives us over other men are undoubtedly so many new titles of servitude to Him who has given them to us. But in His sight, the exter-

---

[4] A reference to Louis's participation in a devotional religious procession.

nal without the internal is nothing at all and serves more to offend Him than to please Him. Judge for yourself, my son, if you should ever find yourself, as it can hardly fail to happen in the course of your life, in the position that is so usual for kings, and in which I have seen myself so often. Even when my rebellious subjects have had the temerity to take up arms against me, they have made me less angry, perhaps, than those who were in the meanwhile remaining at my side being more dutiful and more attentive to me than all the others, while I was aware that they were betraying me and had neither true respect nor true affection for me in their heart. . . .

For indeed, my son, we must consider the good of our subjects far more than our own. They are almost a part of ourselves, since we are the head of a body and they are its members. It is only for their own advantage that we must give them laws, and our power over them must only be used by us in order to work more effectively for their happiness. It is wonderful to deserve from them the name of father along with that of master, and if the one belongs to us by right of birth, the other must be the sweetest object of our ambition. I am well aware that such a wonderful title is not obtained without a great deal of effort, but in praiseworthy undertakings one must not be stopped by the idea of difficulty. Work only dismays weak souls, and when a plan is advantageous and just, it is weakness not to execute it. . . .

I hope that I shall leave you with still more power and more greatness than I possess, and I want to believe that you will make still better use of it than I. But when everything that will surround you will conspire to fill you with nothing but yourself, don't compare yourself, my son, to lesser princes than you or to those who have borne or who may still unworthily bear the title of king. It is no great advantage to be a little better; think rather about all those who have furnished the greatest cause for esteem in past times, who from a private station or with very limited power have managed by the sole force of their merit to found great empires, have passed like comets from one part of the world to another, charmed the whole earth by their great qualities, and left, after so many centuries, a long and lasting memory of themselves that seems, instead of fading, to intensify and to gain strength with every passing day.[5] If this does not suffice, be still more fair to yourself and consider for how many things you will be praised that you will perhaps owe entirely to fortune or to those whom it has itself placed in your service. Get down to some serious consideration of your own weaknesses, for even though you may

[5] Louis was probably thinking of Alexander the Great here.

imagine that all men, and even the greatest, have similar ones, nevertheless, since you would find this harder to imagine and to believe of them than of yourself, it would undoubtedly diminish your conceit, which is the usual pitfall of brilliance and of fame.

Thereby, my son, and in this respect you will be humble. But when it will be a question, as on the occasion that I have just described to you, of your rank in the world, of the rights of your crown, of the king, finally, and not of the private individual, boldly assume as much loftiness of heart and of spirit as you can, and do not betray the glory of your predecessors nor the interest of your successors, whose trustee you are. . . .

PART THREE

Conclusion

Absolutism was a system of government that was especially suited to the particular kind of society that existed in seventeenth-century France. The documents we have examined tell us quite a bit about the nature of that society and the impact Louis XIV had on it. We have looked at domestic affairs because that is where we can best analyze the workings of the system, and we have concentrated on the first thirty years of Louis's personal reign so as to see this system at its peak. Here are some distinguishing characteristics of French absolutism.

First is the principle of absolute power. The king's authority was absolute in the theoretical sense that no other institution had the constitutional capacity to contradict him. In particular, there was no regular national representative assembly, and the existing provincial estates met only when called by the king. Nevertheless, the overwhelming conclusion that emerges from the documents presented here is that despite his authority, the king could rule only by making compromises with preexisting power centers and by persuading influential notables to go along with his reforms. That is why his grandeur and personal authority were so important. The king was still viewed as a divinely inspired individual who ruled by superior birth and calling, but he also ruled in conjunction with others who combined authority delegated by him with their own independently derived sources of influence. How the king held the reins of power made all the difference. If he failed to live up to expectations, he left room for others to step in with their own claims of shared power. We have seen the consequences of such a shortcoming in the Fronde: The Parlement of Paris resisted the crown to the point that Parisian crowds began to talk back to the parlementaires; councillors from the Parlement led riots in the streets of Aix; the princes raised armies to oppose the first minister; the people of Agen took sides for or against the king by throwing up barricades in the streets of their city; and the citizens of Bordeaux seized power in their city and expelled the Parlement. Similar acts of insubordination occurred around the country.

A second distinguishing feature of France at this time was the corporative nature of the society with which the king interacted and of which he was a part. Louis XIV had to deal with a landed nobility that enjoyed privileged status and strong connections in the provinces; a semi-independent Catholic Church with vast wealth and international connections; a collection of cities and provinces, each claiming its own set of rights and proper procedures, which it considered to be inviolable; and powerful companies of royal officers who owned their positions and believed that they also owned the right to pull their weight in public affairs.

This system of venality of office, which created the robe nobility, was a third part of the French situation. Venality slowed social change by linking family fortunes to ownership of office and the acquisition of nobility. The robe nobles supported the monarchy most of the time because they derived their local influence from the offices they occupied and the royal authority they wielded. But at the same time these officers, such as the councillors in the parlements, were not easily removed and tended to oppose measures that went against regional or class interests, as Bouchu was always complaining. From the standpoint of social advancement, the wealthy regional families, who in another society might have devoted their energies to trade and entrepreneurial skills, had their sights set on buying landed estates, acquiring titles and privileges, and finding a niche in the royal administration. Their cousins the financiers also invested in the state through tax farms, loans, and financial offices. Thus much of France's talent and accumulated wealth was channeled away from business and manufacturing and was instead devoted to investment in the royal state machine.

Fourth was the king's and his ministers' active and systematic coordination of the government at the center. To influence a corporative society, the king had to combine constancy of direction with conciliation of powerful social groups. We have seen that he was capable of disciplining his institutions and imposing new programs with a degree of regularity across France, which he accomplished by using the decrees of the royal council and the management of the intendants. He used judges from the recently rehabilitated Parlement of Paris to bring a measure of order to Auvergne by holding the Grands Jours. The trials had a big impact on local society, even though most of the guilty parties, especially the more violent nobles, fled and were executed in effigy. We have read the impressive surveys and instructions issued by Colbert, and in Burgundy we have seen the heroic efforts by the intendant Bouchu to regularize local debts and institute reforms of hospitals, manufacturing operations, and even local elections. But we have also seen the resistance put up by existing authorities, the rivalry between local agencies, and the delays that made Bouchu almost cry out in exasperation.

Fifth, Louis perfected court life to an unprecedented degree. We have seen through the eyes of Primi Visconti and Saint Maurice how grand life at court could be, and conversely, through the eyes of Liselotte, how cruel it could become. We have discovered that the court was a vicious, competitive arena that placed value on differences of rank and put a premium on royal favor. But the court was just a reflection of the values of the high nobility, and Louis XIV's genius was his ability to focus their attention on himself and away from their independent sources of power. No monarch before or since has achieved such an effective combination of hard work and socializing, of dealing with ministers on the one hand and entertaining grandees on the other, without letting the two influence each other unduly. After the reign of the Sun King, those aspiring to oppose the crown always had to take over the state rather than go into armed rebellion against it.

Sixth, Louis's monarchy was based on a divine right theory that required him to associate his power with the established Catholic Church. This association meant that he could not tolerate dissidence, either from within the church or from Protestant alternatives, and that he would face an ongoing dilemma over how to deal with the competing power of the pope in Rome. Not only did this sacred bond draw him into difficult and contradictory measures, such as the régale dispute with the pope and his persecution of the Jansenists, but it ultimately presented the risk of having the monarchy discredited if public opinion took a different view of what was holy and proper. The later desacralization of the monarchy owed something to the opposition of the Jansenists and to Europe's revulsion at the revocation of the Edict of Nantes.

Seventh, it is worth mentioning that the absolute monarchy was patriarchal. The king's power was derived from the Salic law, which decreed that the throne could pass only through the male line and only to men. This principle was clearly enunciated by Bossuet, who considered women to be "that sex which is born to obey" and saw the French system as "the most in conformity to that which God himself has established." In the eyes of Louis's contemporaries, the king's power over society was mirrored by men's control over governing institutions and fathers' control over wives and children. Women were considered incapable of exercising political authority, although they could have great influence at the royal court, in families, and in protesting crowds, as we have seen. This gendering of the monarchy is an aspect that is just being explored by historians. No doubt they will have more to say about it in the future.

Finally, we must never forget the king's relationship to the vast majority of the population — the peasants, artisans, laborers, and poor, who tend to be overlooked in a "top-down" discussion of the people who hold power. These people, too, interacted with absolutism. They accepted the principle of kingship and believed in the king, although they usually suspected that he was being badly advised and demanded that he do more to defend their basic rights to live and die decently. It was they who generated most of the wealth that went to the taxes we viewed statistically in chapter 3. We have glimpsed their daily problems of poverty, deviance, and economic regulation in Dijon, and we have seen them rebel, following elite leaders during the Fronde and on their own behalf in 1675. We have also seen the fate of the Huguenots, as they struggled against the gradual suppression of their way of life, and the suffering of the nuns of Port Royal, who can represent other Catholic dissidents unwilling to bow to the dominant doctrines supported by the king.

These, then, are some of the distinctive characteristics of French absolutism. A full picture of the Sun King's reign would explore other aspects, such as the development of the army (Louis's largest single expense and his biggest organizational project), Louis's position in Europe, his patronage of the arts, his wars against his neighbors, and the changes that took place in the second half of his very long personal reign. But you now have the basis for an appreciation of many key modalities: life at court, the central administration, tax flows, the interplay with provincial interests, venality of office, religious policies, the construction of the royal image, and the occurrence of popular protest. Louis's monarchy was imitated all over Europe, but no other country had exactly France's combination of social forces and royal responses. Finally, the king's memoirs help us to begin to assess how much of his success was real and how much was a legend created from the beginning of his personal reign, making the image of Louis XIV an essential element in his success.

A Louis XIV Chronology (1638–1715)

1638   Birth of Louis XIV.

1643   Death of Louis XIII; Anne of Austria, Louis XIV's mother, be-comes regent and governs, with Cardinal Mazarin as her first minister.

1648   Peace of Westphalia; end of the Thirty Years' War in Germany.

1648–53 The Fronde.

1648   *May*   Chamber of Saint Louis in Paris draws up demands for reform.

   August   Arrest of Broussel; Parisians rise up against Séguier and the queen.

1649   *January*   Revolt of the Parlement of Aix.

1651–53 Rise of the Ormée movement in Bordeaux.

1652   *March*   Agen raises barricades against the prince of Condé.

   May   Confrontation in Bordeaux between the Ormée and the Parlement.

1654   Coronation of Louis XIV.

1654–82 Bouchu is intendant in Burgundy.

1659   Peace of the Pyrenees between France and Spain.

1660   Condé returns to favor and is renamed governor of Burgundy.

1661   Death of Cardinal Mazarin. Louis XIV assumes personal power.

   Priests are required to sign a formulary against Jansenism.

1661–67 Height of influence of Louise de La Vallière over the king.

1662   Chapelain discusses glorifying the king.

1663   Colbert sends out his call for information about the kingdom.

   Bouchu works on municipal debts in Burgundy.

   Commission investigates Protestant worship in Languedoc.

1664   Trial and banishment of Finance Minister Fouquet, orches-trated by Colbert.

1665	Holding of Grands Jours in Auvergne.
	Riot in Noyers (Burgundy) over Bouchu's reforms.
1667	Bouchu works on manufacturing in Burgundy.
1667–68	War of Devolution.
1667–73	Saint Maurice writes his letters about the court.
1667–81	Height of influence of Madame de Montespan over the king.
1669	Forest Reform Ordinance is issued.
1670	Colbert sends his memorandum on finances to the king.
	Louis XIV completes his memoirs in conjunction with others.
	Bossuet named tutor of the Dauphin.
1671	Arrival of the Princess Palatine (Liselotte) at court.
1672–78	The Dutch War.
1673	King tells parlements not to remonstrate.
	King claims the régale for all French bishoprics.
1673–83	Primi Visconti writes about the court.
1674	La Vallière retires to a convent.
1675	Bossuet chides Louis XIV about his adultery with Madame de Montespan.
	Serious revolts in the west of France, especially Bordeaux and Brittany.
1677–79	Bossuet writes most of his *Politics Drawn from the Very Words of Holy Scripture.*
1679	Pope Innocent XI protests to Louis about the régale.
	Intendant d'Aguesseau writes his memo on converting the Huguenots in Languedoc.
1679–80	Intendant Foucault fights resistance to the régale in the diocese of Pamiers.
1681	Louis XIV annexes the city of Strasbourg in Alsace.
1682	French bishops issue the Four Gallican Articles.
	Demolition of the main Protestant temple in Montpellier.
	The court moves permanently to Versailles.
	Liselotte describes the *jour d'appartement.*
1683	Death of Colbert.
	Louis XIV secretly marries Madame de Maintenon.
1684	Revolt of the winegrowers of Dijon.
1685	Revocation of the Edict of Nantes; dragoons in Languedoc.

1688–97	War of the League of Augsburg (Nine Years' War).
1690	Spanheim describes the somber court of the late eighties.
1692	Liselotte bemoans the marriage of her son to Mademoiselle de Blois.
1693	King makes peace with the new pope, Innocent XII.
1693–94	Bad harvests and famine.
1695	Institution of capitation (head tax).
1701–14	War of the Spanish Succession.
1702–10	War of the Camisards (king fights diehard Protestants in the Cévennes Mountains).
1709	King shuts down the convent of Port Royal.
	Bad harvests and famine.
1713	Louis accepts papal bull *Unigenitus* against Jansenism.
1715	Death of Louis XIV. He is succeeded by his great-grandson, Louis XV. The duke of Orléans, Liselotte's son, becomes regent.

Questions for Consideration

1. How would you define absolutism? In what ways was the king's power absolute? In what ways was it limited?

2. What were Louis XIV's strengths and weaknesses as a person and as a monarch? How did the life at his court reflect those strengths and weaknesses?

3. How would you compare the qualities needed to be a successful political leader today with those needed by an absolute monarch? If there are differences, how would you explain them?

4. Analyze Louis's relationship with each of the following groups: grandees, Catholic Church hierarchy, robe nobility, peasants, urban lower classes. Why might he have felt threatened by each group? What did he hope to gain from each group? What reasons might each group have had to support the king?

5. What governmental conditions made the Fronde possible? What were the grievances of those who rebelled, and how did those grievances relate to the situation at the royal court?

6. When Louis XIV and Colbert set out to collect information about various people and events, what kinds of reports were most important to them? Why? How were their concerns different from those of a twentieth-century government?

7. Who benefited the most and who benefited the least from the tax system described in the tables in chapter 3? Explain.

8. What can we learn about the relationship between lords and peasants in backward provinces from Fléchier's tales of the Grands Jours in Auvergne?

9. How would you describe the power structure of the province of Burgundy at the time of Louis XIV? Who was in charge, what kinds of conflicts emerged among those in charge, and what influence did Louis XIV's government have on the situation?

10. How did Louis's role as a monarch by divine right influence his treatment of the Jansenists, the Gallican church, and the pope? How do you

explain the fact that all these good Catholic parties were constantly in conflict with one another?

11. Why was Louis XIV intolerant toward the Huguenots? How was the position presented in his memoirs different from his policy in the 1680s? How did Catholics and Protestants react to one another in Languedoc?

12. Judging by the documents provided, what was likely to induce common people to riot against the authorities? What kinds of issues brought them into the streets? Once they got there, how would you analyze their motives and their actions? Whom were they likely to attack, how did they do it, and why?

13. To what extent do you think the reputation of Louis XIV was consciously created? How and why was it created? Is the Louis of the king's memoirs different from the Louis described in the memoirs of the royal court? Do you find the same objectives and attitudes in the memoirs drawn up by Colbert as in the king's memoirs?

Selected Bibliography

ABSOLUTISM

Anderson, Perry. *Lineages of the Absolutist State.* London: Verso Books, 1984. A broad, Europe-wide argument using a sophisticated Marxist approach.

Bonney, Richard. "Absolutism: What's in a Name?" *French History* 1 (1987): 93–117. A review of the literature.

Henshall, Nicholas. *The Myth of Absolutism: Change and Continuity in Early Modern European Monarchy.* London: Longman, 1992. Debunks the whole concept.

Lossky, Andrew. "The Absolutism of Louis XIV: Reality or Myth?" *Canadian Journal of History* 19 (1984), 1–16. Classic statement.

Rowan, Herbert. *The King's State: Proprietary Dynasticism in Early Modern France.* New Brunswick, N.J.: Rutgers University Press, 1980.

MINORITY OF LOUIS XIV AND THE FRONDE

Bonney, Richard. *Political Change in France under Richelieu and Mazarin, 1624–1661.* Oxford: Oxford University Press, 1978. A magisterial study of the functioning of absolute monarchy before Louis XIV.

Kettering, Sharon. *Judicial Politics and Urban Revolt: The Parlement of Aix, 1629–1659.* Princeton, N.J.: Princeton University Press, 1978. Study of a particularly rebellious parlement.

Moote, A. Lloyd. *The Revolt of the Judges: The Parlement of Paris and the Fronde, 1643–1652.* Princeton, N.J.: Princeton University Press, 1971.

Ranum, Orest. *The Fronde: A French Revolution, 1648–1652.* New York: Norton, 1993. The best narrative history of the Fronde.

Treasure, G. R. R. *Mazarin: The Crisis of Absolutism in France.* London: Routledge, 1995.

BIOGRAPHIES OF THE KING AND HISTORIES OF THE REIGN

Bluche, François. *Louis XIV.* Abridged and translated by Mark Greengrass. Oxford: Blackwell, 1990. A long, detailed history from a conservative, laudatory perspective.

Campbell, Peter Robert. *Louis XIV, 1661–1715*. London: Longman, 1993. A brief study, including some documents.

Goubert, Pierre. *Louis XIV and Twenty Million Frenchmen*. New York: Pantheon Books, 1966. An account stressing social and demographic forces by a master of the *Annales* school.

Hatton, Ragnhild, ed. *Louis XIV and Absolutism*. Columbus: Ohio State University Press, 1976. An older set of analytical essays.

Lossky, Andrew. *Louis XIV and the French Monarchy*. New Brunswick, N.J.: Rutgers University Press, 1994. An expert study featuring foreign policy.

Mettam, Roger. *Power and Faction in Louis XIV's France*. Oxford: Basil Blackwell, 1988. A minimalist interpretation of absolutism that is especially useful on Louis's relations with the high aristocracy.

Parker, David. *Class and State in Ancien Régime France: The Road to Modernity?* London: Routledge, 1996. A cogent Marxist analysis of the nature of French absolute monarchy with a helpful English comparison.

Sonnino, Paul, ed. *The Reign of Louis XIV*. Atlantic Highlands, N.J.: Humanities Press, 1990. Useful introductory essays on themes.

Sturdy, David J. *Louis XIV*. New York: St. Martin's Press, 1998. An excellent, short, up-to-date account.

Wolf, John B. *Louis XIV*. New York: Norton, 1968. The best longer biography of the king in English.

STUDIES OF ABSOLUTISM IN PRACTICE

Beik, William. *Absolutism and Society in Seventeenth-Century France: State Power and Provincial Aristocracy in Languedoc*. Cambridge: Cambridge University Press, 1985.

Cole, Charles Woolsey. *Colbert and a Century of French Mercantilism*. 2 vols. New York: Columbia University Press, 1939.

———. *French Mercantilism, 1683–1700*. New York: Columbia University Press, 1943.

Collins, James. *Classes, Estates and Order in Early Modern Brittany*. Cambridge: Cambridge University Press, 1994.

Hamscher, Albert. *The Conseil Privé and the Parlements in the Age of Louis XIV: A Study of French Absolutism*. Transactions of the American Philosophical Society 77, part 2. Philadelphia: American Philosophical Society, 1987.

———. *The Parlement of Paris after the Fronde, 1653–1673*. Pittsburgh: University of Pittsburgh Press, 1977.

Hickey, Daniel. *Local Hospitals in Ancien Régime France: Rationalization, Resistance, Renewal, 1530–1789*. Montreal: McGill-Queens University Press, 1997.

Kettering, Sharon. *Patrons, Brokers, and Clients in Seventeenth-Century France*. Oxford: Oxford University Press, 1986.

Lynn, John A. *Giant of the Grand Siècle: The French Army, 1610–1715.* Cambridge: Cambridge University Press, 1997.

Smedley-Weill, Anette. *Les intendants de Louis XIV.* Paris: Fayard, 1995.

Smith, Jay M. *The Culture of Merit: Nobility, Royal Service and the Making of Absolute Monarchy in France, 1600–1789.* Ann Arbor: University of Michigan Press, 1996.

Sonnino, Paul. *Louis XIV and the Origins of the Dutch War.* Cambridge: Cambridge University Press, 1988.

COURT SOCIETY

Barker, Nancy Nichols. *Brother to the Sun King: Philippe, Duke of Orléans.* Baltimore: Johns Hopkins University Press, 1989.

Berger, Robert W. *A Royal Passion: Louis XIV as Patron of Architecture.* Cambridge: Cambridge University Press, 1994.

———. *Versailles: The Château of Louis XIV.* University Park: Pennsylvania State University Press, 1985.

Elias, Norbert. *The Court Society.* New York: Pantheon Books, 1983. A famous sociological study of the system of Louis XIV's court.

Kettering, Sharon. "Brokerage at the Court of Louis XIV." *Historical Journal* 36 (1993): 69–88.

———. "The Decline of Great Noble Clientage during the Reign of Louis XIV." *Canadian Journal of History* 24 (1989): 157–77.

Le Roy Ladurie, Emmanuel. *Saint-Simon ou le système de la Cour.* Paris: Fayard, 1997. An extensive study, in French, of ranks and hierarchy at the late court of Louis XIV.

Motley, Mark. *Becoming a French Aristocrat: The Education of the Court Nobility, 1580–1715.* Princeton, N.J.: Princeton University Press, 1990.

Solnon, Jean-François. *La cour de France.* Paris: Fayard, 1987. The best comprehensive history of the French court, in French.

Walton, Guy. *Louis XIV's Versailles.* Chicago: University of Chicago Press, 1986.

SYMBOLIC REPRESENTATIONS OF THE KING

Apostolidès, Jean-Marie. *Le roi-machine: Spectacle et politique au temps de Louis XIV.* Paris: Éditions du Minuit, 1981. Explores the symbolism in the king's entertainments.

Burke, Peter. *The Fabrication of Louis XIV.* New Haven, Conn.: Yale University Press, 1992. A lavishly illustrated examination of the creation of the king's image.

Isherwood, Robert M. *Music in the Service of the King.* Ithaca, N.Y.: Cornell University Press, 1973.

Klaits, Joseph. *Printed Propaganda under Louis XIV.* Princeton, N.J.: Princeton University Press, 1976.

Melzer, Sara E., and Kathryn Norberg, eds. *From the Royal tô the Republican Body: Incorporating the Political in Seventeenth- and Eighteenth-Century France.* Berkeley: University of California Press, 1998. Innovative essays, some concerning the body of Louis XIV.

Zanger, Abby E. *Scenes from the Marriage of Louis XIV: Nuptial Fictions and the Making of Absolutist Power.* Stanford, Calif.: Stanford University Press, 1997. An anthropological analysis of the meanings conveyed in accounts of the royal marriage.

THE GENDERED MONARCHY

Farr, James R. *Authority and Sexuality in Early-Modern Burgundy (1550– 1730).* Oxford: Oxford University Press, 1995. Explores the gendered assumptions of the councillors in the Parlement of Dijon.

Hanley, Sarah. "Engendering the State: Family Formation and State Building in Early Modern France." *French Historical Studies* 16 (1989): 4–27. Gives the basic argument that will be laid out in a forthcoming book.

Lougee, Carolyn. *Le Paradis des Femmes: Women, Salons, and Social Stratification in Seventeenth-Century France.* Princeton, N.J.: Princeton University Press, 1976.

Rapley, Elizabeth. *The Dévotes: Women and Church in Seventeenth-Century France.* Montreal: McGill-Queens University Press, 1990.

FRENCH SOCIETY AND SOCIAL GROUPS

Beik, William. *Urban Protest in Seventeenth-Century France: The Culture of Retribution.* Cambridge: Cambridge University Press, 1997.

Bercé, Yves-Marie. *History of Peasant Revolts: The Social Origins of Rebellion in Early Modern France.* Translated by Amanda Whitmore. Ithaca, N.Y.: Cornell University Press, 1990.

Bernard, Leon. *The Emerging City: Paris in the Age of Louis XIV.* Durham, N.C.: Duke University Press, 1970.

Billaçois, François. *The Duel: Its Rise and Fall in Early Modern France.* New Haven, Conn.: Yale University Press, 1990.

Dewald, Jonathan. *Pont-Saint-Pierre, 1398–1789: Lordship, Community and Capitalism in Early Modern France.* Berkeley: University of California Press, 1987.

Farr, James R. *Hands of Honor: Artisans and Their World in Dijon, 1550– 1650.* Ithaca, N.Y.: Cornell University Press, 1988.

Goubert, Pierre. *The French Peasantry in the Seventeenth Century.* Cambridge: Cambridge University Press, 1986.

Le Roy Ladurie, Emmanuel. *The Peasants of Languedoc.* Translated by John Day. Urbana: University of Illinois Press, 1974.

Monahan, W. Gregory. *Year of Sorrows: The Great Famine of 1709 in Lyon.* Columbus: Ohio State University Press, 1993.

Schneider, Robert A. *Public Life in Toulouse, 1463–1789: From Municipal Republic to Cosmopolitan City.* Ithaca, N.Y.: Cornell University Press, 1989.

RELIGIOUS HISTORY

Briggs, Robin. *Communities of Belief: Cultural and Social Tensions in Early Modern France.* Oxford: Oxford University Press, 1989. Valuable essays on church and state, Jansenism, and Catholic reform.

Hanlon, Gregory. *Confession and Community in Seventeenth-Century France: Catholic and Protestant Coexistence in Aquitaine.* Philadelphia: University of Pennsylvania Press, 1993.

Mentzer, Raymond. *Blood and Belief: Family Survival and Confessional Identity among the Provincial Huguenot Nobility.* West Lafayette, Ind.: Purdue University Press, 1994.

Sedgwick, Alexander. *Jansenism in Seventeenth-Century France.* Charlottesville: University of Virginia Press, 1977.

Van Kley, Dale. *The Religious Origins of the French Revolution: From Calvin to the Civil Constitution, 1560–1791.* New Haven, Conn.: Yale University Press, 1996. Treats the religious foundations of absolutism.

ORIGINAL SOURCES IN ENGLISH

Bossuet, Jacques-Benigne. *Politics Drawn from the Very Words of Holy Scripture.* Translated and edited by Patrick Riley. Cambridge: Cambridge University Press, 1990.

Church, William F., ed. *The Impact of Absolutism in France: National Experience under Richelieu, Mazarin, and Louis XIV.* New York: Wiley, 1969. A few short documents.

Judge, H. G., ed. *Louis XIV.* New York: Barnes & Noble, 1965. Another set of brief selections.

Lafayette, Madame de. *The Secret History of Henrietta, Princess of England, Together with Memoirs of the Court of France for the Years 1688–89.* Edited by J. M. Shelmerdine. New York: Howard Fertig, 1993.

Locke, John. *Travels in France in 1675–1679.* Edited by John Lough. Cambridge: Cambridge University Press, 1953. The famous British philosopher's travels, including the court.

Louis XIV. *Mémoires for the Instruction of the Dauphin.* Translated and edited by Paul Sonnino. New York: Free Press, 1970.

Mettam, Roger, ed. *Government and Society in Louis XIV's France.* London: Macmillan, 1977. An excellent collection of administrative documents.

Orléans, Elisabeth Charlotte, duchesse d'. *A Woman's Life in the Court of the Sun King: Letters of Liselotte von der Pfanz, 1652–1722.* Translated by Elborg Forster. Baltimore: Johns Hopkins University Press, 1984. There are other versions of her letters.

Perrault, Charles. *Memoirs of My Life*. Edited and translated by Jeanne Morgan Zarucchi. Columbia: University of Missouri Press, 1989. Perrault was one of Colbert's cultural advisers.

Ranum, Orest and Patricia, eds. *The Century of Louis XIV*. New York: Harper & Row, 1972. The finest collection of documents from the period.

Rule, John C., ed. *Louis XIV*. Englewood Cliffs, N.J.: Prentice-Hall, 1974. Short documents.

Saint-Simon, Louis, duc de. *Historical Memoirs of the duc de Saint-Simon: A Shortened Version*. Edited and translated by Lucy Norton. 2 vols. London: Hamish Hamilton, 1967. This is one of any number of published selections from Saint Simon, who was the most famous commentator on the court at the end of the reign of Louis XIV.

Sévigné, Madame de. *Selected Letters*. Edited and translated by Leonard Tancock. New York: Penguin Books, 1982. Letters by an aristocratic lady who disliked the court but sometimes talked about it. There are many editions.

Smith, David L., ed. *Louis XIV*. Cambridge: Cambridge University Press, 1992. Designed for secondary schools, this collection nevertheless is well constructed and useful.

Ziegler, Gilette, ed. *At the Court of Versailles: Eyewitness Reports from the Reign of Louis XIV*. Translated by Simon Watson Taylor. New York: Dutton, 1968.

Acknowledgments

"A Mazarinade against the Queen and the Cardinal." From *Entretien familier du roy et de la reine régente sa mère sur les affaires du temps* (Rouen, 1649). Pamphlet selected, edited, and translated by Amy Enright, with revisions by William Beik. From *French Political Pamphlets 1560–1653,* a microfilm collection, #1182, compiled by Doris Varner Welsh, Newbury Library, Chicago, Illinois. (312) 943-9090.

"Agen Seduced by the Princes, 1652, Narrated by Bru." 19th century copy from A. L. Calbet, teacher at Bon-Encontre. Courtesy Archives departementales de Lot-et-Garonne, 2J 67.

"The Princess Palatine." Excerpts from Elisabeth Charlotte Orléans, *A Woman's Life in the Court of the Sun King: Letters of Liselotte von der Pfanz, 1652–1722* translated by Elborg Forster, pp. 3–4, 31–36, 44–45, 67, 83, 104–105, 214, 250–253, 255–256, 258–260, 271–272. © 1984 Johns Hopkins University Press. Reprinted by permission.

"Meeting the People of Dijon." Selected unnumbered documents: I 110, I 119, I 123, I 130, I 143. From Archives Municipales de Dijon. Courtesy AM Dijon.

Excerpts from *Politics Drawn from the Very Words of the Holy Scripture* by Jacques-Benigne Bossuet, edited and translated by Patrick Riley, pp. 51, 57–60, 62–66, 81, 83–85, 87, 103, 115–116. Courtesy of Cambridge University Press.

"Bossuet Chides Louis XIV about the State of His Soul." Excerpt from *Politique de Bossuet* by Jacques Truchet. © Armand Colin, Paris, 1966. Reprinted by permission of the publisher.

Excerpt from letter by Pope Innocent IX to Louis XIV, December 29, 1679 from *Louis XIV* edited by David L. Smith, 1992, p. 61. Courtesy of Cambridge University Press.

"Verbal Abuse, Protestants to Catholics, 1678." Courtesy AD Gard, G450.

"Verbal Abuse, Catholics to Protestants, 1680." Document TT256B, fol.56. Courtesy of Centre Historique des Archives Nationales (C.A.R.N.).

"Royal Dragoons in Languedoc." From *Histoire de Languedoc* edited by Philippe Wolff. © 1967 Privat, Toulouse. Courtesy of the publisher.

"Bordeaux 1675, Eyewitness Account." Melanges Colbert 171, fols. 126–194; Clairambault 796. Cliché Bibliotheque nationale de France, Paris.

Excerpt from Charles Perrault, *Memoirs of My Life,* edited and translated by Jeanne Morgan Zarucchi, pp. 41–42, 89. Copyright © 1989 by the Curators of the University of Missouri. Reprinted by permission of the University of Missouri Press.

Excerpts from *Louis XIV King of France and of Navarre: Mémoires for the Instruction of the Dauphin,* translated and edited by Paul Sonnino. Copyright © 1970 by The Free Press. Reprinted with the permission of The Free Press, a Division of Simon & Schuster.

Index